CHILDREN'S LIVES AND SCHOOLING ACROSS SOCIETIES

RESEARCH IN SOCIOLOGY OF EDUCATION

(Formerly Research in Sociology of Education and Socialization)

Series Editors: Emily Hannum and Bruce Fuller

Previous Volumes:

Volume 10: Research in Sociology of Education and Socialization – Edited by Aaron M. Pallas

Volume 11: Research in Sociology of Education and Socialization – Edited by Aaron M. Pallas

Volume 12: Research in Sociology of Education and Socialization – Edited by Aaron M. Pallas

Volume 13: Schooling and Social Capital in Diverse Cultures – Edited by Bruce Fuller and Emily Hannum

Volume 14: Inequality Across Societies: Families, Schools and Persisting Stratification – Edited by David Baker, Bruce Fuller, Emily Hannum and Regina Werum

RESEARCH IN SOCIOLOGY OF EDUCATION   VOLUME 15
(Formerly Research in Sociology of Education and Socialization)

CHILDREN'S LIVES AND SCHOOLING ACROSS SOCIETIES

EDITED BY

EMILY HANNUM
University of Pennsylvania, USA

BRUCE FULLER
University of California, Berkeley, USA

ELSEVIER
JAI

Amsterdam – Boston – Heidelberg – London – New York – Oxford
Paris – San Diego – San Francisco – Singapore – Sydney – Tokyo
JAI Press is an imprint of Elsevier

JAI Press is an imprint of Elsevier
The Boulevard, Langford Lane, Kidlington, Oxford OX5 1GB, UK
Radarweg 29, PO Box 211, 1000 AE Amsterdam, The Netherlands
525 B Street, Suite 1900, San Diego, CA 92101-4495, USA

First edition 2006

Copyright © 2006 Elsevier Ltd. All rights reserved

No part of this publication may be reproduced, stored in a retrieval system
or transmitted in any form or by any means electronic, mechanical, photocopying,
recording or otherwise without the prior written permission of the publisher

Permissions may be sought directly from Elsevier's Science & Technology Rights
Department in Oxford, UK: phone (+44) (0) 1865 843830; fax (+44) (0) 1865 853333;
email: permissions@elsevier.com. Alternatively you can submit your request online by
visiting the Elsevier web site at http://elsevier.com/locate/permissions, and selecting
Obtaining permission to use Elsevier material

Notice
No responsibility is assumed by the publisher for any injury and/or damage to persons
or property as a matter of products liability, negligence or otherwise, or from any use
or operation of any methods, products, instructions or ideas contained in the material
herein. Because of rapid advances in the medical sciences, in particular, independent
verification of diagnoses and drug dosages should be made

British Library Cataloguing in Publication Data
A catalogue record for this book is available from the British Library

ISBN-13:   978-0-7623-1291-7
ISBN-10:   0-7623-1291-2
ISSN: 1479-3539 (Series)

For information on all JAI Press publications
visit our website at books.elsevier.com

Printed and bound in The Netherlands

06 07 08 09 10   10 9 8 7 6 5 4 3 2 1

Working together to grow
libraries in developing countries

www.elsevier.com | www.bookaid.org | www.sabre.org

ELSEVIER   BOOK AID International   Sabre Foundation

CONTENTS

ACKNOWLEDGMENTS — vii

OVERVIEW: CHILDREN'S LIVES AND SCHOOLING ACROSS SOCIETIES
  Emily Hannum and Bruce Fuller — 1

COMMUNITY MATTERS IN CHINA
  Jennifer H. Adams — 15

SOCIAL CAPITAL FORMATION THROUGH CHINESE SCHOOL COMMUNITIES
  Heidi Ross and Jing Lin — 43

GIRLS' SCHOOLING AND MARRIAGE IN RURAL BANGLADESH
  Simeen Mahmud and Sajeda Amin — 71

GENDERED HOMES AND CLASSROOMS: SCHOOLING IN RURAL NEPAL
  Jennifer Rothchild — 101

FAMILIES, SCHOOLS, AND READING IN ASIA AND LATIN AMERICA
  Hyunjoon Park and Gary D. Sandefur — 133

THE CONTEXTS OF CHILDREN'S LIVES IN ASIA: FAMILIES, SCHOOLS, AND COMMUNITIES COMMENTARY ON ADAMS, ROSS AND LIN, MAHMUD AND AMIN, ROTHCHILD, AND PARK AND SANDEFUR
  Emily Hannum — 163

CHILDREN'S WORK AND SCHOOL ATTENDANCE IN GHANA
Niels-Hugo Blunch   *177*

DEMAND FOR SCHOOLING AMONG ORPHANS IN ZIMBABWE
Craig Gundersen, Thomas Kelly and Kyle Jemison   *207*

CHILDREN'S WORK, HEALTH, AND SCHOOL DEMAND
COMMENTARY ON BLUNCH AND GUNDERSEN ET AL. PAPERS
Bruce Fuller   *231*

ALIENATION FROM LEARNING – POOR ETHIOPIAN CHILDREN IN ISRAEL
Gad Yair and Orit Gazit   *239*

HOME ENVIRONS AND ALIENATION FROM SCHOOLING
COMMENTARY ON YAIR AND GAZIT
Daniel Bekele   *265*

ABOUT THE EDITORS AND AUTHORS   *271*

SUBJECT INDEX   *277*

ACKNOWLEDGMENTS

We thank all who have contributed manuscripts to *Research in Sociology of Education* in recent years. This is the third edition that we have co-edited. Readers do not get to see all the fine work that is submitted and discussed with our reviewers, only a portion of which appears on these pages.

We express appreciation to our editorial board members who share the bittersweet task of whittling down submissions to fit the annual theme and those that stand out in their quality. They include Fran Vavrus, Annette Lareau, Sara Lawrence-Lightfoot, Pedro Noguera, Aaron Pallas, Chiqui Ramirez, Steve Raudenbush, and Yoshi Shavit. Several additional colleagues served as reviewers for this volume, including David Baker, Daniel Bekele, Alex Weinreb, and Scott Yabiku.

Elizabeth King helped us design the volume and invite a diverse set of papers from economists who are working on issues of childhood and school attainment. Bob Hass, again this year, thoughtfully edited each paper and commentary, along with corralling our authors and keeping their feet to the fire in delivering elegant prose. Thank you all.

Emily Hannum
Bruce Fuller
Editors

OVERVIEW: CHILDREN'S LIVES AND SCHOOLING ACROSS SOCIETIES

Emily Hannum and Bruce Fuller

THE CASE FOR CONSIDERING CHILDREN'S LIVES OUTSIDE OF SCHOOLS

A key tenet of the modern nation-state – embedded in the notion of progress – is the belief that our children can lead better lives than our own. Trust in the possibility of upward mobility for future generations drives movements of families around the world, and, indeed, drives the spirit of capitalism. In today's world, the notion of mass access to educational opportunity is a key element of the dream of upward mobility. This ideal is manifest in the huge public investment in schools that all nations must make, no matter how rich or poor, to signify membership in modern society.

But how much does schooling really contribute to the mobility of children? Four decades of studies in sociology of education have taught us much, at least in the U.S. and Europe, about the school's ability to lend a hand in pulling some graduates up by their bootstraps. This work also has moved some sociologists to glance back at the family, since the household's social-class position is most often the main driver of the quality of schools children enter, and their adult destinations. If nothing else, modern schooling legitimates the reproduction of class differences and enables parents to prevent their children from backsliding down the class hierarchy.

Social scientists moved up a level of analysis, over a generation ago, to assess whether the spread of schooling helped nations, not just individuals, become upwardly mobile. That is, did the historical spread of mass schooling help power economic growth, greater income equality, or the rise of democratic institutions? This elevation in level of analysis provided fresh thinking about the school's society-level effects. The news was pretty good, at least in early historical periods of commercialized agriculture, then early industrialization in the West (for a review, see Fuller & Rubinson, 1992). Yet, recent research suggests a less sanguine perspective: whether educational expansions drive national economic productivity and democratization remain topics of debate, and stratification research suggests that educational expansions often seem to preserve families' class positions, more than loosen class boundaries (for a review, see Hannum & Buchmann, 2005).

A separate strand of sociological research on schooling in comparative perspective arose from neoinstitutional theorists. Led by the likes of John Boli, John W. Meyer, and Francisco Ramirez, this line of thinking has come to view schooling as a world institution, replete with an isomorphic organizational form around the globe (e.g., Thomas, Meyer, Ramirez, & Boli, 1987). Building schools came to be viewed as a phenomenological celebration of shared symbols, rather than as delivering mobility for families or material progress for nations. Every nation-state, big and small, had to borrow from the World Bank to build a system of mass schooling. Like Levi's or Coca Cola, mass schooling was what modernity was now all about.

Yet, as sociologists have inventively examined the nature of the school institution and its uneven effects on the progress of families, societies, and the global community, another world has been largely left out: the family institution – the most basic context in which childhood is constructed; tacitly organized around diverse social ideals and material realities. Yes, mass schooling is a second context, and one that takes up an increasing amount of children's time. But as sociologists have been busy empirically gauging the school's effects, the character of childhood and the power of home practices have been largely ignored.

Comparative sociologists and economists do occasionally glance at the family. The production-function tradition seeks to identify school inputs or human processes that predict higher school achievement. Scholars working along this line of analysis rather incidentally add measures of family background into their regression models, typically putting in maternal education or parents' occupational status (Fuller & Clarke, 1994). When Steve

Heyneman and Bill Loxley endeavored to prove James Coleman wrong when it came to explaining student achievement in developing countries – eager to show that school institutions mattered more than student background – they tossed in conventional Western markers of class position as statistical controls (Heyneman & Loxley, 1982, 1983). When some of us revisited this issue of family versus school, and included culturally situated measures of household resources or parental practices, guess what? The variance in achievement explained by family factors rose, as the slice explained by school qualities diminished (Lockheed, Fuller, & Nyirongo, 1989).

Our aim in collecting the new papers that follow is not to settle this debate around the relative force of family and school in determining children's life chances – a question that prompts many different empirical answers around the globe. Rather, we have solicited diverse set of papers that illustrate the particularistic, non-school contexts of childhood – community as well as family – that shape and constrain educational outcomes in different parts of the world. Collectively, these studies illustrate significant challenges for efforts to develop meaningful comparative research about how families, schools, and communities affect education. We return to this issue in our discussion.

THE COMPARATIVE FORCE OF CHILDHOOD, FAMILY, AND SCHOOLING

One recent casting of the tandem institutions of family and school, advanced by David Baker and Gerald LeTendre (2005), argues a close and "symbiotic" relationship. The infamous Coleman Report (Coleman et al., 1966), published by the U.S. government in 1966, found that the lion's share of variance in children's achievement was explained not by disparities in school spending or features of quality, but by parents' social-class background.

Subsequent interpretations claimed that schooling did not matter. In fact, schooling exerts sizeable effects in raising the average level of literacy observed among a population (e.g., Ceci, 1991). We continue to observe this phenomenon in developing countries. Modern schooling also significantly alters dominant ways in which youngsters are socialized, in part to fit into industrial-like workplaces.

What Coleman actually found was that variation in school achievement was more strongly attributable to class and ethnic membership than to between-school differences in quality. Still, the finding was not encouraging for reformers and educators who believed they could boost schooling to reduce class inequality.

By the late 1970s, the World Bank was swept into the argument that the state and school could successfully combat family poverty and provide upward mobility across developing societies. But if Coleman's findings applied outside of the U.S., then would larger investments in educational expansion and school quality be wise? Steve Heyneman, a graduate student at the University of Chicago, was eager to prove Coleman wrong when it came to the school's effects in poor and middle-income nations. In a remarkable line of cross-national studies, Heyneman and his associate, Bill Loxley, found that children's achievement was substantially more sensitive to school quality differences than to the class background of students (e.g., Heyneman & Loxley, 1982, 1983).

What is intriguing is that the clout associated with between-school differences in school quality vanished in all but the poorest societies by the mid-1990s (Baker, Goesling, & LeTendre, 2002; Baker & LeTendre, 2005). Cross-national differences in average achievement are probably still related to a nation's overall wealth, and presumably to the quality of its schools. But the relative force of family and school in explaining achievement is no longer conditioned by the wealth of a nation or the class structure associated with industrialization, according to Baker and LeTendre's (2005, p. 41) most recent analysis. Baker and LeTendre (2005) argue that the Coleman effect has spread throughout the world: large family effects and small school effects are the dominant pattern in explaining variation in outcomes.

As sociologists and others rediscover the force of family, we also realize that a 40-year obsession with school effects has constrained our knowledge of both families and communities as contexts of childhood across diverse societies. Allied fields have flourished in the U.S. and Europe, from the broad study of children's development, to ethnographic work on childhood and families, to cross-cultural investigations into socialization practices across ethnic and social-class groups. But much less is known about the varying experiences of children in diverse urban and rural settings in developing and transitional societies. This persisting ignorance is what sparked interest in the present volume. We are pleased to offer new scholarship that examines the contexts of children's daily lives in disparate national settings.

DIFFERING CHILDHOODS, DIVERSE SCHOOLS, AND UNEVEN ATTAINMENT

We travel first to East and South Asia, to look into the nature of childhood in rural villages and urban centers, and to compare the factors that shape children's school participation and attainment across Asian societies. From China, Bangladesh, and Nepal, we present qualitative and quantitative studies about how family and community resources and norms shape children's school experiences and outcomes. We turn next to a comparative analysis of East Asian and Latin American countries that adds a striking new result to the families versus schools debate. We then move to Africa, peering into the everyday conditions facing children in Ghana and Zimbabwe, from the pressure to work as young child, to the pressure to make it on one's own after being orphaned by the HIV-AIDS epidemic. We offer regional commentaries following the Asia and Africa papers. Finally, we present a paper and commentary on how poverty and poor housing conditions impact the education of Ethiopian immigrant children in Israel.

Community Resources and Schools in China

As noted in the Asia commentary in this volume, a theme that emerges in both the China and South Asia papers is that local, not just national, contexts shape the experience of education, and its desired and actual outcomes. Jennifer Adams, drawing on surveys conducted among rural families in China, highlights the role of educational policies as a context for understanding the how family and community factors in driving school attainment. That is, the evolving nature of childhood is shaped jointly by state action and a priori local conditions. Adams argues that as Beijing has decentralized control of schools – and growing parts of the fiscal burden – certain communities have greater resources to pay for higher quality teachers and richer instructional materials. Moreover, Adams shows that the quality of children's educational achievement can be linked, in part, to the strength of social bonds within communities.

Heidi Ross and Jing Lin further illuminate the links between community social resources and schooling in China, through portraits of four schools, complemented by observations and interviews conducted in schools across the country over many years. Ross and Lin explore how a community's social resources shape the educational experiences of its children. Their paper builds on Adams' findings by making the point that communities with social resources offer children not just better academic learning, but also a brighter vision of future possibilities.

Ross and Lin also upturn conventional thinking on community disparities in schooling by considering whether the kind of schooling on offer is likely to promote future social cohesion and social empowerment in these different communities. Interestingly, Ross and Lin's field-based study leads to an insight that parallels a recent argument made by Steve Heyneman (2005) in a critique of global survey research on schooling. Both Heyneman and Ross and Lin argue that notions of school accountability need to broaden from a focus on whether schools narrow the gap in achievement (or by extension, adult incomes) to whether schools are effective in fostering social cohesion.

Gender, Family Organization, and Education in Rural South Asia

Childhood in many societies continues to be organized along gender lines. Feminist theory in the West has altered how we think about social classes and the determinants of opportunity. Scholars working in developing countries, over the past generation, have also detailed how disparities persist in girls' ability to rise in the modern-wage sector, relative to boys. School expansion and affirmative efforts to incorporate girls have become favored policy strategies around the world.

The two pieces in this volume on South Asia illustrate some significant limiting factors to the likely reach of these strategies, at least in the short term. Simeen Mahmud and Sajeda Amin, analyzing panel data in rural Bangladesh, argue that marriage markets, rather than labor markets, continue to be the favored next step after schooling for most girls. In these rural communities, marital considerations, more than potential for earnings, seem to serve as a basis for parental educational decisions for girls.

How can it be that norms around girls' education are changing, with more girls entering schools, yet traditional norms about gender, marriage, and work seem to persist? While the papers here cannot address this question for the case of rural Bangladesh, Jennifer Rothchild's study suggests some answers for the case of rural Nepal. Drawing from rich qualitative interviews and extensive observations in a rural village, she shows how formal schooling can act to reinforce, as often as transform, traditional, local gender norms. She shows how gender is socially constructed and reproduced in a rural village, which in turn shapes the treatment of boys and girls inside schools. Her provocative findings raise the possibility that modernizing institutions may not be as liberal and equitable as their architects claim, and suggest that schooling may not be as uniform as neoinstitutional scholars believe.

Family and School Effects in East Asia and Latin America

The chapter by Hyunjoon Park and Gary D. Sandefur moves up a level of analysis, to ask where the relative influence of home and school varies across societies. They advance the line of cross-national analysis pioneered by sociologist John W. Meyer and colleagues, then pursued by David Baker and Gerald LeTendre as introduced above. The new Park–Sandefur paper shows that the influence of children's social-class background is significantly weaker in East Asian societies than in Latin America.

This finding appears to be due not so much to differing structures of class and income, but rather to the fact that East Asian school systems are more inclusive of a wider variety of families – less vertically differentiated – than those in Latin America, where a family's class position is more readily reproduced through the public school system. The most elite Latin American families send their children to even better-resourced private schools, while in East Asia, the private sector offers schooling of lower quality. This fascinating paper illuminates how the reproduction of class differences can be altered through school structures, and how cross-national variability is being revealed with fresh global data. This chapter moves beyond vertical and deterministic renditions of class, recognizing that healthy or pallid forms of social organization can mediate the effects of a family's class position.

Child Labor, Orphanhood, and Educational Opportunities in Africa

The next set of papers takes us to Ghana and Zimbabwe, to focus on two important and distressing aspects of children's lives that shape education in many settings in Africa: child labor and orphanhood. As the commentary on the Africa papers points out, one key contribution lies in highlighting the agency of families – through coping strategies such as labor allocation decisions and the decision to foster and invest in non-biological children – in the face of extreme poverty and disease. These strategies have important implications for educational attainment.

Work still fills the everyday lives of many children in poor societies, particularly in Africa (Siddiqi & Patrinos, n.d.). International Labor Organization data indicate that more than 40 percent of African children work (World Bank, 2001). Yet, household surveys in Africa suggest that over 95 percent of child labor takes place in and around private households, and thus may not impinge on schooling (World Bank, 2001).

Niels-Hugo Blunch addresses the complexity of the relationship between child labor and education in Ghana. As elsewhere in Africa, child work remains a significant phenomenon in Ghana. In 2001, the Ghana Statistical Service estimated that approximately 27.7 percent of children ages 5–14 years were working (Department of Labor, 2004). Blunch finds that many children who engage in household labor do not consider themselves as working. Yet, even using a restrictive definition of work in which children report their main status in the preceding four weeks as being a worker (rather than a student), more than one in 10 children in Ghana ages 8–14 are working and not attending school. Most are contributing to the family farm or working to help support an urban household.

Children's contexts, including the presence of school institutions, matter when it comes to the propensity to work. Blunch found that child workers in Ghana tend to be older and are usually females, and reside in rural areas and farther from government schools, compared with children not working. Rural children are more likely to work when families own cattle. The opportunity cost of not working and remaining in school is higher if child labor can generate significant income for the family. This point highlights the complexity of class and wealth impacts on schooling, and of developing meaningful cross-national definitions of class and wealth.

In addition to the intensity of child labor in Africa, another unusual feature of the family context of schooling in this region is that many children face orphanhood. In sub-Saharan Africa, more than 11 million children under age 15 have lost at least one parent to AIDS (Atwine, Cantor-Graae, & Bajunirwe, 2005). Indeed, Zimbabwe now has the highest level of orphanhood in the continent, with UNAIDS estimating that about 14 percent of children under 15 in the year 2000 had lost one or both parents (Bicego, Rutstein, & Johnson, 2003; Kobiane, Calves, & Marcoux, 2005). Recent analyses of Demographic and Health Survey from 10 countries in sub-Saharan Africa indicate that orphans are significantly less likely than non-orphans to be enrolled in school (Case, Paxson, & Ableidinger, 2004).

Craig Gundersen and his colleagues examine the influence of orphanhood on the likelihood that six to 16-year-old children in Zimbabwe stay in school. Sharp changes in the health conditions facing children can dramatically alter their propensity to enter school and pursue better futures. We have long known this for individual, unfortunate families. But the HIV-AIDS epidemic still besetting wide swathes of the African continent has brought the nexus between health and education attainment into an unprecedented focus.

Gundersen et al.'s findings are disturbing. The immediate impact of orphanhood is modest, as young children initially stay in school, in line with high enrollment rates achieved in Zimbabwe soon after independence. But as orphaned children grow older, by age 11, they leave school at significantly higher rates. Over one-fourth of all orphaned children are out of school in the 11–16 age group, compared to about 12 percent of non-orphans. This finding highlights the point that the ongoing health crisis in much of Africa will leave a mark on successive generations, as the life chances of orphans shrink over time. Gundersen et al.'s paper makes the sad point that in parts of Africa, children's orphanhood status must now be considered a standard predictor – on a par with economic status, parental education, and sibship – in studies of educational attainment.

Home Environment and Schooling for Ethiopian Immigrants in Israel

The final paper in this volume, by Gad Yair and Orit Gazit, takes us deep into the daily lives of Ethiopian children of immigrants to Israel. Ethiopians are among the most vulnerable populations in Israel, in socio-economic terms: they have substantially lower educational and occupational attainments than members of other ethnic groups in Israeli society (Offer, 2004). Yair and Gazit focus on an important, seemingly prosaic issue facing this community: poor and cramped housing conditions, and the logistical challenges such conditions present for children's studies. Overcrowding and dismal, poorly lit spaces for studying directly undercut these children's ability to keep pace with their studies.

Yet, the study offers a much more broad set of insights into the ways that these children's lives outside of school color opportunities for social mobility. Yair and Gazit's informants – research assistants who wrote reports about tutors' experiences working in homes to help children – paint a disturbingly bleak portrait of chaotic physical environments and social interactions.

What are the roots of these environments? Yair and Gazit make a strong structural argument linking the home environment to conditions of economic deprivation, poor housing stock, overcrowding, and cultural difficulties with adjusting to modes of social organization in Israel. Daniel Bekele's commentary on this paper underscores the importance of housing conditions and cultural dislocation. Bekele also suggests additional contributing factors. Daily social interactions colored by perceptions of class and migrant status probably weigh heavily on these families' ability to muster the resources needed to support their children's schooling. Race is probably also at play here. Bekele's commentary is consistent with earlier research on the Ethiopian community suggesting that racial differentiation contributes to disaffection among Ethiopians in Israel (for evidence and discussion, see Offer, 2004).[1]

More broadly, Yair and Gazit richly, disturbingly illuminate how the circumstances of marginalized children's lives can severely constrain their life chances – even within an affluent society. Yair and Gazit argue effectively that not just the school lives, but the home lives of children must be fully considered by policy makers in Israel, if they wish to address the significant educational disadvantages faced by Ethiopian immigrants. Bekele suggests that important next steps for research include studies designed to identify strengths in these immigrant families, and studies of successful upward mobility. Such approaches might suggest promising strategies for supporting the integration of this community into Israeli society. Both Yair and Gazit and Bekele stress that policy makers and the research community must think in much broader terms about how policies affecting the family, and not just educational policies, constrain and enable children's schooling.

LESSONS FROM NEW STUDIES OF CHILDHOOD

These papers offer new perspectives on how to conceive of childhood and school attainment, cross-nationally. One important point that comes through in these papers is a caveat about the transformative capacity of education. Children face disturbing basic conditions in many settings around the world. This point comes through most poignantly in the examples of orphans' limited enrollments in Zimbabwe, immigrants' dismal housing conditions in Israel, and children facing pressure to work at young ages in Ghana. These findings call into question accepted notions of what a modern school system might do for a society, in terms of promoting mobility. School expansion alone will not equalize opportunities for social integration and a decent quality of life for children facing such fundamental life problems outside of schools. A similar caveat emerges in the papers about girls in rural Nepal and Bangladesh, where schooling is increasing, but still leads mainly to marriage, rather than the workplace. More broadly, in many societies, there are constraints to full social participation for some groups of children that are deep-seated, and strategies for addressing these constraints will require creative thinking and multi-sectoral approaches. Yet, the comparative study of family and school effects in Latin America and East Asia offers the more hopeful perspective that there are settings where the institutions of schooling are organized in ways that reduce the impact of home circumstances on educational outcomes.

These papers also make the point that nature of childhood can also vary greatly *within* a given society, for males and females, by family circumstances, and across communities. This statement is illustrated in rural Bangladesh and rural Nepal, where family roles are highly differentiated on the basis of gender: local norms about workplace gender segregation and family gender roles color the educational choices of parents in rural Bangladesh, and shape the daily activities of girls in rural Nepal. It is illustrated in the case of Israel by family migrant status and in Zimbabwe by orphanhood status. Finally, the China papers illustrate how communities shape the schools children attend, children's likely future labor markets, and the kinds of interactions that children will have with peers and role models.

Why does the diversity of childhood experience – across and within societies – matter for comparative educational research? It presents a real quandary for cross-national projects. At an abstract level, there are certainly many similarities in the attributes of home life, communities, and schools that should matter for children's educational outcomes. Yet, many salient concepts – orphan status, work status, community of residence, migrant status, and gender, for example – vary in their relevance and meaning across societies. This reality poses a significant challenge to interpretations and generalizations.

More problematic, however, is that even when concepts are relevant across societies, it is difficult to operationalize them in ways that are both valid and standard: how does one measure social class or poverty in a way that is both comparable across and meaningful within societies? This challenge is one of research design: what proxy for socio-economic status would work in both Korea and Zimbabwe? Would it be better to use a common measure, with limited in-country validity, or different measures that better approximate the concept of interest, but are not comparable? The particularistic dimensions of children's lives, even in the limited sample of national settings represented in this volume, highlight the challenge inherent in developing global research about how families, schools, and communities affect education.

We urge social scientists, policy makers, and advocates to think more carefully about how the evolving, diverse nature of childhood around the world shapes demand for modern schooling, and resulting disparities in attainment. Rather than sprinkling crude proxies for social class into estimation models, or ignoring the child's household and community settings in qualitative studies, the research in this volume suggests the need to carefully investigate evolving contexts of childhood – from the varying degrees of social cohesion in Chinese communities, to cultural norms about gender in rural South Asia, to orphanhood and child labor among African youngsters, to the crowded, bleak housing conditions faced by children Ethiopian immigrants in Israel, to the stratified schools that confront families in Latin America. These local settings, at times preserved or transformed by policies of the state, are where the tacit socialization and the explicit forms of schooling are shaping children's futures, for better or for worse.

NOTES

1. For example, Offer (2004) shows that Ethiopians have lower returns to education in the labor market in Israel, possibly because of discrimination. Offer suggests that this circumstance, together with the extremely low levels of education among Ethiopian immigrants, places them at risk of becoming a marginalized group within the Jewish population.

REFERENCES

Atwine, B., Cantor-Graae, E., & Bajunirwe, F. (2005). Psychological distress among AIDS orphans in rural Uganda. *Social Science & Medicine, 61,* 555–564.

Baker, D. P., Goesling, B., & LeTendre, G. K. (2002). Socioeconomic status, school quality, and national economic development: A cross-national analysis of the "Heyneman-Loxley effect" on mathematics and science achievement. *Comparative Education Review, 46*(3), 291–312.

Baker, D. P., & LeTendre, G. K. (2005). *National differences, global similarities: World culture and the future of schooling.* Palo Alto: Stanford University Press.

Bicego, G., Rutstein, S., & Johnson, K. (2003). Dimensions of the emerging orphan crisis in sub-Saharan Africa. *Social Science & Medicine, 56,* 1235–1247.

Case, A., Paxson, C., & Ableidinger, J. (2004). Orphans in Africa: Parental death, poverty, and school enrollment. *Demography, 41*(3), 483–508.

Ceci, S. J. (1991). How much does schooling influence general intelligence and its cognitive components? A reassessment of the evidence. *Developmental Psychology, 24,* 703–722.

Coleman, J., Campbell, E., Hobson, C., McPartland, J., Mood, A., Weinfield, F., & York, R. (1966). *Equality of educational opportunity.* Washington, DC: U.S. Government Printing Office.

Department of Labor. (2004). *The department of labor's 2004 findings on the worst forms of child labor.* Report prepared by the United States Department of Labor, Bureau of International Affairs, Washington, DC. http://www.dol.gov/ILAB/media/reports/iclp/tda2004/overview.htm

Fuller, B., & Clarke, P. (1994). Raising school effects while ignoring culture? *Review of Educational Research, 64*(1), 119–157.

Fuller, B., & Rubinson, R. (Eds). (1992). *The political construction of education: The state, school expansion, and economic change.* New York: Praeger.

Hannum, E., & Buchmann, C. (2005). Global educational expansion and socio-economic development: An assessment of findings from the social sciences. *World Development, 33*(3), 333–354.

Heyneman, S. P. (2005). Student background and student achievement: What is the right question? *American Journal of Education, 112*(1), 1–9.

Heyneman, S. P., & Loxley, W. A. (1982). Influences on academic-achievement across high and low income countries – a reanalysis of IEA data. *Sociology of Education, 55*(1), 13–21.

Heyneman, S. P., & Loxley, W. A. (1983). The effect of primary-school quality on academic-achievement across 29 high-income and low-income countries. *American Journal of Sociology, 88*(6), 1162–1194.

Kobiane, J., Calves, A. E., & Marcoux, R. (2005). Parental death and children's schooling in Burkina Faso. *Comparative Education Review*, 49(4), 468–489.

Lockheed, M., Fuller, B., & Nyirongo, R. (1989). Family effects on student achievement in Thailand and Malawi. *Sociology of Education*, 62, 239–256.

Offer, S. (2004). The socio-economic integration of the Ethiopian community in Israel. *International Migration*, 42(3), 29–55.

Siddiqi, F., & Patrinos, H. A. (n.d.) *Child labor: Issues, causes and interventions.* World Bank HCO Working Paper 56. Washington, DC: World Bank. http://www.worldbank.org/html/extdr/hnp/hddflash/workp/wp_00056.html

Thomas, G., Meyer, J., Ramirez, F., & Boli, J. (Eds) (1987). *Institutional structure: Constituting state, society, and the individual.* Newbury Park, CA: Sage.

World Bank. (2001). *Child labor in Africa: Issues and challenges.* World Bank Africa Region, knowledge and learning center report 194. Washington, DC: World Bank. http://www.worldbank.org/afr/findings/english/find194.pdf

COMMUNITY MATTERS IN CHINA

Jennifer H. Adams

ABSTRACT

In China, a growing awareness that many areas have been left behind during an era characterized by market reform has raised concerns about the impact of community disadvantage on schooling. In this paper, I investigate whether villages exert distinct influences on student achievement. Building on these results, I explore the relationship between student achievement and resources present in the community. Results indicate that children who live in communities with higher levels of economic and social resources have higher mathematics scores, on average.

INTRODUCTION

In the past decade, educational policy trends around the globe, which have decentralized school finance, and management by shifting responsibilities from central governments to local communities and schools, have raised important questions about whether differences across communities might be linked with disparities in children's schooling (Bray, 1996a, b; Hanson, 2000). Local governments in many nations have become responsible for the provision and administration of basic education, and in turn, are expected to raise their own funds, hire their own teachers, and run local schools (Hanson, 2000; Patrinos & Lakshmanan, 1997; Bray, 1996a, 1996b). In this way, decentralization policies have fashioned community schools that are even more local – now tied to community economies, leadership, and social organizations (Cheng, 2001). The increasingly local nature of schooling is sometimes credited with increasing real national expenditures for education, inspiring educational innovation, and encouraging community involvement (Tsang, 1996; Bray, 1996a, 1996b; Eskeland & Filmer, 2002). But this praise must be tempered by evidence from some nations, such as China, that shows concurrent increases in educational inequality (Tsang, 1996, 2003; Park, Li, & Wang, 2003).

In China, there is a growing awareness that many areas have been left behind during an era characterized by market reform, which has raised concerns about the impact of community disadvantage on schooling (West & Wong, 1995; Ross & Lin, 2002; Adams, 2001; Adams & Hannum, 2005). In recent years, researchers have linked community economic indicators to tangible measures of education, such as enrollment and the provision of schools (Connelly & Zheng, 2003; Adams, 2001; Park et al., 2003; Hannum, 2003). Evidence has also established a connection between both province and county-level economic conditions and local investment in education (Park et al., 2003). Moreover, recent research indicates that both local revenue and community donations vary across provinces, within provinces, and sometimes even within counties (Park et al., 2003; Tsang, 2003). While researchers have successfully documented the extent of variation in community financial resources available for schooling in China, little is known about whether differences in these economic resources directly influence student achievement. Moreover, the connection between social conditions in the community and local schooling is poorly understood.

This paper examines the links between community conditions and student achievement in one rural interior province in China. In it I address the following questions: First, after controlling for child background, does student achievement depend on where the child lives? Second, do children who live in villages with better economic and social conditions achieve more? If so, does the effect of social conditions differ depending on the economic resources available in the community?

I begin by describing a framework for understanding the effect of community conditions on schooling. Next I describe educational reform during the decentralization era in China, in order to provide a backdrop for a synthesis of studies that have linked dimensions of communities and educational outcomes in the Chinese context. This is followed by a presentation of my data and methodological approach, an analysis of the data, and an interpretation of findings.

The results of this study clarify our understanding of the linkages between where children live and their achievement in school, not only by connecting community conditions with local student achievement empirically, but also by identifying specific dimensions of communities that influence achievement. As educational policies focused on decentralization intermingle with the financial limitations of an economy in transition, research that reveals significant geographic inequalities becomes increasingly important to policymakers, in China and abroad, who are concerned with reducing educational inequality and improving the quality of schooling in poor areas.

BACKGROUND AND CONTEXT

The Importance of Place: Understanding the Effect of Communities on Schooling

In the last decade, several researchers have linked the socioeconomic and structural differences across communities with the individual outcomes of the children who live in them (Duncan, 1994; Dornbusch, Ritter, & Steinberg, 1991; Garner & Raudenbush, 1991). Even more notable is research that suggests that the influence of communities on children's social welfare is *separate* from family characteristics. For example, Ho and Willms' (1996) study of eighth graders in the United States found that parental participation measured at the school level had a positive effect on student achievement, net of individual parental participation, indicating that even those children whose parents did not participate in school activities achieved higher scores when they went to a school where a greater percentage of community parents were involved. Similarly, using data from the National Education Longitudinal Study (NELS), Pong (1998) also found that strong social networks within a school positively affected mathematics achievement. Strikingly, one study of adolescent females in the Panel Study of Income Dynamics suggested that neighborhood effects on school leaving sometimes rivaled the influence of family characteristics (Brooks-Gunn, Duncan, Klebanov, & Sealand, 1993).

Research also demonstrates that community economic indicators – such as mean community income and the percentage of families in poverty – exert distinct effects on student achievement (Duncan, 1994). In the United States, several researchers found that the presence of affluent neighbors is a significant predictor of school leaving (Brooks-Gunn et al., 1993; Clark, 1992). In addition, Dornbusch et al. (1991) found that low neighborhood socioeconomic status has a negative effect on student grades, even after controlling for individual family background. Similarly, Binder (1999) explains that average community earnings are a significant predictor of desired schooling in Mexico. Corman's (2003) study uses data from four waves of the National Household Education Survey to provide evidence that community wealth decreases the probability of grade repetition for U.S. students ages 6–15. Children in richer neighborhoods are less likely to repeat a grade than children living in poorer neighborhoods. In short, one of the most clearly established sources of community disadvantage is economic constraints present in the community.

International studies have documented that schools in many communities are constrained by local financing (Bray, 1996a, 1996b; Tsang, 1994). In many nations, communities are required to raise funds for schooling to supplement the inadequate funds provided by national governments (Bray, 1996a, 1996b). However, faced with a weak tax-base, many local governments in poor communities are unable to adequately finance their local schools (Bray, 1996a, 1996b). Accordingly, resource-constrained local schools must rely increasingly upon local sources of funds generated by community donations, revenue from school businesses, and student fees (Cheng, 1994; Ross, 1999; Hannum & Park, 2002). Often, poor communities are unable to pay teacher salaries, provide school supplies, or fund the costs of basic amenities such as heat and water (Tsang, 1994; Cheng, 1996). In many countries, as the burden of raising school funds falls increasingly on local communities, local economic resources are likely to become increasingly important determinants of local school quality.

In more recent investigations of community effects, primarily in the United States, scholars have extended their explorations of the role community resources play in shaping educational advantage and disadvantage beyond issues of local economics, to consider the social contexts in which children learn. For example, Stanton-Salázar and Dornbusch's (1995) investigation of Mexican high school students in the San Francisco area revealed a positive correlation between social networks and academic achievement. Similarly, in their study of at-risk youth, Furstenberg and Hughes (1995) find that social capital, broadly defined, is positively associated with socioeconomic success in early adulthood. Coleman and Hoffer (1987) also credit differences in the social capital of the communities surrounding schools with the extant differences in student achievement that we observe between public and Catholic schools.

In explaining how the presence of social capital might influence student performance in school, Coleman (1988) contributed the concept of "intergenerational closure," or the relationship of an individual student's parents with their children's friends' parents. Coleman explains that when parents are in relationships with other parents, they are more likely to exchange information that may foster children's schooling. The following example illustrates how intergenerational closure may operate. Suppose two students develop a plan to avoid studying for a test: one student tells her mother she is studying at the other child's home and vice versa. Instead of studying, the two students are actually at a third child's home listening to a new CD. However, if the children's parents know each other and communicate regularly, the children's ruse will be uncovered quickly – perhaps even in time for their parents to get the children to study for the test. In this way, intergenerational closure helps parents garner the information needed to enforce norms and shape expectations about schooling.

The results from empirical examinations linking intergenerational closure with educational outcomes have been mixed. Consistent with the illustration provided, Sandefur and Lauman (1998) found that information about their children's efforts and successes at school can help parents influence their children to engage with school. Similarly, using the 1988 NELS data, Carbonaro (1998) found that intergenerational closure is positively associated with both student math achievement and school retention. However, a more recent investigation of the 1988 NELS data that treats social capital as a collective asset indicates that intergenerational closure in public schools is negatively associated with gains in mathematics achievement, when controlling for friendship density (Morgan & Sørenson, 1999). These researchers argue that it is friendships between students, rather than parents of students, that positively influence learning.

Taken as a whole, the existing literature on community effects suggests that the differences in educational outcomes across communities may arise from various characteristics and processes operating at the community level. First, local economic resources influence enrollment, attainment, and achievement. The reviewed research emphasizes that it is not only the economic resources at home that matter, but also the average wealth of the surrounding families. Community economic resources may influence educational outcomes by shaping the quality of local schooling. In addition, community wealth affects the quality of after-school activities available to community youth – activities that may also affect aspirations, effort, and learning. Second, the extent and quality of community social relationships influence the ways communities shape expectations, share information, and enforce rules. In this way, communities with more social resources are more likely to influence student behavior and beliefs both in and out of the classroom.[1]

Educational Reform During Decentralization Era in China

Nearly two decades of decentralization reforms have made China an informative case study for investigating the relationship between community resources and schooling. The shift of financial responsibilities from the central government to local levels was the foundation of the country's decentralization reforms in education (Cheng, 1996). Based on the *Decision on the Reform of the Educational Structure* in 1985, local governments were given the responsibility for raising and spending educational revenue. In practice, the state retained control of curriculum and teacher development, but withdrew its financial and administrative commitments. This decision was strengthened by several educational policies published in the 1990s, which reaffirmed the state's commitment to a more decentralized system with a more diversified resource base.[2] Typically, provincial governments are now responsible for the provision of higher education, county governments finance and manage secondary schools, and villages pay for and run primary schools.

As a result of these policies, local governments were required not only to raise their own funds for schools, but also to mobilize nongovernmental and community resources. First, schools were encouraged to set up school-run enterprises, such as orchards, bakeries, or bicycle repair shops. By 1993, school-run enterprises were generating 5.4% of the total national expenditure on education (Tsang, 1996). Next, schools were encouraged to solicit social contributions from local citizens and businesses. And finally, many schools made up the difference between their revenue and costs by charging a variety of school fees (Paine, 1998; Bray, 1996a, 1996b; Tsang, 1994). In this way, decentralization may be responsible for the increasingly local nature of Chinese schooling, now tied to local economies and social organizations.

Community Resources and Schooling in Rural China

Not surprisingly, scholars who study schooling in China have also discovered connections between economic resource constraints in the community and educational disadvantage (World Bank, 1992; Connelly & Zheng, 2003; Adams & Hannum, 2005). Connelly and Zheng (2003) demonstrate that school enrollment is directly linked to county per capita income. Furthermore, their results indicate that community circumstances affect enrollment even when family background is taken into account. Adams' (2001) examination of children in the China Health and Nutrition Survey in the early

1990s reveals a positive relationship between village wealth and enrollment. Adams and Hannum's (2005) analysis of China Health and Nutrition Survey data through the 1990s illustrates that village infrastructure is also important in the provision of social services. Perhaps more telling, children who live in communities where village enterprises contribute financial resources to schools are always more likely to be enrolled in school. Although this research empirically links community resources and education in rural China, it is limited by both an emphasis on enrollment probabilities and a narrow definition of community conditions.

Few studies have sought to link local economic differences to children's experiences once they are in school. Policies that have emphasized both financial decentralization and the expansion of compulsory education, taken together with data limitations, have prompted researchers to focus on enrollment as a primary outcome of interest. In recent years, some researchers have widened the scope of their investigations by exploring the connections between community resources and a more complex outcome, grade-for-age student attainment (Adams, 2001; Adams & Hannum, 2005).

Another strand of research focuses on the connection between community differences and indicators of school quality, such as educational expenditure. For example, Park, Li, and Wang's study (2003) of school equity in rural China reveals that village income per capita is positively associated with both the percentage of qualified teachers in the village and the percentage of students with desks and chairs. Yet, their research falls short of establishing how these differences across villages affect what children learn in school. A knowledge gap exists concerning the influence that communities exert on achievement once children are enrolled in village schools. A more detailed understanding of the ways in which local community resources affect student achievement is particularly needed now, as school enrollment rates rise in China's poor interior and educational policy refocuses on issues of quality.

Even less well established are the particular facets of communities that influence children's experiences in school. Previous research in the Chinese context has linked general indicators of economic development, such as village per capita income or the presence of electricity to improved educational outcomes (Adams, 2001; Adams & Hannum, 2005). However, this work is limited by a narrow definition of community that captures only the most basic economic characteristics in a village and overlooks the social resources available for cultivating education. Two notable exceptions are Connelly and Zheng (2003), who constructed a variable to represent community norms for education, and the qualitative investigations of Ross and Lin (2006, in this volume), who reveal the importance of communities' ability to use social networks to bring together resources to support local schools.

On this foundation, individuals in some villages may benefit from the existence of community norms that support education. For example, in some communities, pressure to enforce child labor laws could encourage children to stay in school and work hard rather than to drop out and seek employment. Connelly and Zheng (2003) found that positive community norms for education, as measured by the proportion of village children in school, positively affected educational outcomes for children in the village. Similarly, some villages have links to social organizations in other communities that they use to generate both financial and human resources for local schools (Ross & Lin, 2006). For instance, rural schools that have relationships with schools in more prosperous areas sometimes "borrow" qualified teachers for a term to improve the skills of local teachers (Lee & Li, 1994). In this way, the strength of social networks – both within and outside some communities – may contribute to the sharing of information or behavior that furthers student achievement.

The current study addresses some of the limitations of previous research and makes several new contributions to scholarly understanding of the influence of community resources on schooling in rural China. First, this is the first study of rural China that links differences across communities with variation in student achievement, rather than enrollment or attainment. Second, by utilizing village and school-level data, I extend my analysis beyond basic indicators of village economic level to the actual differences in school revenue garnered within the village. Third, drawing on social capital theory and specifically Coleman's concept of intergenerational closure, I test empirically whether social relationships in the community matter for student achievement. Each of the above contributions is possible because of a rich data set collected during the summer of 2000 in rural Gansu Province, China.

DATA AND METHODOLOGICAL APPROACH

Data: Gansu Survey of Children and Families

To examine community influences on children's schooling outcomes in rural China, I use data from the Gansu Survey of Children and Families (GSCF-1), a multi-level survey of children aged 9–12, which was conducted during the summer of 2000 in 100 villages in Gansu province. Gansu, located in

China's northwest, embodies the geographic diversity and poor economic conditions that characterize China's interior provinces. Poverty rates are high and economic growth is slow (Gansu Statistics Yearbook, 2001). Although rural industries have slowly emerged, for the most part, residents are employed in subsistence farming. The average annual per capita income of rural residents was only 63% of the national average in 2000 (Gansu Statistics Yearbook, 2001). The illiteracy rate, approximately 14%, is more than double the national average in China (Gansu Statistics Yearbook, 2001).

Most children in Gansu attend primary school in their village. Provincial educational statistics indicate that nearly 99% of school-aged children are enrolled in school (Gansu Educational Statistics Yearbook, 2000). However, this figure masks the numerous children who start school late and drop out early. Many children leave school because of health problems or financial constraints, only to enroll again another time. Poor families often lack the resources to pay school fees (Hannum & Park, 2002; Bray, Ding, & Huang, 2004). In addition, persistent poverty negatively affects children's health and nutrition, and in turn, their ability to regularly attend and learn in school.[3] Moreover, in some communities, children leave school because of general attitudes toward schooling. For example, if enrollment rates in a particular community are generally low, families who do not choose to send their children to school are not considered unusual, and in turn, are not pressured by other village members to support schooling (Bray et al., 2004).

In this setting, schools also reflect poverty. While most rural villages have a local primary school, many rural villages lack the capacity to raise the funds required to adequately finance education. Funds collected locally, including student fees, pay for nearly all school expenses (Bray et al., 2004). Many teachers in Gansu have little training or access to professional support. Even more alarming, it is common for teacher wages to be three months late.

The GSCF-1 examines children's schooling, achievement, and welfare in the context of rural poverty by integrating a primary sample of 2000 children with secondary samples of children's mothers, homeroom teachers, school principals, and village leaders. In addition, a teacher questionnaire was administered to all teachers in schools attended by sample children; providing a sample of more than 1,000 primary school teachers. A multistage cluster sample was drawn, selecting counties, townships, villages, and finally, school-aged children in selected villages. Achievement tests in mathematics or Chinese language, designed by specialists at the Gansu Educational Commission, were administered to all children in the sample. On a random basis, half of the children were administered the mathematics examination; the remaining half were administered the Chinese language examination. Different exams were administered to children in grades 3 and below and to children in grades 4 and above, to ensure that the tests assessed an appropriate range of knowledge.

Analytic Sample

This study used an analytic sample of 436 students in grades 1–3, all of whom were given the mathematics exam. All of the students also attended school in their own village.[4] This sample was chosen to address both methodological and substantive concerns. First, I limit the study to the children who were administered the mathematics exam.[5] Within this group of students, some of the students were administered the math exam for children in grades 1–3, and some were given the exam for grades 4 and above. Accordingly, I exclude the children in grades 4 and above. Next, in an attempt to find out more about whether community resources influence schooling at the local village school, I limited the sample in two additional ways. I excluded villages with more than one primary school.[6] I also restricted the sample to children who attended school in their own village.[7] Children who were enrolled at boarding schools or attended a school in another village were not included in the sample.

Measurement

This investigation focuses on a subset of questionnaire items that measure individual level and village level characteristics. The data was collected through questionnaires administered to the children, their mothers, the village leaders, and also through village primary school instruments.

Table 1 presents descriptive statistics for all variables included in the analyses. The student level data consists of controls for the children's socioeconomic background and other factors that are hypothesized to affect learning. The village level data include variables detailing the economic and social resources in the village, as well as controls for village population and topography. Table 1 also contains data on student mathematics achievement.

This paper examines the effect of community on children's achievement in mathematics as measured by a test developed by the Gansu Educational Commission. The test, which was scored on a scale of 0–100, was developed to examine an appropriate range of the primary school curriculum for students in first, second, and third grades. The mathematics exam scores in the

Table 1. Descriptive Statistics for 436 1st, 2nd, and 3rd Graders in 85 Villages in Gansu Province, China.

Variable	Mean	Standard Deviation	N
OUTCOME VARIABLE			
MATH (Grades 1–3)	42.44	(27.92)	436
STUDENT-LEVEL CONTROL VARIABLES			
GRADE 1	0.14	(0.34)	436
GRADE 2	0.38	(0.49)	436
GRADE 3	0.48	(0.50)	436
AGE	10.04	(0.95)	436
AGE-SQUARED	101.77	(19.48)	436
GENDER (FEMALE = 0, MALE = 1)	0.51	(0.50)	436
LOG FAMILY WEALTH	8.95	(0.94)	436
DAYS ABSENT	0.32	(1.04)	436
BOOKS	17.82	(14.95)	436
VILLAGE-LEVEL CONTROL VARIABLES			
VILLAGE POPULATION	1574.62	(796.13)	85
TOPOGRAPHY (HILLY = 1)	0.20	(0.40)	85
LOG GOVT PER PUPIL EXP.	1.08	(1.51)	85
VILLAGE-LEVEL PREDICTOR VARIABLES			
LOG NONGOVT PER PUPIL EXP	1.52	(1.52)	85
VILLAGE SOCIAL CAPITAL (0–1)	0.73	(0.20)	85

Source: GSCF-1, 2000.

analytic sample range from 0 to 99, with an average score of 42.44. As expected, the average score for second grade students of 29.91 is higher than the average score for first grade students of 15.54. Similarly, the mean score for third graders of 59.64 was higher than scores for students in grades one and two.

Child background measures included as controls include a categorical variable for grade level, and the children's ages, which range from 7 to 13. Because previous research findings reveal that girls may experience more constraints to schooling in rural China (Hannum, 1998; Zhang, 1998), I also include student gender (coded 0 if female and 1 if male) as a control predictor. As indicated in Table 1, 49% of the analytic sample, or 214 students, are female. Family wealth is also included as a control predictor, because of previous research that connects financial resources in the home to schooling in rural China (Brown and Park, 2003; Adams, 2001). The sample average value for the log of family wealth is 8.95, and this variable has a standard deviation of 0.94.

In addition, I include two predictors to control for children's opportunity to learn. The first is the variable, absent, that captures the number of days a child has missed school during the previous semester. The average number of days absent in the sample is less than one, indicating that many students do not miss much schooling at all. However, as suggested by a standard deviation that is more than three times as large as the mean, there is large variation in days absent across children. For the students who have missed school during the semester, the number of days absent ranges from 1 to 8. These absences may limit children's opportunity to learn, and in turn, influence their achievement. I also control for the number of books that the family purchased that semester, as an indicator of support for education in the home. Books in the home can be regarded as a form of cultural capital in the family. Hannum and Park (2001) found that the presence of books in the home supports the child's educational aspirations and academic confidence.

Table 1 also contains descriptive statistics on the village-level variables selected to control for the effect of community when estimating differences in student achievement in mathematics. In this study, I control for both village population and village topography. Finally, the majority of village primary schools do not receive financing from the government; rather, they rely completely on financial resources collected at the village level. In my analytic sample, 32 schools (less than half) received some funding from the government.[8] I control for the presence of these funds by including the log of per pupil expenditure from government funds as a predictor in my analyses. The untransformed version of this variable varies widely, ranging from 1 to 125 yuan.

Most importantly, Table 1 also presents descriptive statistics on two carefully selected village-level question predictor variables – economic resources and social resources. Based on research findings that suggest the increasing importance of community economic resources for local schools (Adams, 2001; Adams & Hannum, 2005; Park et al., 2003; Tsang, 2003), I use the log of per pupil expenditure from nongovernmental or extrabudgetary resources to represent community economic resources.[9] Park, Li, and Wang's research (2003) indicates that extrabudgetary financing increased during the mid- and late-1990s.

To capture the effect of social resources in the community, I draw on the work of James Coleman (1988, 1991) in creating a variable to represent "community closure." Coleman identified the concept of "intergenerational closure," which can be defined as the relationship of an individual student's parents with the parents of their children's friends. In the Gansu Survey of Children and Families, mothers were asked if they knew the parents of their children's friends. I use the average response of mothers in the village to this question to capture "the community closure" in the village. This variable ranges from 0 to 1, with villages that score closer to 0 having less social capital and villages with scores closer to 1 having more social capital. As displayed in Table 1, the average score is 0.73. In communities with more social capital, more parents know the parents of their children's friends, and as a result can garner information about school-related matters, shape and share behavioral norms, and monitor child behavior.

Analytic Strategy

The following analysis presents figures accompanied by regression analyses of student math achievement. In the first set of fitted regression models presented in this paper, I use a fixed effects analysis to examine whether there is an overall relationship between student mathematics achievement and the village in which the student lives, net of family poverty and other individual characteristics. After controlling for selected child and family characteristics, I ask whether children who live in some villages in Gansu have higher mathematics achievement than children who live in other villages, on average. To conduct this fixed effects analysis, I regress the student mathematics outcome on a system of 85 dummy variables, V_1 through V_{85}, representing the 85 different villages in the analytic sample, controlling for individual-level variables. In this model, each group of children who live in the same village shares a unique intercept parameter or "village fixed effect." An examination of the heterogeneity among these distinct intercepts indicates whether villages differ in students' mathematics achievement, on average, controlling for child background. The hypothesized fixed-effects model is as follows:

$$\text{MATH}_{ij} = \beta_1 V_1 \ldots + \beta_{85} V_{85} + \delta Z + \varepsilon_{ij}$$

for the ith student in the jth village. Regression parameters β_1 through β_{85} represent the main effects of the village fixed effects, and the δ coefficient represents the effect of the vector of control variable, Z, and ε is the usual regression residual. I fit this model to my data using OLS multiple regression analysis to estimate and test model parameters. I begin by estimating the model containing only the student-level control predictors. Next, I estimate a model containing the system of village dummies. I compare models on the overall goodness of fit, using the R^2 statistic. Additionally, I use a general linear hypothesis test to test a joint null hypothesis that the regression parameters, β_1 through β_{85}, the village fixed-effects, were simultaneously equal. Rejecting this joint null hypothesis will indicate that the community where a child lives does affect math achievement, and consequently sets the stage for a second phase of the analysis in which I investigate what kind of community characteristics affect the village effects.

In the second set of hypothesized regression models, I explore the effect of community economic and social resources on student mathematics achievement by replacing the fixed effects of village by their equivalent random effects, and including selected predictors that describe the presence of community level resources in a new taxonomy of fitted regression models. In these analyses, I ask, on average, do children who live in villages with higher levels of economic and social resources have higher math achievement, controlling for child background? I fit these models using GLS regression analysis in order to account for the random effects of village now residing in the residuals. I use GLS regression and a multi-level model because standard OLS regression analysis does not account naturally for the nesting of the students within village. An examination of the estimated coefficients associated with each of the community-level main effects then indicates whether the selected community resources influence mathematics achievement in Gansu, net of child background. An example of a typical random effects model is

$$MATH_{ij} = \gamma_{00} + \gamma_{01}VILPOP_j + \gamma_{02}VILTOP_j + \gamma_{03}LGOVPPE_j$$
$$+ \gamma_{04}LNGOVPPE_j + \gamma_{05}CLOSURE_j + \gamma_{10}LWEALTH_{ij}$$
$$+ \gamma_{20}AGE_{ij} + \gamma_{30}AGESQ_{ij} + \gamma_{40}GENDER_{ij}$$
$$+ \gamma_{50}GRADE2_{ij} + \gamma_{60}GRADE3_{ij} + \gamma_{80}BOOKS_{ij} + u_j + \varepsilon_{ij}$$

where MATH is the math achievement score for the ith child in the jth village. γ_{00} represents the estimated average math score in the population provided all variables are centered on their grand mean, $\gamma_{01}, \gamma_{02}, \gamma_{03} \ldots$ are regression parameters representing the main effects of community level predictors on student achievement, and $\gamma_{10}, \gamma_{20}, \gamma_{30} \ldots$ are the regression parameters associated with individual level control variables. Residual ε is the unique error term associated with student i in village j and u is a random effect, representing the common unobserved characteristics that distinguish village j.

I begin by fitting the model containing the student-level controls. Next, I fit several models that include predictor variables that represent community economic and social resources. Models are compared on overall goodness of fit, using the R^2 statistic. A statistically significant and positive coefficient associated with any of the community-level variables ($\gamma_{01}, \gamma_{02}, \gamma_{03} \ldots$) demonstrates that children who live in villages with higher levels of that particular community characteristic are associated with higher mathematics scores, on average, taking into account the other community and individual characteristics in the model.

Then, I fit a final model to examine the interaction between village economic resources and village social resources. A statistically significant coefficient on the interaction term reveals that the effect of social resources on student mathematics achievement differs according to the economic resources present in the village. For example, the effect of social capital may be more pronounced in villages with less economic resources. Alternatively, the coefficient on the interaction term may not be significant, indicating that the effect of social and economic resources may be additive.

RESEARCH FINDINGS

The average mathematics exam scores in the analytic sample is 42.44. The scores vary widely, as suggested by the range from 0 to 99 and a standard deviation of nearly 28. Fig. 1 provides a schematic plot illustrating variation in average unadjusted village mathematics scores by grade. Not surprisingly, the figure suggests that average math scores vary widely across villages even when we take grade into account. For example, average village mathematic scores range across 83 points for first and second graders, and 86 points for third graders. An examination of the interquartile ranges for students in grades one, two, and three also illustrates the extent of the variation in average mathematics scores across villages. For first graders, the middle 50% of average village mathematics scores also spread widely, falling between 26 points of each other, from approximately 3 to 29 points. Among second and third grade students, the interquartile range is not as large, or approximately 23 points, as among first graders, yet it continues to demonstrate ample variation in average village mathematics scores.

In order to determine whether there is an overall relationship between student mathematics achievement and the village in which the student lives, we now turn to regression analysis, and examine the fixed effects of villages on student mathematics achievement.

Examining Mathematics Achievement Across Rural Villages in Gansu: Does it Matter Where a Child Lives?

Table 2 displays the parameter estimates for a selection of fitted models predicting the influence of where a child lives on student mathematics

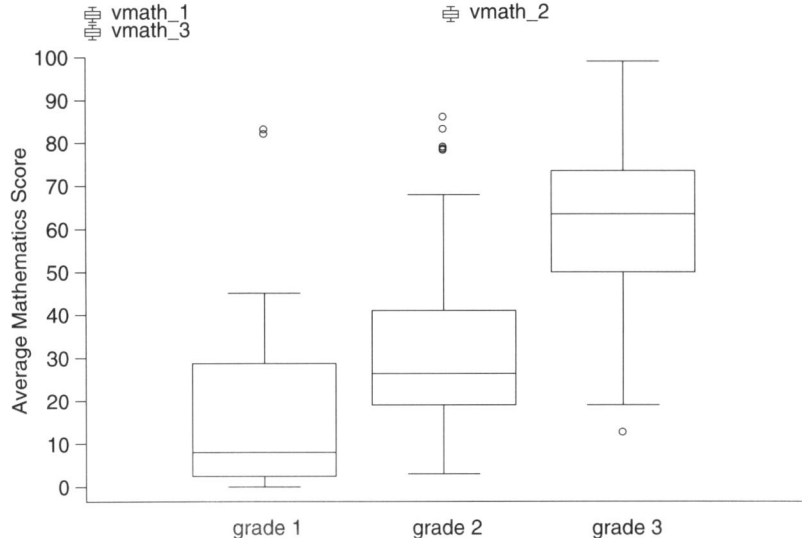

Fig. 1. Variation in Village Mathematic Achievement, Represented by Village-Specific Intercepts (n village = 85, n students = 436).

achievement, controlling for child socioeconomic background, days absent from school, and the number of books purchased that semester.

Model 1 controls only for the individual characteristics of the student. This fitted model suggests that the only statistically significant student level predictor of math achievement included in the fitted model represents the student's grade in school. In addition, in this model, approximately 40% of the variation in mathematics achievement is predicted by the student level characteristics, leaving a substantial portion of the variation unexplained.

Model 2 presents the results of a fixed effects regression analysis in which student mathematics achievement is predicted by a system of dummy variables representing villages, controlling for student background and other individual characteristics. Most of the student-level control predictors that represent student socioeconomic background continue to show the same relationship as in fitted Model 1. In addition, however, the results in Model 2 suggest that student mathematics achievement depends on both school attendance and books purchased in the last semester. All else being equal, each day a student was absent in the last semester is associated with a decline of 2.1 points in the mathematics test score, on average. Like students

Table 2. Regression of Student Mathematics Achievement on Socioeconomic Controls and Village Fixed Effects (n students $= 436$; n villages $= 85$).

	Model 1		Model 2	
STUDENT-LEVEL SOCIOECONOMIC CONTROL PREDICTORS				
GRADE 2	14.381***		17.187***	
GRADE 3	44.988***		48.716***	
AGE	−20.910		0.848	
AGE-SQUARED	0.999		−0.048	
GENDER	−0.680		−0.013	
LOG FAMILY WEALTH	1.884		1.537	
DAYS ABS	−0.569		−2.159*	
BOOKS	0.061		0.158*	
VILLAGE FIXED EFFECTS				
VILLAGE 1			32.624**	
VILLAGE 2			36.283***	
VILLAGE 3			33.086**	
VILLAGE 4			37.997***	
VILLAGE 5			13.127	
VILLAGE 6			13.544	
VILLAGE 7			11.359	
VILLAGE 8			51.378***	
....				
VILLAGE 78			18.395	
VILLAGE 79			25.007	
VILLAGE 80			25.110*	
VILLAGE 81			54.984***	
VILLAGE 82			46.383***	
VILLAGE 83			53.133***	
VILLAGE 84			55.739***	
Goodness of fit	R^2	0.416	R^2 within	0.545
			R^2 between	0.249
			R^2 overall	0.409
			Test of equality of VILLAGE coefficients	$F_{84,343} = 4.12$***

Source: GSCF-1, 2000.
*$p<0.05$.
**$p<0.01$.
***$p<0.001$.

who usually attend school, children who have purchased more books in the last semester are likely to have higher mathematics achievement. Perhaps most importantly, all else being equal, the village in which a child lives influences his or her mathematics score.

But what is the magnitude of the differences in average mathematics achievement across villages? After controlling for the effect of student background, I found that the estimated variance of the estimated village fixed effects is 239.5. However, to provide a more reliable estimate of the magnitude of these differences, I need to take into account measurement error in the village-specific fixed effects displayed in Table 2.[10] After controlling for student background and adjusting for measurement error, I found that the estimated variance of the true village effects is 153.1. Thus, one standard deviation difference in the true village effects is associated with an estimated difference in student mathematics achievement of approximately 12 points. These results support my hypothesis that where a child lives matters, and suggest that differences in village level characteristics influence student mathematics achievement. In the next section, I investigate whether economic and social resources in the village affect individual student achievement.

Do Children Who Live in Communities With Higher Levels of Economic and Social Resources Achieve Higher Mathematics Scores?

In the fitted models presented in Table 3, I replaced the village fixed effects present in the previous taxonomy of models with their equivalent random effects, and added selected predictors to represent village characteristics to the regression models. I continued to control for the individual characteristics of the child and also take into account the village population, village topography, and per pupil expenditure from government funds.

In Model 3, I include the log of per pupil expenditure from nongovernmental or extrabudgetary resources to represent community economic resources. The coefficient on this variable indicates that students who live in villages that have higher per pupil expenditures from extrabudgetary, or locally generated, resources have higher mathematics scores, on average, controlling for student characteristics and other village characteristics with the exception of village social capital. The coefficient on the log of per pupil expenditure from nongovernmental funds in Model 5, which controls for village social capital, is only slightly different from the coefficient in Model 3, indicating that this measure of village economic resources exerts a distinct influence on student achievement, and operates separately from the effect of the measure of village social resources.

Models 4 and 5 display the effect of village social capital as measured by "community closure." The coefficient on this variable in Model 4 indicates that on average, children who live in villages with higher levels of social

Table 3. Regression of Student Mathematics Achievement on Socioeconomic Controls, Village Controls, and Village Predictors (n students $= 436$; n villages $= 85$).

		Model 1	Model 2	Model 3	Model 4	Model 5	Model 6
STUDENT-LEVEL SOCIOECONOMIC CONTROL VARIABLES							
GRADE 2		16.645***	16.068***	15.713***	15.745***	15.347***	15.419***
GRADE 3		47.657***	47.460***	47.105**	46.856***	46.431***	46.546***
AGE		−8.412	−6.899	−5.615	−6.374	−4.986	−4.973
AGE-SQUARED		0.389	0.310	0.240	0.296	0.222	0.220
GENDER		0.020	−0.020	0.043	0.008	0.074	0.051
LOG FAMILY WEALTH		1.578	1.568	1.323	1.520	1.264	1.278
DAYS ABSENT		−1.632†	−1.558†	−1.498†	−1.652†	−1.601†	−1.630†
BOOKS		0.125†	0.126†	0.112†	0.122	0.108	0.110†
VILLAGE-LEVEL CONTROL VARIABLES							
L VIL POP			4.167	4.965†	5.018	5.827*	5.825*
VIL TOP			12.050**	14.339***	12.301***	14.481***	14.776***
LGOVPPE				0.996	−0.025	1.305	1.320
VILLAGE-LEVEL PREDICTOR VARIABLES							
LNGOVPPE				2.960**		2.895**	4.736
COMMUNITY CLOSURE					16.059*	16.147*	19.447*
INTERACTION							
LNGOVPPE*CLOSURE							−2.366
Goodness of fit	R^2 within	0.544	0.544	0.544	0.544	0.544	0.544
	R^2 between	0.256	0.326	0.374	0.367	0.415	0.416
	R^2 overall	0.412	0.444	0.467	0.459	0.481	0.481

Source: GSCF-1, 2000.
† <0.10.
*$p<0.05$.
**$p<0.01$.
***$p<0.001$.

capital, or where more mothers know the parents of her child's friends, children have higher mathematics scores, controlling for individual and village characteristics. The coefficient on community closure in Model 5, which also controls for a measure of village economic resources – namely the log of per pupil expenditure from nongovernmental funds – is nearly identical to the coefficient on this variable in Model 4, indicating that the effect of village social capital remains the same even when accounting for village economic resources.

The fitted models presented in Table 3 lead to two important findings. First, on average, children who live in communities that have a higher per pupil expenditure from nongovernmental resources have higher mathematics achievement, net of controls. Similarly, children who live in villages with a higher level of community closure, i.e., where more parents know the parents of their children's friends, have higher mathematics scores, on average. These findings support my hypothesis that differences in economic and social resources at the community level partially explain the difference across villages in mathematics achievement.

The specific effects of village economic and social resources can be better appreciated in Fig. 2, which illustrates fitted math achievement as a function of per pupil expenditure from nongovernmental resources and community closure. In this plot, child background and other village level characteristics remain constant. The figure shows the estimated mathematics achievement for a female student, age 10, in grade 3, who has not been absent from school in the last semester, and who purchased the mean number of books during this period. She lives in a small village in the mountains or plains and her school, like many village primary schools, does not receive funding from

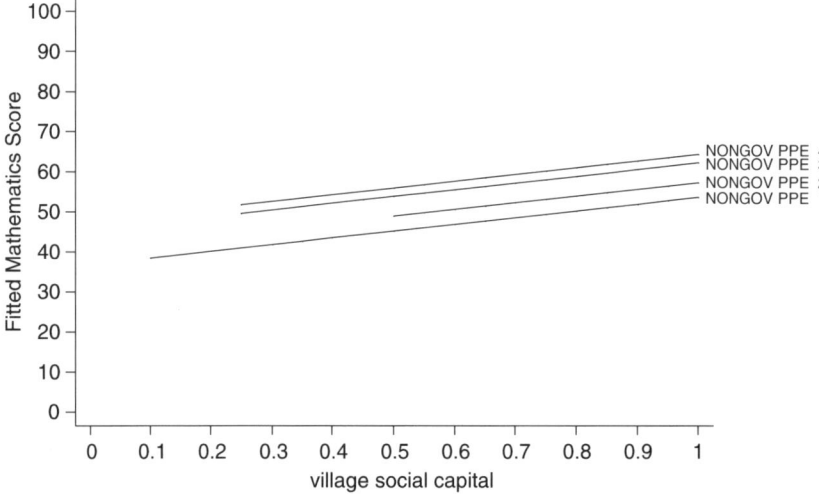

Fig. 2. Fitted Mathematics Achievement as a Function of Village School Per Pupil Expenditure Funded by Nongovernmental Resources and Village Social Capital for a Prototypical Female Student, Age 10, and is in Grade 3 (n students $= 436$, n villages $= 85$). (*The student has not been absent from school in the last semester, and purchased the mean number of books during this period. She lives in a small village in the mountains or plains and her school, like many village primary schools, does not receive funding from the state*).

the state. Village social capital, as measured by community closure, is displayed on the horizontal axis with a scale of 0 to 1; villages that are closer to 1 have more social capital. The four sloping lines represent prototypical students in villages at the quartiles for per pupil expenditure from nongovernmental resources.

Fig. 2 shows that there is a positive relationship between village social capital and math achievement when per pupil expenditure is held constant. All else being equal, the data show that villages with more social capital have higher mathematics scores. For example, in a village with low per pupil expenditure from nongovernmental resources and low village social capital (0.3), a child could have an estimated math score of 42 points. If the same child lived in a village with average social capital (0.73), her score would be six points higher, and if she lived in a village with high levels of social capital it would be even higher.

The prototypical fitted plot in Fig. 2 also displays the effect of village economic resources. When we hold village social capital constant, the gaps between the sloping lines represent the effect of per pupil expenditure. For example, in a village where social capital is average (0.73), a child might have an estimated mathematics score of 48 points, net of other controls, if she lived in a village with low per pupil expenditure from nongovernmental resources. If the same child lived in the same type of village, but one with high (top quartile) per pupil expenditure, her estimated mathematics score would be 59 points, or a difference of 11 points between the poorest and wealthiest villages.

The effect of village resources is even more striking if we compare the differences in estimated mathematics achievement between a child who lives in a village with the highest levels of social and economic resources with a comparable child who lives in a village with the lowest levels of social and economic resources. The gap in estimated mathematics achievement is 21 points.

Does the Effect of Village Social Capital Differ Depending on the Economic Resources Available in the Community?

The final question posed in this paper examines whether the effect of village social capital operates differently on student mathematics achievement depending on the village economic resources. Model 6 in Table 3 sheds light on this hypothesis by interacting community closure with the per pupil expenditure from nongovernmental (i.e., community generated) funds. As displayed in Model 6, the coefficient associated with the interaction term is not significant, suggesting that the effect of village social capital, as measured by community closure, was not conditioned by the economic resources in the village. In other words, village social capital exerted the same effect on student mathematics achievement regardless of whether the student lived in a village with more or less economic resources.

DISCUSSION AND CONCLUSION

Community Matters: Where a Child Lives and the Resources Present in the Village Influence Student Achievement

The results presented in this paper reveal important new insights regarding the relationship between communities and schooling in rural China. One of the most striking findings is that where a child lives definitely affects student achievement. There are large differences across villages in average mathematics achievement. In addition, these analyses reveal that the differences in educational outcomes across communities arise, at least in part, from specific characteristics and processes operating at the village level. In other words, economic and social resources in the village influence student achievement.

More specifically, children who live in villages with higher per pupil expenditures from nongovernmental resources have higher mathematics scores, on average, even when taking individual background and other village characteristics into account. In this way, the economic resources available to spend on schooling in a particular village may influence educational outcomes by shaping school quality. This finding resonates with the concerns expressed by children and parents in rural Gansu during interviews. One child said that the problem with his school is that it did not have any money. He went on to explain, "Our village doesn't have any money, so there's no money to go to the school." Villages with more economic resources may have a higher percentage of qualified teachers working at the village school and a higher percentage of students with adequate materials for learning. In addition, community economic resources may also affect the quality of afterschool activities available for children in the community and may, in turn, indirectly shape student aspirations, effort, and attitudes about schooling.

An additional avenue of community influence is social relationships. These results indicate that net of child background and other village characteristics, children who were living in communities where a greater number of parents knew the parents of their children's friends had higher math scores, on average. It is important to note that it is probably not the actual friendships between parents that affect student achievement. Rather, children who live in this kind of community may be advantaged by the support, guidance, and common values created by these relationships among parents.

This finding also echoes the explanations provided by Gansu parents during interviews. When parents described their conversations with other parents, they talked about collaborating on common rules for their children, such as having the children finish all of their homework before they can play. In addition, they talked about how they should reprimand village children who did not follow these guidelines. One mother recounted the story of a time when one of her daughter's friends was not studying well or paying attention in class. The woman called the young girl to her house and told the child "to focus on studying and not to play too much ... or she would not test into junior high." In this way, social pressure from parents helps to promote behavior that may improve student achievement in some villages. Interestingly, this study's results indicate that in the case of rural China, the effect of village social and economic resources are additive rather than interactive. Village social capital effects did not vary according to the economic resources present in the village.

As in many other parts of the world, community matters for children's schooling in rural China. This paper demonstrates that village differences in the economic and social resources available to support local schools have consequences for the students who live in these communities and attend village schools. The decentralization of school funding and management has served to create schools that are increasingly local institutions, reflecting the economic and social resources of the communities they are a part of. As schools become more local, they also become more diverse, reflecting different levels of economic resources to draw on, different kinds of physical infrastructure to facilitate schooling, and different social resources to mobilize. Cross-community inequality is linked to the quality of village schools, and, ultimately, to student achievement.

NOTES

1. Despite the findings described above, the conclusion that communities "matter" is not reached without difficulty. One frequently argued problem when discussing community effects in the United States is that people are not randomly assigned to their neighborhood. Instead, similar types of people tend to choose or self-select into the same communities – the Tiebout process. However, this process of choice is less relevant in rural China where geographic mobility is restricted.

2. Please see Central Committee of the Community Party (1993), Education Law (Jiao yu fa) Beijing and Central Committee of the Community Party (1995), Education Law (Jiao yu fa) Beijing.

3. For example, many children in Gansu consume low levels of nutrients, which affect cognitive development, such as Vitamin A, iron, and zinc. See Emily Hannum and Albert Park, "Educating China's Rural Children in the 21st Century."

4. This sample size provides me with sufficient statistical power (>0.80) to detect small effects at the usual levels of Type I error (Light, Singer, & Willett, 1991).

5. Previous research indicates that mathematics is more sensitive to differences in school characteristics than language achievement. See Richard J. Murnane (1975), "The Impact of School Resources on Inner City Children."

6. For example, some communities have an incomplete primary school, serving children in grades 1–4, and a complete primary school, enrolling students in grades 1–6. Due to data limitations, I cannot determine how the village allocates financial resources between these schools. Eight villages were dropped from the sample because they had more than one village primary school. As a result, 47 children were excluded from the analytic sample.

7. China has a system of residency laws that require most children to attend schools in their official residences. However, most children walk to school, and so may attend school in a neighboring village if it is closer to their home. Similarly, some children attend boarding schools if their homes are so remote that they are unable to commute to school daily. Due to these circumstances, I excluded 16 children from the analysis.

8. The variable representing the funds received by village schools from the state (GOV) was missing for 31% of villages. I regressed 15 variables from the village and village school surveys on GOV. The R^2 statistic from the regression was 0.97, indicating that the variables included in the regression explain 97% of the variation in GOV. Given the high R^2 statistic, I decided that using the imputed values would result in estimates that were less biased than either excluding the cases with missing data or using the mean value of GOV to replace the missing values.

9. The variable representing the funds received by village schools from the villages, social organization, school's own revenue, and donations from students, teachers, and officials (NONGOV) was missing for 45.2% of villages. I regressed 27 variables from the village and village school surveys on NONGOV. The R^2 statistic from the regression was 0.88, indicating that the variables included in the regression explain 88% of the variation in NONGOV. Given the high R^2 statistic, I decided that using the imputed values would result in estimates that were less biased than either excluding the cases with missing data or using the mean value of NONGOV to replace the missing values.

10. In order to adjust for measurement error and estimate the variance of the true village effects, I fit a random-effects model, and found that the estimated variance of the true village effects is 153.1. I used a Breusch-Pagan Lagrangian Multiplier Test to test the null hypothesis that the variance of the true fixed-effects is zero. The estimated variance of the village fixed-effects is 239.5, which is considerably higher than the estimated true variance obtained from the random-effects model. Thus, the estimated reliability of the measurement of the village fixed-effects is 0.64.

ACKNOWLEDGMENTS

This research was generously funded by the Spencer Foundation. The author was supported while conducting this research by a Spencer Research and Training Grant. In addition, data collection for the Gansu Survey of Children and Families was supported by grants from The Spencer Foundation Small and Major Grants Programs.

REFERENCES

Adams, J. (2001). Educational opportunity and school finance reform in China: Is the right to education increasingly dependent on family income and community wealth? Paper presented at the annual meeting of the comparative and international education society, Washington, DC.

Adams, J., & Hannum, E. (2005). Children's social welfare in post-reform China: Access to health insurance and education, 1989–1997. *The China Quarterly, 181*, 100–121.

Binder, M. (1999). Community effects and desired schooling of parents and children in Mexico. *Economics of Education Review, 18*, 311–325.

Bray, M. (1996a). *Decentralization of education: Community financing*. Washington, DC: World Bank.

Bray, M. (1996b). *Counting the full cost: Parental and community financing of education in East Asia*. Washington, DC: World Bank.

Bray, M., Ding, X. H., & Huang, P. (2004). *Reducing the financial burden on poor households: Review of cost-reduction strategies in the Gansu basic education project*. Comparative Education Research Centre, Faculty of Education, University of Hong Kong.

Brooks-Gunn, J., Duncan, G., Klebanov, K., & Sealand, N. (1993). Do neighborhoods influence child and adolescent development? *American Journal of Sociology, 99*, 353–395.

Carbonaro, W. J. (1998). A little help from my friend's parents: Intergenerational closure and educational outcomes. *Sociology of Education, 71*, 295–313.

Central Committee of the Communist Party. (1985). *Decisions on the reform of the education structure (Guanyu jiaoyu tizhi gaige jueding)*. Beijing.

Central Committee of the Communist Party. (1993). *Education Law (1993 Jiaoyu fa)*. Beijing.

Central Committee of the Communist Party. (1995). *Education Law (1995 jiaoyu fa)*. Beijing.

Cheng, K. M. (1994). Education, decentralization, and regional disparity in China. In: G. Postiglione & W. O. Lee (Eds), *Social change and educational development: Mainland, China, Taiwan, and Hong Kong* (pp. 53–56). Hong Kong: Hong Kong Centre for Asian Studies, University of Hong Kong.

Cheng, K. M. (1996). *The quality of primary education: A case study of Zhejiang province, China*. Paris: International Institute for Educational Planning.

Cheng, K. M. (2001). Invited lecture at the Harvard conference on Chinese education. Cambridge, MA.

Clark, R. L. (1992). *Neighborhood effects on dropping out of school among teenage boys*. Washington, DC: Urban Institute Mimeograph.

Coleman, J. (1988). Social capital in the creation of human capital. *American Journal of Sociology, Supplement 94*, S95–S120.

Coleman, J. (1991). *Parental Involvement in Education*. Washington, DC: Educational Research and Improvement, U.S. Department of Education.
Coleman, J., & Hoffer, T. (1987). *Public and private high schools: The impact of communities*. New York: Basic.
Connelly, R., & Zheng, Z. (2003). Determinants of primary and middle school enrollment of 10–18 year-olds in China. *Economics of Education Review, 22*, 379–388.
Corman, H. (2003). The effects of state policies, individual characteristics, family characteristics, and neighborhood characteristics on grade repetition in the United States. *Economics of Education Review, 22*, 409–420.
Dornbusch, S. M., Ritter, L. P., & Steinberg, L. (1991). Community influences on the relation of family status to adolescent school performance: Differences between African Americans and non-Hispanic Whites. *American Journal of Education, 38*, 543–567.
Duncan, G. (1994). Families and neighbors as sources of disadvantage in the schooling decisions of White and Black adolescents. *American Journal of Education, 103*, 20–53.
Eskeland, G., & Filmer, D. (2002). *Autonomy, participation, and learning in Argentine schools: Findings and their implications for decentralization*. Washington, DC: World Bank.
Furstenberg, F., & Hughes, M. E. (1995). Social capital and successful development among at-risk youth. *Journal of Marriage and Family, 57*, 580–592.
Gansu Educational Statistics Yearbook. (2000).
Gansu Statistics Yearbook. (2001).
Garner, C., & Raudenbush, S. (1991). Neighborhood effects on educational attainment: A multilevel analysis. *Sociology of Education, 64*, 251–262.
Hannum, E. (1998). *Educational inequality: Hidden consequences of the reform era in rural China*. Unpublished doctoral dissertation, University of Michigan, Ann Arbor.
Hannum, E. (2003). Poverty and basic education in rural China: Villages, households, and girls' and boys' enrollment. *Comparative Education Review, 47*, 141–159.
Hannum, E., & Park, A. (2001). Families, classrooms, and educational engagement in rural Gansu, China. Paper presented at the conference on education reform in China, Harvard University, Cambridge, MA, July 2001.
Hannum, E., & Park, A. (2002). Educating China's rural children in the 21st century. *Harvard China Review, 3*, 8–14.
Hanson, M. (2000). Educational decentralization around the pacific rim. www1.worldbank.org/education/globaleducationreform/Hawkins.pdf, August 14, 2000.
Ho, E., & Willms, D. (1996). Effects of parental involvement on eighth-grade achievement. *Sociology of Education, 69*, 126–141.
Lee, W. O., & Li, Z. (1994). Education, development, and regional disparity in Guangzhou. In: G. Postiglione & W. O. Lee (Eds), *Social change and educational development: Mainland, China, Taiwan, and Hong Kong*. Hong Kong: Hong Kong Centre for Asian Studies, University of Hong Kong.
Light, R. J., Singer, J. D., & Willett, J. B. (1991). *By design: Planning research on higher education*. Cambridge, MA: Harvard University Press.
Morgan, S. L., & Sørenson, A. B. (1999). Parental networks, social closure, and mathematics learning: A test of Coleman's social capital explanation of school effects. *American Sociological Review, 64*, 661–681.
Murnane, R. J. (1975). *The impact of school resources on inner city children*. Cambridge, MA: Ballinger Publishing Company.

Paine, L. (1998). Making schools modern. In: A. Walder (Ed.), *Zouping in transition: The process of reform in rural north China*. Cambridge, MA: Harvard University Press.
Park, A., Li, W., & Wang. S. G. (2003). School equity in rural china. Paper presented at the international conference on educational reform in China, teachers college, Columbia University, New York, NY.
Patrinos, H., & Lakshmanan, D. (1997). *Decentralization of education: Demand side financing*. Washington, DC: World Bank.
Pong, S. L. (1998). The school compositional effect of single parenthood on 10th grade achievement. *Sociology of Education, 71*, 24–43.
Ross, H. (1999). History, memory, community service, and project hope: Reclaiming the social purposes of education for the Shanghai McTyeire school for girls. In: G. Petersen & R. Hayhoe (Eds), *Education and society in 20th century China*. Ann Arbor, MI: The University of Michigan.
Ross, H., & Lin, J. (2006). Social capital and Chinese school communities. *Research in Sociology of Education: Children's Lives and Schooling Across Societies, 15*, 43–70.
Sandefur, R., & Lauman, E. (1998). A paradigm for social capital. *Rationality and Society, 10*, 481–501.
Stanton-Salázar, R., & Dornbusch, S. (1995). Social capital and the reproduction of inequality: Information networks and Mexican origin high school students. *Sociology of Education, 68*(2), 116–135.
Tsang, M. (1994). Costs of education in China: Issues of resource mobilization, equality, equity, and efficiency. *Education Economics, 2*, 287–312.
Tsang, M. (1996). Financial reform of basic education in China. *Economics of Education Review, 15*, 423–444.
Tsang, M. (2003). Financial disparities and intergovernmental grants in compulsory education. Paper presented at the international conference on educational reform in China, Teachers College, Columbia University, New York, NY.
West, L., & Wong, C. (1995). Fiscal decentralization and growing regional disparities in China: Some evidence in the provision of social services. *Oxford Review of Economics, 11*, 7–85.
World Bank. (1992). *China: Strategies for reducing poverty in the 1990s*. Washington, DC: World Bank.
Zhang, Y. H. (1998). *Determinants of enrollment in basic education in China: Evidence from three provinces*. Unpublished doctoral dissertation, Harvard University, Cambridge, MA.

SOCIAL CAPITAL FORMATION THROUGH CHINESE SCHOOL COMMUNITIES

Heidi Ross and Jing Lin

ABSTRACT

We investigate how communities in China use schools to create and reproduce the values, knowledge, and social expectations that engender social capital. We focus on private and girls' education, and report on the experiences of four schools between 1995 and 2005. We argue that, beyond schools' contribution to the skills acquired by individual students, whether they promote the formation of social capital within communities should be a part of our assessment of their effectiveness. Schools as centers of activism can provide communities a forum for formulating their social demands and identities. In this context, social capital formation provides a useful heuristic for reclaiming the language of social justice and considering the human ends of education.

INTRODUCTION

Social capital can be conceptualized as collective, fluid resources that schools draw from communities and magnify in complex ways as they transfer those resources to students. We define social capital broadly as the cumulative capacity of social groups to cooperate and work together for a common good.[1] The concepts of "social group," "cumulative capacity," and "common good," are informed by Chinese scholarship and shaped by the economic and socio-political transformations associated with market socialism.

Cumulative capacity – the level of resources available to social groups, overall – has increased dramatically in China during the past two decades. Yet, great disparities have also emerged between social groups, such that some benefit greatly, and some little at all, from that capacity (Study Group, 2005). Furthermore, until recently, schooling has been conceived in China as a public good, not just or even primarily as an individual "investment." As the socialist narrative of public good is replaced by a market narrative of private interest, just what "common good" implies is hotly contested.

Three central themes emerge from our analysis. First, the extent to which schools harness social capital is inextricably related to their communities' cultural, economic, and political resources. In other research, we have shown that the distribution of such resources is influenced by reform era policies that have altered social class formation and perceptions about the role of schooling in the construction of social advantage and efficacy (Lin & Ross, 1998; Ross & Lin, 2004).[2] For example, as schools are required to marshal an increasing proportion of funding from local communities, they become more tied to the needs of local constituencies and particularistic interests. Prestigious academic, technical, and private schools, recognized for their ability to prepare students for college-level training or employment, are positioned to take advantage of local material and cultural resources. These resources come not only from a community's economic infrastructure, but also from the social and professional networks of students' parents and energetic alumni supporters. The direct financial resources (from fund raisers and direct donations for teacher bonuses, student scholarships, and school equipment) and "in-kind" (travel, instructional technology, tutoring, and co-curricular) services that these informal networks channel to schools currently provide one of the most significant catalysts for pedagogical and curricular reform in China (Lin & Ross, 1998; Ross & Lin, 2001). In contrast, vocational and rural schools, generally serving poorer and less-educated communities, have much less political, intellectual, and economic capital upon which to draw, and are increasingly disadvantaged in their search for "multi-channeled" school support (Lewin & Wang, 1994; Cheng, 1994).

Second, the relationship between social capital formation and schooling is influenced by the growing gap between China's haves and have-nots. China's successes during the last 10 years in reducing illiteracy among youths and middle-aged adults, providing near-universal access to basic education, and raising the living standards of hundreds of millions of

Chinese citizens are extraordinary (Ross, 2005). China's 2005 Human Development Index ranking of 85 (out of 177 countries) is 20 places higher than it was in 1990 (UNDP, 2005). However, in 1985, the disposable income of urban citizens was on average 1.89 times that of the rural population. By 2003, the disparity had reached 3.1 (Ross, 2005). In 2003, the percentage of the Chinese population with primary education or below in rural areas was 3.2 times that in urban areas. In contrast, percentages of urban residents with senior middle school education, junior college education, and a four-year college education are respectively 3.5, 55.5, and 281.55 times the percentages in rural areas (Subject Group, 2005).

Despite China's turbulent educational history of Cultural Revolution and state corporatism, there may be no developing country more predisposed to favor schools as potential sites for the cultivation of individual talents and mutual social action.[3] The high value placed on formal schooling is reinforced by policies of decentralization implemented since the 1980s, which made basic education the most important responsibility (in both administrative and financial terms) of local governments. There is also a cultural tendency to put high value on moral education. This tendency has sometimes made education vulnerable to political indoctrination, but has also prevented it from becoming a mere provider of knowledge and skills (Cheng, 1996, p. 74). The near universal faith in schooling for social mobility and progress in Chinese communities is the primary source of social capital, which the state exploits to justify cost-recovery policies that have made affording even compulsory education a struggle for China's poorest citizens.

Third, social capital formation provides a useful heuristic for reclaiming the language of social justice, and considering the human ends of education. We suggest that the tension between how trust in formal education is manipulated by the Chinese state and how local leaders, teachers, and parents expect much from their schools may erode the Chinese state's continuing success in maintaining public legitimacy through policies of "holistic control" (Cheng, 2001). This problem, hardly unique to China, stems from conceptualizing the outcomes of schooling in utilitarian terms and neglecting the role of schooling in the construction of social identity, community responsibility, and social justice.

PORTRAITS OF FOUR SCHOOL COMMUNITIES

We explore these themes through case studies of four school communities. The schools include one exceptional private school in Beijing that offers preschool through 12th-grade programs; one private suburban comprehensive secondary school in Jiangxi; and two rural primary schools in Guangxi. The communities served by these schools provide teachers, parents, and students with very different capacities for creating the enabling environments that nurture social networks and stability. With the exception of the schools associated with the "Yu Cai-Shanghai #3 Partnership," the names of schools have been changed to protect their anonymity.

We have chosen private and girls' schools as case studies. These kinds of schools began to re-emerge in China in the 1980s, and illustrate the new plurality of Chinese school experiences. While such schools have opened in urban areas for the children of small business owners, entrepreneurs and professionals, they also serve migrant and rural children with limited access to public schools. The missions of these schools vary as dramatically as the communities they serve. Some programs for girls, like the two profiled in this article, are designed to help pupils resist gender stereotyping. Others explicitly train female students for service-related careers "naturally" appropriate for girls (Ross & Lin, 2001). Some private schools are crassly proprietary, while others attempt to redress inadequate state funding, irrelevance of the public school curriculum to students' lives and employment opportunities, and restricted access to quality education (Lin, 1999). The state's plan to encourage, support, guide, and effectively administer private schools is motivated by a complex set of policies designed to support greater educational opportunity, institutional accountability, and quality. Private schooling likewise aids the state's effort to boost China's economy by prompting families to use their savings on the one commodity they consistently desire – education for their children.

Our discussion draws from analysis of in-depth, open-ended interviews and intensive observations at the schools during a combined total of six months of fieldwork conducted between 1996 and 1999. In addition, our discussion is informed by fieldwork on private and girls' education conducted in 20 schools through 2005, including the four case study schools. In the larger sample of 20 schools, six are primary level and 14 are secondary level. Although primary schools are the focus of this article, our discussion is also informed by on-going research on senior secondary education, the most significant bottleneck of education opportunity in China.[4] The 20 schools include private and public institutions administered at the village, county, city district, and municipal levels, and are located within a 100 km distance from Beijing, Dalian, Shanghai, Guilin, Nanchang, and Jiangxi. The schools were selected for their representation of a wide range of regional and material settings in which to explore how gender and social class intersect to influence the purposes and consequences of schooling.

Our adoption of a qualitative research design allowed us to integrate system-level data with portraits of how schools respond to the social backgrounds and interests of their students.[5] Our model of educational stratification, and of how schools might inhibit or advance social capital, draws from discussions based on a set of related questions that we shared with teachers and administrators at our study schools.[6]

Bright Light School: A "First World" Urban Private School on the Privileged Periphery

Bright Light's white buildings, framed by expansive gates, rise pristinely from a flat, unfinished suburban Beijing landscape. Corridors and open spaces catch pools of light from large windows, casting shadows on children's paintings, awards, and photographs. Students, dressed in colorful, stylish uniforms, move purposefully among classrooms, gardens, and playing fields, catching the eyes of visitors with relaxed grins.

Bright Light was established in 1985 as the first private preschool in Beijing. The founder loved Chinese traditional music and wished to use music and the arts to help students learn academically. Bright Light quickly made a reputation for itself, although its shaky beginning paralleled the contentious re-introduction of China's private schools, which were promoted by individuals and investors well in advance of governmental recognition, and regulation (Lin, 1999). Local government officials, not knowing how to deal with a new school structure outside their range of control, sought opportunities to force Bright Light to close. The biggest challenge came when Bright Light outgrew its leased facilities, and school leaders embarked on the construction of new buildings. Before completion, city officials pulled down the structures, citing violation of construction codes. Undeterred and supported by parents, Bright Light's principal (and primary owner) moved Bright Light, along with some 200 students and teachers, south to Guangdong Province. Through considerable profits from two companies, the principal eventually moved Bright Light back to Beijing. In 1995, Bright Light was housed in a new suburban campus with a full range of facilities, including a new secondary school program.

Larger facilities allowed Bright Light to expand its programs and cultivate relations with a college that provides Bright Light graduates with short-term training in English, commerce, administration, and accounting. In 1999,

Bright Light's secondary school had a total enrollment of 600 pupils, recruited primarily through referrals from parents with children already studying at the school. "We do not need to advertise, we never do! Word of mouth among parents is good enough for us to get students," the principal proudly informed us. Most students were Beijing residents, although a small number of pupils came from other cities and provinces. Over 90% of these students were single children, and those who had siblings were primarily from minority backgrounds. About 50% were female, unanimously characterized by the principal as "our most hard-working students." The principal, knowing full well that the school could not rely on just tuition to survive, had become a shrewd entrepreneur, owning several companies. However, operating expenses were primarily drawn from student tuition, which in 1999 was 18,000 yuan (approximately 2,250 USD), well over the average annual wage of a Beijing resident.

The spirit of Bright Light has been shaped by the principal. He founded the school to bring, as he put it, "the light of love" into children's lives, because during the Cultural Revolution he had "suffered too much from lack of love." The school's motto is "*bo-ai*," or "universal love," which is carved on a stone in front of the school. Fully dedicated to his dream, the principal is highly respected by parents and staff for his "pioneering spirit," charisma, hard work, and commitment.

Bright Light's educational goal is the all-round development of students, a holistic, moral view of teaching central to Chinese educational philosophy (Watkins & Biggs, 1996). The principal believes that this aim can only be achieved by "providing students opportunities to develop themselves according to their characteristics and interests. Every student has unique qualities and these deserve respect." The principal advocates placing students at the center of teaching, helping them achieve "creative independence." He is extremely critical of "the traditional way of teaching" which overwhelmingly emphasizes rote learning. Ultimately, Bright Light will have succeeded in this mission, he believes, if students "have true abilities that are directed outward toward serving society, students who can respond and adapt to the changes of a new era."

The school's signature program is Chinese music. All primary school students study one or two Chinese musical instruments during three weekly lessons, and are encouraged to take optional lessons in piano, Chinese folk music, or "military music." Students may also study other "generative arts," which include chess, drawing, painting, and dancing. The principal dreams that his students will come to appreciate China's traditional musical heritage. "We aim for the students to become culturally educated," the principal explained.

To develop continuity across the curriculum, Bright Light's kindergarten and early elementary curricula are connected. The students begin what might be called pre-academic activities at age 3, through carefully articulated lessons designed to "eliminate redundancy" from student learning experiences. Four-year-olds are praised for completing learning tasks ordinarily assigned to first graders in public schools. The vocabulary of competitive efficiency that pervades descriptions of skill development is meant to complement Bright Light's emphasis on artistic and individual expression. Through the efforts of "connected learning between kindergarten and primary school," which is aimed at "saving students' time," the school aspires to provide students an advantage in their future academic learning.

Teachers are hired directly on contract by the principal. Their yearly evaluations are used to determine merit bonuses and reconsideration of employment terms. As is common in private schools, teachers have much less time than their public school counterparts for life outside the school environment. With the exception of a few who live nearby the suburban campus or close enough to the staff bus line to commute, most teachers leave the school campus only on weekends. In our conversations, teachers shared that they followed the principal wherever he went, because they agreed with his educational ideals. At Bright Light, they felt that they could achieve their life values. Although they have little time for themselves, they felt respected and wished to do their best to help their students and Bright Light succeed.

Bright Light could not exist without affluent urban parents and their high expectations for their children, their expendable incomes, and their changing work and familial relationships. Bright Light's parents come from all walks of life, but are primarily the privileged members of China's middle and professional classes (Lin & Ross, 1998). The principal is frank about his need to gain parents' cooperation. While parent–school interactions appear relatively free and open, they are based on the mutual (and to parents acceptable) recognition that Bright Light must sometimes implement "corrective policies" to ameliorate problems that develop in the home. Parents are fined, for example, if students return to school sick from excessive weekend eating – perceived to be a common ailment of only spoilt children. Professional parents are widely believed to indulge their children to "make up for living their simple life at school."

Unlike some other elite private schools in Beijing, Bright Light deliberately does not provide students with an overly comfortable material environment. The principal believed that single children need to learn to live cooperatively with others. Bright Light's explicit curriculum, again considered to be corrective of parental behavior, emphasizes frugality, self-reliance, and collective action. In the primary school student dormitory, 20 pupils share one large "family room." Students we spoke with enjoy their close school friendships. But they also were critical of how adults intentionally controlled their lives, leaving them no time to call their own.[7]

The principal identified his biggest challenges as "competition" for good pupils and meeting parental demands that Bright Light help children succeed in external examinations. Bright Light has gained a reputation for its rich arts program. However, Bright Light must also recruit students within a broader culture of schooling that is highly competitive. As their children reach secondary school, Bright Light parents expect that teachers will devote more time in the explicit curriculum to academic subjects tested in examinations. Teachers feel caught in the middle of pressures to nurture individual capabilities and model test-taking skills. Even elite private schools like Bright Light are often considered "second chances" for students who cannot enter excellent public schools, either because they have failed to pass entrance examinations or because they reside in neighborhoods with poor local schools. As one principal stated, "Parents pay large sums of money for their children's education here. And even though the children may be less qualified than pupils in public key schools, we must turn them into high achievers." Parents demand to know how their children "measure up" to public school students. Teachers respond that they cannot guarantee specific futures. They can only guarantee that students will make progress in their studies. When we visited in 1999, teachers expressed a feeling of desperation, because regardless of their efforts they faced the destiny of "the tyranny of admission ratios" to universities. Although a much higher proportion of Beijing high school graduates enter college, admission ratios (particularly to highly selective elite universities) remain society's chief criterion for measuring "school effectiveness."

Not far from Bright Light's campus, a public vocational school straddles agricultural fields and a ramshackle suburb. Like Bright Light, the school has 600 students. Teacher salaries, class size, and perceptions of students (in need of remediation due to previous mediocre schooling) do not vary greatly from Bright Light. However, upon learning that we had been interviewing Bright Light pupils, the school's dispirited teachers sighed, "Ah, but *we* are a third world school." They meant that students' parents, most of whom had quit farming to engage in small enterprises, were generally poor members of a bleak, rootless neighborhood. The teachers may have meant to suggest also the extent of their alienation from teaching in a vocational school, generally considered to be the third-class citizens (after academic and specialized technical schools) of China's educational community. A poorly financed vocational school located in a make-shift town of transient families was completely out of step with Bright Light's "first world" catch phrases for educational reform – progressive, market driven, and learning for a global information age.

West Bend and Willow Path: Private Schools for the Rural Poor

West Bend: A Community without Bridges
West Bend Private School was founded in 1993 by villagers who knew "third world" schools firsthand and understood how profoundly their children were marginalized. West Bend had a long history of running private schools, including a well-known academy established at the end of the 19th century. The high-quality education children were thought to receive in that institution gave the village an outstanding local reputation, and villagers were proud of themselves. In 1949, the academy became a public school and in 1969 was moved to a site 30 km away from the village. The only local school left to West Bend children was a day's walk from the village.

Prior to West Bend's establishment, public school tuition for students amounted to 300 yuan per semester, in addition to extra fees for school uniforms, power, water, examinations, and transportation. Parents report receiving no accounting of how such fees were used. When they refused to pay disputed fees, their children were not expelled from school but were given a hard time by teachers, including being ridiculed in front of classmates. Families, some with four children and less than one acre of land, had little cash income, except money generated from raising a few pigs. Most onerous to parents was a state-mandated "additional fee for education," based on 2% of their annual household incomes. Villagers accused county officials of inflating village incomes in order to strengthen their opportunity for job promotion, angrily concluding: "They don't care whether we live or die."

West Bend became a reality through the money and networking abilities of a local businessman frustrated by paying the fees for his five children. "We must take into our own hands our children's education or we will have no future," the businessman said. With small donations from village representatives, the school's founder covered most of the school's start-up costs, in addition to one year of teachers' salaries, from his own savings.

Upon receiving news of the construction of West Bend, the county government issued an order to demolish the building. In response, 400 villagers mobilized at the construction site, "even the youngest child carrying a brick in each hand." By the time county officers arrived on the scene, the building was nearly completed. It was saved by the intervention of prefecture officials who supported the project.

West Bend's school board was made up of seven village representatives, who determine tuition and teachers' salaries. Tuition was intentionally fixed at well below the local public school's 300 yuan per semester fees: 36 yuan for preschool, 110 yuan for grades 1–4, 115 yuan for grade 5, and 125 yuan for grade 6. The teaching staff, hired on a contract basis, comprised retired teachers and senior secondary school graduates from surrounding villages and towns. Salary for them was meager, "enough to buy rice but nothing leftover to buy meat and vegetables," a teacher complained. Nevertheless, the onus was placed on West Bend teachers to enable whole classes of students to succeed in countywide examinations. A merit system rewarded students and teachers of a class who achieved an average score of 90% or higher. This measure was designed to encourage teachers to work together to insure that all students received a solid foundation of knowledge that would be tested on external exams. Because West Bend students outperformed their public school counterparts at the end of year examinations, the school began to draw students from villages far enough away to require boarding facilities.

West Bend provided pragmatic teacher and text-directed lessons that would be criticized as narrowly utilitarian by the Bright Light community. The differential access to cultures of power that shaped these teaching and learning strategies is similar to differences in U.S. schools studied by scholars like Lisa Delpit (1995). West Bend parents wanted what Bright Light parents wanted – good schools that respect their children and connect them to the resources of successful adulthood. But they expressed this desire in relationship to the structures of discrimination that as poor, rural parents they experienced on a daily basis. They wanted their children "disciplined," to receive a basic education "so they will not be bullied" in business, trade, or in social interactions when they grow up. They wanted their children to be competent in reading, negotiating legal disputes, and business contracts.

The mud classrooms their children studied in contained only tables and chairs. There were no tape recorders for learning English, which meant students would be severely disadvantaged in listening comprehension. The school had no laboratory equipment, another obstacle to mastery of the basic science curriculum. These two disadvantages effectively eliminated the dream of peasants to help their children to "leap the rural gate" and use entrance to universities to receive a higher education as a way of achieving social mobility. Frankly, without social networks beyond the county level,

West Bend parents and educators could do little more to enhance students' educational opportunities, nor to create bridges for bringing more resources back into the community. And there was no one on the horizon, a powerful sponsor, or the state, who would make that happen.

Willow Path: A School Community with Bridges
Willow Path was established in 1994 in the context of prolonged village dissatisfaction with the local public school. Educational officials had been perceived as simply gouging villagers for their personal benefit. The school's quality was suspect, as well, since villagers believed (rightly it seems) that teachers obtained their positions through kinship connections or "backdoor" maneuvering. We were told of a joke that one teacher, the wife of a village official, could not even write her own name correctly. Angry and anguished parents told us that: "Our heart is burning with pain when we see our children wasting their lives in this way."

The director of Willow Path's school committee was a highly respected village head. Having worked as a salaried salesman all his life, he returned to his village at the age of 60 and encouraged village leaders to raise funds for a private school. The village head also contacted a prominent villager who served for two decades as chief education officer on Hainan Island. Bored with retirement and searching for "something useful to do with his life," he accepted the village head's offer to become Willow Path's principal.

As word of the enterprise spread, villagers working in other provinces and cities sent money back to support the school's construction. Assistance from the village's "public welfare savings fund," normally used for road maintenance or to help villagers in need, was designated for the construction of the school. In addition, the school committee requested that every household donate 10 yuan for constructing the school's 6-room elementary school. The year following the school's establishment, the village head worked for the school gratis, appreciative that his 10 grandchildren would be attending. With donations from villagers, Willow Path bought a closed public school building in 1996 and began a secondary education program.

Willow Path's classrooms were crowded with 50–70 students. Tuition, approximately half the amount charged by local public schools, was progressively calculated depending upon family income. The teaching staff was led by three retired teachers from the local village. Other teachers, selected from among high school graduates in the nine local brigades, attended one-month training programs before entering the classroom.

Villagers judged Willow Path's success primarily by examination results. In 1995, grade 5 students did so well on their examinations that pupils began to transfer from the nearest public school to Willow Path. As the school began drawing students and their school fees from as far away as neighboring Guangdong Province, county officials notified the village that the school must close. They feared that having a large number of students outside the domain of their control would create problems for them and jeopardize their careers. To apply pressure, the county education bureau stopped pension payments to the three retired teachers on Willow Path's staff and refused to allow Willow Path graduates to sit for county matriculation examinations. Willow Path's leaders would not back down. "We believe we are doing the right thing, and justice is on our side," they told us. They appealed to district and provincial education officials as well as the provincial Chinese Communist Party committee. "The multiple trips cost us 3,000 yuan, all we have saved in the last year, but it is worth it!" They won the sympathy of the prefecture head, who issued an official criticism of the local education administration for its resistance to private education.

Assessing West Bend and Willow Path
Government resistance to both West Bend and Willow Path illustrates that the formation of social capital by and in support of the poor does not happen in a social–political vacuum. Being at odds with local government authorities ultimately limits a school's ability to build social capital. A school outside the public system may act as a catalyst for public sector reform, but only if that school can create strong external linkages that connect its community members to more distant forms of material and social capital. Willow Path was able to find such linkages in native sons. West Bend had no such benefactor.

A related conclusion from West Bend and Willow Path is that to block the integrative functions of social capital that might dismantle social hierarchies, state agents do not have to be hostile. They can simply remain indifferent to the consequences of decentralization. Recently, for example, official reports document that decentralization has led to a divorce of financial powers (located with county-level government) from powers of office (located with villages and townships), with adverse effects on poor communities. In addition, decentralization policies ostensibly designed to provide local communities with flexibility to raise school funds from multiple sources obscure the fact that government support of compulsory education has declined as a percentage of total education expenditures (Education for All, 2000; Kroeber & Miller, 2005).

Finally, the West Bend and Willow Path cases indicate that schools can be more than state agent or vehicle of the market. The desire for schools that serve and respect their children pressed villagers to take collective action. This collective action extended educational opportunity and provided villagers a public space for voicing concerns that went well beyond the education of their children. Villagers' resistance was not directed at "the government" per se. While the level of trust between villagers and the county government was low, villagers turned to authorities at the prefectural level, removed from immediate financial responsibility, to act on their behalf. Although this lack of coordination among levels of government is a troubling sign for participatory citizenship in the long run, the villagers' reliance on the state for mediating a conflict with its local representatives suggests that civic trust in rural China has not been exhausted.

The Yu Cai-Shanghai #3 Partnership: Bridging Social Capital through Chinese Transnationalism

> Any one individual's abilities have limits, just as the contributions one person can make for one's country during one's lifetime are small in the scheme of things. Nevertheless, through the power of education one can nurture a thousand able individuals, whose combined force can contribute to the goodness of the nation. (Xue Zheng)

The transnational community of girls and women represented by the Yu Cai-#3 partnership provides our clearest example of how schooling can be used for the construction of social capital. The Shanghai #3 Girls' Secondary School was established in 1893 by Southern Methodist missionaries and is today China's most prestigious all-female public college preparatory institution.[8] Shanghai #3's insistence on quality education for girls, summarized in the acronym, IACE (independence, ability, care, and elegance), has become a national model for girls' schools established by educators and parents eager to provide appropriate educational opportunities for their daughters. With stained glass windows, an expansive lawn, and on-line library catalog, Shanghai #3 exudes an atmosphere of cultural power, grace, and high educational expectations. Accompanying her husband to China in the summer of 1998, Hillary Clinton delivered an impassioned address on girls' schooling at Shanghai #3.

In 1992, Shanghai #3 became a partner of the Yu Cai Private Secondary School, the first private secondary school to be founded in Jiangxi Province since 1949. Housed in a cluster of rundown buildings in the outskirts of Nanchang, Jiangxi's capital, Yu Cai appears a world away from the cosmopolitan campus of Shanghai #3. Classrooms are packed front to back with battered desks and chairs. Many students have struggled and failed in their exams, and turned to Yu Cai as a last resort to continue their schooling.

The Yu Cai Xue Zheng Project Hope for Girls that brought these two schools together was initiated in 1995 to extend the opportunity of senior secondary schooling to impoverished girls residing in rural communities.[9] The partnership was named in memory of Xue Zheng, Shanghai #3's late honorary principal. Xue Zheng's conviction (quoted above) in the power of schooling provides the epigraph for Project Hope, which was conceived by overseas Shanghai #3 alumnae. Their aim was "to help reverse the tragic trend of high illiteracy among Chinese women in impoverished villages, to promote our legacy of Live, Love, and Grow beyond the Shanghai #3 Girls' School to those young girls struggling for their high school education." Specifically, alumnae donors were asked to fund, at an initial annual per pupil cost of $350 US, the tuition, room and board, and book fees of 42 girls who would study for three years at Yu Cai. A condition of joining the project was that donors must personally welcome Yu Cai girls – through letters, photographs, and encouragement – into a transnational community of extraordinarily accomplished, advantaged women.

The recruitment region for scholarship recipients consisted of 11 of Jiangxi's poorest counties. Candidates were selected from families whose annual per capita incomes ranged from an extremely low 100–800 yuan. With no non-agricultural incomes or remittances from relatives working in cities, these families struggled to make ends meet in the face of declining agricultural infrastructure and few village and township enterprises. In addition to meeting the economic criteria outlined above, students had to have graduated from junior secondary school and attained a high combined score on their senior secondary school entrance examination. Without a scholarship, none of the 42 girls could have continued their education, because their families could not afford public high school fees.

The transition to high school life in Jiangxi's capital city proved difficult for most students. One student explained, "Usually, countryside students feel inadequate ... when they come to big cities, which are very different from the countryside where they used to be. Just as how 'Grandma Liu entering the Garden of Daguan' is described in 'The Dream of the Red Mansion.'... After three years in senior high ... I knew more about society and people. I didn't have that kind of feeling." Language was often identified as a negative identity marker. "When I entered this school, I don't know how they [other students] felt about me, but I had a little bit of a sense of inferiority. For example, when I first came, I could not speak *Putonghua* [the national language] well. So, they [the urban students] look down on us a little bit."

The longer she was in school, another girl remarked, the more she was "unsure," "confused" about what her village had come to mean to her. She (and her parents) perceived "success in school" as an overwhelmingly positive yet contradictory resource; one that would produce skills, desires, and associations that would both complicate and enhance her future identity, family relationships, and career opportunities. "[My parents] want me to go out of the countryside so that I will not be like them."

Yu Cai students were painfully aware of the high costs of their educational opportunities. One student related the following story:

> Both my parents are farmers but in order to earn enough money for my brother and me to go to school, my father, at the age of 40, went out to take on a part time job. You can't really earn money by cultivating fields. Nowadays, tuition is very high, so my father has to go out to work at this age. Then my mother couldn't handle all the farming. So she simply went out with my father to work and also to take care of my father. Since I've always been a top student, my parents always ask my brother to learn from me and work hard. Maybe because of this kind of psychological pressure – or because boys in elementary school like to play a lot – he simply went out and played around – and turned bad. So he couldn't go on with his learning, and because he didn't have the money to buy things like snacks in school, he began to play truant. He hated school and refused to go when he entered junior middle school. But my parents forced him to go. They thought, well, he is a boy and if he doesn't get educated he will have no opportunities to develop in the future. But still he couldn't learn – and now he has followed my parents out to work. So I am the only one that studies in my family, and all the others are earning to pay for my learning.

Yu Cai graduates expressed sadness that their schooling, coupled with the intense physical demands of rural life, meant sacrificing family welfare. One girl explained, "I wanted very much to go to senior high but my parents asked me to go to a vocational high school so that I could start work earlier." Another remarked, "Nowadays, tuition is very high ... I am the only one that studies in my family and all the other three are earning to pay for my learning." On hearing this exchange, a third student interrupted, "I have an elder sister who stopped schooling after junior high because we didn't have enough money ... [My parents] asked me to apply for vocational high school when I finished junior high so that I could start work earlier."

Students also worried about the impact of their choices on parents struggling to cope with chronic health problems. "[My mother's] health is so poor that she can't work in the fields. So, the economic burden is completely on my father's shoulders." A student recalled, "My mother has heart problems ... [When her health was at its worst], I had to get up at 6:00 to cook for the whole family, feed the pigs and rush to school afterwards ... sometimes, I had to leave for school without eating. That was also the most intense period in my schooling because I was preparing for the senior high entrance exam."

Yu Cai students expressed ambivalence about the distance that now separates their experiences from those of their families, and some of them resented the complications and pain of their "in-between lives." "We live in a village with feudal, traditional ideas. Since boys are more valued than girls in the countryside, and my parents only had girls at first, my grandparents looked down upon them and drove them out of the family."

On the one hand, the students saw themselves as living examples of "confronting the legacy of 'feudal thinking.'" As one student put it, "People were saying that a girl didn't need to go to senior high ... It's really fortunate for me to study here because people in my hometown have feudal ideas and they discriminate against girls. They think that boys are learning for their careers while girls only need to know the knowledge that is needed in their domestic life."

On the other, the girls remained unsure about their abilities as young educated Chinese women. "It is often said that women are narrow-minded ... I feel that if ever boys become hard working, they are going to be much more successful than girls. They are also stronger in their practical use of knowledge." "With an increase in age, girls have a tougher time studying than boys. If we want to do as well as they do, we have to work harder. Boys are stronger in abstract thinking while girls are stronger in memorizing." "My major is mathematics. It is said that girls have a hard time learning math and I feel it personally sometimes. And we have few female students in this department ... It is said that it's difficult for girls to learn and teach math ... I must learn it well so I won't be baffled by their questions." "It is said that some companies prefer a mediocre male graduate than an excellent female student. I don't know why. Maybe they think boys are more capable than girls. It is often said that female graduates from computer science usually work as secretaries." "I am a medical student. Usually patients don't trust female doctors, especially female surgeons. I wanted to choose surgery as my major, but *they* told me that girls are not suited to being surgeons. *They* suggested that we become gynecologists."

Grappling with such contradictions, Yu Cai graduates reported a sea change in their lives, and the goal of Shanghai #3 donors to make Yu Cai girls a part of their extended, transnational Chinese community seems to be succeeding. The majority of Yu Cai graduates talked about female role models in their interviews. They recognized and spoke out forcefully against sexist practices and values. Furthermore, they expressed their desire to emulate the passion and strength with which He Jing, the recently deceased founding principal of Yu Cai, pursued her goals. Students admired Principal He because she was "well educated," "loving to others," "talented," and "successful." "Principal He is the person I admire most and first ... I admire how she treated others and how devoted she was to her career. I can learn a lot from her life experience. It was not until I entered this school that I realized how powerful love is. I hope I can be like her."

Finally, the girls discussed Shanghai #3's illustrious past and overseas alumnae, who had "given so much back to their community," with admiration. Becoming part of that community's history has given Yu Cai graduates and students a powerful collective identity with which to replace their previous self-understanding as backward rural girls in need of welfare. "It was really precious for me to study in Yu Cai and I treasure it very much." "I am very grateful to the alumni abroad who give us financial assistance." "I treasure the opportunity of going to senior high very much because it was not easily earned."

Identity transformation, of course, does not necessarily lead to the formation of social capital. In fact, equating collective change with individual transformation is a proven strategy for reproducing, not dismantling, hierarchies. Hecht's (1998, p. 91) discouraging analysis of how China's state-dominated educational law erects barriers to women's rights being "expressed and activated from a broader social basis" provides a compelling example. However, "individual change" has a powerful connotation in contemporary China, with the re-invigoration of community imagined through the authenticity of autonomous voices. Feminist theorist Li Xiaojiang has pointed out that while the words liberation and liberty are related in the English language, there is no such connection in the Chinese word for liberation (*jiefang*). In fact, "lack of freedom to be an individual is precisely one of the important critiques of the state project of women's liberation" (Li, 1999, p. 273). Critical of the communist project that pitted political consciousness (*juewu*) against self-consciousness (*yishi*) and individual agency, Li argues that recognition of self-consciousness is a necessary precondition for social change in China.

The teachers and administrators in China's girls' schools look to educational and occupational mobility as what one principal called "obvious measures of success." "But," she continued, "It is really identity transformation that we are after." Borrowing a Buddhist phrase, another educational researcher called what happened to rural girls in schools "sudden enlightenment." "The changes in girls are not obvious but profound. It is their openness to the world, their sense of opportunity. These girls are the biggest risk takers that Chinese schools are producing. Their very presence is transgressive. They surprise us all." By saying the girls' presence was transgressive, the administrator meant that their presence changes the nature of what happens in the classroom, and what the purpose of schooling is.

By both standards, the Yu Cai-Shanghai #3 partnership has achieved remarkable results. By 2005, 28 of the 42 students of the class of 1998 have graduated from colleges and universities – a very high matriculation rate.[10] Thirteen of these graduates were accepted into three- and four-year tertiary institutions in the autumn of 1998. The remaining young women, who scored poorly the first time they sat for the college entrance examination, were supported for another year by Shanghai #3 alumnae, so they could retake the examination. Available information on 39 of the 42 graduates of the class of 1998 indicates that 10 students remain in Jiangxi, while the rest have followed educational and occupational opportunities to cities in the eastern third of China, from Beijing to Guangzhou, and from Ningbo to Chengdu. Five are currently in graduate school. One graduate has gone back to college and is in her third year of study. In addition to the six students currently in college or graduate school, five are professionals and teachers in colleges and research institutes, five are workers in enterprises, two are mid-level service personnel in factories, eight are teachers at the precollege level, primarily in mathematics and the sciences, two are physicians, two are engineers, six are accountants and financial analysts, one is a lawyer, one is a legal aid, and one is an English language translator. Based on the experiences of these "girl pioneers," Yu Cai administrators raised money to support another cohort of 40 students for three years of senior secondary schooling. Each graduate of the class of 1998 became an "elder sister" to a student of the new group, serving as an informal advisor, confidant, and big-city informant.

Although several of the graduates are volunteering as mentors in girls' education projects in rural Shaanxi and Jiangxi, the Shanghai #3-Yu Cai partnership goal of training female leaders for rural areas is not really being achieved. Graduates have not returned to the countryside to settle down. In the eyes of supportive parents, Yu Cai provided a new possibility of future access for their daughters to both academic training and career opportunities, to "leap the rural gate." Only one student training to be a teacher explicitly spoke about going back to the village to become a "bridge builder." The transnational connections graduates have made through their Shanghai #3 alumnae sponsors have offered them a powerful source of imagination and social capital; what anthropologist Xin Liu has called spatial extroversion. In contrast, it is unlikely that their expanded horizons will enhance the complementary process that Liu terms spatial introversion; that is, enriching the villages in which they once lived (Liu, 2000).

SOCIAL CAPITAL AND EDUCATIONAL OPPORTUNITY

The concept of social capital offers the possibility to critique functionalist accommodations to transnational capitalism. To apply a phrase used by John Montgomery (1998), the concept of social capital pushes us to consider how schools and research on schools might advance possibilities to pursue moral values.

Both public and private schools in China can and do channel material and social forms of capitals in ways that disproportionately disadvantage students who are female, rural, and ethnic minority. From our point of view, however, negative social capital is an oxymoron whose manifestations should be met with a critique of exclusionary policies. Thus, we limit our designation of social capital to those processes that have the potential *to lessen social hierarchies*. We believe that this affirmative definition is in keeping with the urgent needs and rights of children in rural communities and with a normative movement by Chinese scholars and educators to find sources of social action that give expanded voice to individuals in poor communities (Study Group, 2005).

From this perspective, Bright Light holds its own in China's competitive educational market as a model of educational initiative created by those who want good schooling for social mobility and prestige, and pool their material and cultural capital to that end. Its adult supporters are connected to professional, educational, and economic networks that they use to serve (and eventually employ) their children, who cannot, because of low marks or neighborhood residency, obtain similar advantages in Beijing's best public schools. The Bright Light community uses its joint financial and information resources on behalf of its children. However, the capital created through that process does not meet our criterion of dismantling social hierarchies, certainly not in the long run. A very expensive alternative to the public school sector, Bright Light is exclusive. When parents cannot meet Bright Light's tuition, the school "saves" their child's place and welcomes him or her back – but only when the parents can pay.

Furthermore, Bright Light is marginalized from its elite public counterparts. It remains in conflict with the local government and provides its students with a route for social mobility outside the state system. As an outsider to the system, Bright Light is unlikely to enrich the larger educational community. If we equate social capital with processes that sustain and invigorate a public community on behalf of all its members, Bright Light is lacking. It also fails to advance social capital for a wider public good, because it perpetuates class-based inequality of educational opportunity.

Nevertheless, Bright Light does offer, along with West Bend and Yu Cai, an important insight about educational reform on the margins. In all three cases, collective action and innovation developed to mitigate or eliminate a perceived threat. In other words, community support for private and girls' schooling was a form of collective resistance to multiple and contradictory pressures of the market, the state, and social inequality.[11] Of course, the manipulation of formal education by social actors (including agents of the state) in a changing and unequal economic environment is not new. Communities seeking alternatives to public schools have been in conflict with state authorities and the professional educational establishment for over a century (Pepper, 1996).

The unequal *and* redistributive opportunities generated by our private school cases illustrate contradictions inherent in social capital theory. On the one hand, private schools are not uniformly exacerbating disparities in educational opportunity, since they have filled educational gaps left by a state unable or unwilling to provide sufficient schooling to meet increasing public demand. Our case study schools illustrate unmet demand among both poor and professional communities. On the other, elite private schools do fuel the dynamics of social group formation for China's "latent" middle class, whose desires for social mobility and status we have identified as one of the driving forces behind educational reform.

Examination of how this emergent group makes use of and is constructed through schooling is central to evaluating social capital formation in China, because it has been identified as the architect of Chinese "civil" or "autonomous" society. Explanations of social capital, and the school as a site for its use to advance social policy, rest squarely upon such assumptions about state–society relations. Whether civil society is a meaningful construct in the Chinese context has been a matter of vigorous debate for well over a decade (Brook, 1997). Some scholars reject its usefulness, maintaining that in China, "the state is not distinguished from the public. It is the public" (Lu & Perry, 1997, p. 10). Others see the Chinese state as "the captive arbiter of competing desires and interests within capitalism" (Brook, 1997, p. 9).

Our research indicates that entrepreneurial and managerial social groups (like those that support Bright Light) do wish to "remake society in their image, and the state in their service" (Brook & Frolic, 1997 14). They also illustrate that pressure on "the state," or, more precisely, representatives of local government, is exerted by villagers who "find themselves at the mercy of market reforms, and are constantly devising means to manipulate and subvert the state and the global processes it seeks to harness" (Brook & Frolic, 1997, p. 14). Some Chinese scholars point to both examples as the seeds of a fledgling civil society. Surely, this is a misnomer if what civil society refers to is social space contested by interest groups. Nevertheless, the concept of civil society can be useful in evaluating the educational sources of social capital in China, particularly if it is "thought of as a formation that exists by virtue of state–society interaction" (Brook & Frolic, 1997, p. 12). It is precisely at the nexus between political economy and society that schools operate. This location explains why schools' centrality to regimes of power and knowledge is always a source of concern to those, including many Chinese educational reformers, who wish to use schools for genuinely communicative as well as instrumental purposes.

Finally, our case study schools illustrate how the power or social capital that comes from interpersonal relationships (sometimes referred to in the Chinese context as "*guanxi* capitalism") intersects in contradictory ways with the cultural and social capital that adheres in schools as institutions. Findings from international research on educational opportunity suggest that rural children's educational experiences are sometimes restricted by conflicts between "protective agents" of family and village and "institutional agents" such as teachers (Reimers, 2000). Conflicts between different stakeholders characterize the experiences of children in West Bend and Willow Path. However, the Yu Cai-Shanghai #3 partnership's alumnae and educators have created interpersonal and institutional relationships for impoverished girls with the explicit purpose of providing social capital to be converted into future opportunities. In this example of sharing educational advantage, social capital emerges through conscious community building. The Yu Cai example suggests that a frequently made distinction between a school's "institutional social capital" and "private social capital" gained through personal networks (Lee & Brinton, 1996) is a false dichotomy. The institutional capital residing in particular schools is directly related to and shaped by its perceived importance and the ability of local parents and students to make use of or resist it in some way.

CONCLUSION

Making social capital formation an explicit, desired outcome of "effective schools" allows us to articulate why educational and community development is not just about securing the means to capitalize upon goods and services. More importantly, schools as centers of activism can provide communities a forum for formulating their social demands and their social identities. In this context, social capital formation provides a useful heuristic for reclaiming the language of social justice and considering the human ends of education.

The experiences of the four school communities discussed above intimate how such a dialog might begin. First, conceptualizing social capital as resistance to perceived problems is not only an accurate description of why people choose to join together for a common purpose. It is also an important analytical move, because it reminds us that successful school policies must be rooted in knowledge of local communities.

Second, the fact that schooling can be wholly supported as a good in itself by villages such as West Bend, even when schools appear to make individuals poorer, not richer, in their local knowledge, raises significant questions about the limits of schools, particularly in rural areas, to fully support children's welfare. We were struck by how frequently the word "survival" bubbled to the surface of conversations with educators, parents, and students in struggling communities. Drawing on their understanding of the commodification of society and human relationships, teachers, administrators, parents, and girls as young as 12 decried how unemployment and the dislocation of migration were impacting the lives of their friends and families. Particularly teachers in private schools reported working "in crisis mode all the time." As contract workers, they were constantly reminded that the quality of their teaching insured students with good job opportunities, upon which their schools' survival ultimately depended. Private school principals also operated "on the edge," scrambling for resources. Success, they noted, depended upon how well they "build community," which one principal described as making connections between the school and "like-minded educators and parents concerned about girls' education and futures." The principal's remarks resonated with interpretations of social capital formation that emphasize how social change emerges from the hard, daily work of maintaining of social relationships (Moi, 1991).

Third, even struggling schools can act as sites for the production and extension of social capital that reaches those most in need. This process is evident at the level of individual transformation, as we have seen in the Yu Cai project. Access to information and knowledge is what drives and then reinforces the collaborative networks at Yu Cai, whose graduates are explicitly asked by their transnational "aunties" to grade their abilities to communicate and build relationships with others, and ultimately to use their schooling "to remake society in their own image."

Fourth, interviews with Chinese children and parents reveal the necessity of developing measures for analyzing social capital formation that reflect local experiences of institutional life, discrimination, and identity. For example, when we described to a private school teacher our understanding of social capital and what people or institutions might do to promote its creation, she burst forth with a furious litany about "the barriers to social capital" that surrounded her. She began locally but quickly expanded her indictment to include "government corruption up to the highest levels." She did not omit the party in her scathing comments. "What about party members?" she pressed. "They're supposed to help us. Surely you wouldn't count them as social capital?!" In a similar conversation with a rural mother, our shared vocabulary faltered altogether. The member of "no group" outside her immediate kinship circle and drained by a schedule of physical labor in the field, she had no response to our question regarding "relationships that helped her solve problems." Looking to her school age daughter for help, she asked, "What should I answer?"

Finally, China's educational reform policies affect social capital formation and investment in contradictory ways, simultaneously promoting a feeling and perhaps the reality of common good in communities supported by marketization and unintentionally restricting such capacity in impoverished communities. The educational and social resources that can be pooled through heroic efforts by poor rural communities are limited, without an infusion of material capital. This is true even in schools such as West Bend, where many students experienced educational success for the first time because of supportive teachers and administrators. Even when parents direct scarce community resources toward the betterment of their children's futures, this does not mean that their abilities are infinitely elastic. Whether or not a group of parents and educators sees its relationship with local authorities as partner, adversary, or watchdog, its efforts at promoting schooling should not provide the state an excuse for draining support from local schools. Likewise, efforts to direct social capital formation toward the dismantling of hierarchies cannot succeed in isolated or fleeting projects. As numerous reviews of NGO activity in China have demonstrated, local initiatives cannot transform structures without external allies, including the state.

It is ironic that three decades after the death of Mao, Chinese scholars are quoting Amartya Sen to remind their leaders that growth does not necessarily lead to greater equality, because "the latter is determined by how the fruits of economic growth are used and distributed" (Subject Group, 2005, p. 1), China's leaders seem to be listening. They have reacted (in a rather functionalist way) to criticism about the economic and social costs of inequality by promoting "people-centered" development, designed to cultivate a "harmonious society" of "five balances": between economic and human development; between the domestic and external economy; between human beings and nature; between rural and urban development; and between coastal and interior development (for a brief discussion of people-centered development in China, see Malik, 2005). Responding both to a perceived skills gap among the young working population and the potential for social unrest, the state has mandated the elimination of tuition for compulsory schooling in rural areas by 2007 and has proposed a number of measures designed to boost village income, including lightening or eliminating agricultural tax burdens and increasing social services. Whether or not the state will be able to continue to rely upon its citizens' collective trust in formal education as a key policy resource will hinge on the success of these policies.

NOTES

1. This definition is derived from conversations with colleagues at the Pacific Basin Research Center at Soka University. We wish to thank the Center as well as Colgate University, McGill University, ASIANetwork, and the Spencer Foundation for supporting various aspects of this study.

2. Our original research approach is built upon the work of two scholars, who have examined educational access and equity across three domains of geography, ethnic or minority membership, and gender. In addition, we draw inspiration from two (contradictory) strands of North American scholarship on social class formation. The first strand points out the inadequacy with which class has been theorized, at home and abroad, and conceptualizes schools as contested institutions in which relationships among class background, educational opportunity, and economic advantage are often unpredictable and always shaped by particular historical and cultural contexts (see Ira Katznelson & Margaret Weir, 1985; Lois Weis & Fine, 1993). The latter study eschews class as a fixed category and analyzes its "nonsynchronous" intersections with gender, ethnicity, and race over time. Conceptualizing class as contextual rather than categorical complements much Chinese scholarship on social identity and underscores our intent to investigate changes in class formation as much as possible from Chinese points of view. However, the work of scholars who insist on the importance of a *categorical* analysis of social class in the U.S. context, such as Annette Lareau (2003), may be becoming more relevant to the Chinese context as income inequalities increase there.

3. Economists argue about whether the resultant internalized desire for education among parents regardless of their own educational background will be strong enough to stave off social instability. See Kroeber and Miller (2005).

4. Our secondary school examples highlight China's diverse and market-driven senior secondary schools; the level of Chinese schooling is most socially stratified and least represented in educational research. Two primary factors have guided our choice of senior secondary schools as the sites for our research. First, the purposefully

stratified nature of senior secondary schooling in China presents high school students with clear messages about whether their school experiences and training will permit the possibility of attending an institution of higher education or lead to an employment upon graduation from high school. In addition, educational development in China is driven, as it is worldwide, not only by the need for increasingly specialized labor, but also by complex interactions between state and class interests. Comparative models of such interaction suggest that when strong state direction of education is reduced, for whatever reasons, schools, once tightly linked to national interests, will be gradually reshaped to reflect a combination of interests derived from powerful social groups and "market" forces (see Insook Jeong & Michael Armer, 1994). We believe that our examination of how different types of Chinese senior secondary schools are influenced by and channel the social values and economic resources of local supporters (including parents) will offer important comparative evidence for refining models of state and class influence in schools.

5. At each field site semi-structured interviews were conducted with the purpose of gaining information in five categories: (1) student outcome data and the number and social characteristics of the school's student body (including gender and ethnic make-up, educational and occupational history of parents, recruitment to the school); (2) the social characteristics, educational background, and organization of the teaching staff; (3) conceptions of the school's relative position and prestige in local and regional educational communities; (4) general and financial administration of the school and its linkages to enterprises or other social and economic units in the local community; and (5) the goals and content of the formal school mission and curriculum.

6. As Chinese affiliate in new ways, how are the social purposes of schooling altered for particular social groups? How are perceptions regarding the power of schooling in shaping one's life chances influencing the stated public missions of schools? How do administrators, teachers, and parents describe the consequences of education for the life chances of children? Are these descriptions contradictory? Are they reflected in actual student outcomes? How/do Chinese educators discuss equality of educational opportunity? How do groups of individuals, identifiable as part of an emerging "middle" class actively use and create schools to support their own interests? Do the processes of schooling (formal curriculum) conform to and re-affirm these interests? Do parents define the purpose of schools and use schools in similar and/or different ways for their sons and daughters? How do diverse girls' schools illuminate such patterns? How does economic/geographical location influence the material conditions and human resources as well as community support, available to schools? How are messages different for or differently received by girls in ways that restrict or enhance their access to political, economic, and intellectual power? Are private schools by definition exclusionary or can they expand access for students with few economic resources and initiate positive debate on the state's responsibility to schooling?

7. This is a comment that boarding school students in China have made for the last two decades (see Heidi Ross, 1993).

8. This case study is drawn from a larger history of #3 (see Heidi Ross, 1997).

9. The name of this project borrows from the national program run by the China Youth Development Foundation, which in the past decade has channeled

donations for educational development to poor rural regions for the establishment of schools.

10. Only 30% of students from Nanchang's college preparatory high schools were admitted to tertiary training in 1998.

11. We do not use "resistance" in the tradition of critical theory to imply a conscious penetration of and rejection of structures of power. Instead, we mean challenging the consequences (poverty, exam-based school placement, discrimination against girls, and rural children) of state policies perceived to work against particular group interests.

REFERENCES

Brook, T. (1997). Auto-organization in Chinese society. In: T. Brook & B. M. Frolic (Eds), *Civil society in China* (pp. 19–45). Armonk, NY: M.E. Sharpe.
Brook, T., & Frolic, B. M. (Eds). (1997). *Civil society in China*. Armonk: M.E. Sharpe.
Cheng, K. M. (1994). Education, decentralization, and regional disparity in China. In: G. Postiglione & W. O. Lee (Eds), *Social change and educational development: Mainland China, Taiwan, and Hong Kong* (pp. 53–65). Hong Kong: Centre for Asian Studies, University of Hong Kong.
Cheng, K. M. (1996). *The quality of primary education, a case study of Zhejiang Province, China*. Paris: International Institute for Educational Planning.
Cheng, K.-M. (2001). China's education reform: Priorities and implications, a brief review of 20 years. Paper presented at the conference on Education Reform in China, Harvard University, July 14–15, p. 14.
Delpit, L. (1995). *Other people's children: Cultural conflict in the classroom*. New York: New Press.
Education for All. (2000). *Education for all: The year assessment final country report of China*. Beijing: UNESCO.
Hecht, J. (1998). Women's rights, state's Law: The role of law in women's rights policy in China. In: J. Montgomery (Ed.), *Human rights, positive policies in Asia and the Pacific Rim* (pp. 71–96). Hollis, NY: Hollis Publishing Co.
Jeong, I., & Armer, J. M. (1994). State, class, and expansion of education in South Korea: A general model. *Comparative Education Review, 38*, 531–545.
Katznelson, I., & Weir, M. (1985). *Schooling for all: Class, race, and the decline of the democratic ideal*. New York: Basic Books.
Kroeber, A., & Miller, T. (2005). Education, schooling for the future. *China Economic Quarterly, (9)*4, (Online).
Lareau, A. (2003). *Unequal childhoods, class, race, and family life*. Berkeley: University of California Press.
Lee, S., & Brinton, M. (1996). Elite education and social capital: The case of South Korea civil society. *Sociology of Education, 69*, 177–192.
Lewin, K., & Wang, Y. J. (1994). *Implementing basic education in China: Progress and prospects in rich, poor and national minority areas*. IIEP Research Report no. 101. International Institute for Educational Planning, Paris.
Li, X. J. (1999). With what discourse do we reflect on Chinese women? In: M. Yang (Ed.), *Spaces of their own, women's public sphere in transnational China*. Minneapolis: University of Minnesota Press.

Lin, J. (1999). *Social transformation and private education in China.* Westport, CN: Praeger Press.
Lin, J., & Ross, H. (1998). The potentials and problems of diversity in Chinese education. *McGill Journal of Education, 33,* 31–49.
Liu, X. (2000). *In one's own shadow: An ethnographic account of the condition of post-reform rural China.* Berkeley: University of California Press.
Lu, X., & Perry, E. (Eds) (1997). *Danwei, the changing Chinese workplace in historical and comparative perspective.* Armonk, NY: M.E. Sharpe.
Malik, K. (2005). Launch of the China Human Development Report 2005: Opening remarks at the launch of the China Human Development Report 2005 by Khalid Malik, UN resident coordinator and UNDP resident representative (December 16, 2005). Retrieved March 9, 2006.
Moi, T. (1991). Appropriating Bourdieu: Feminist theory and Pierre Bourdieu's sociology of culture, gender, communities. *New Literary History, 22*(4), 1017–1049.
Montgomery, J. (1998). *Human rights, positive policies in Asia and the Pacific Rim.* Hollis, NY: Hollis Publishing Co.
Pepper, S. (1996). *Radicalism and education reform in 20th-century China, the search for an ideal development model.* Cambridge: Cambridge University Press.
Reimers, F. (2000). *Unequal schools, unequal chances: The challenges to equal opportunity in the Americas.* Cambridge: Harvard University Press.
Ross, H. (1993). *China learns English.* New Haven: Yale University Press.
Ross, H. (1997). Cradle of female talent: The McTyeire home and school for girls, 1892–1937. In: D. Bays (Ed.), *Christianity in China: From the eighteenth century to the present* (pp. 209–227). Stanford: Stanford University Press.
Ross, H. with contributions by Lou, J., Yang, L., Rybakova, O., & Wakhungu, P. (2005). *Where and who are the World's illiterates: China.* A Background Paper Submitted to UNESCO Global Monitoring Report.
Ross, H., & Lin, J. (Eds.), (2001). Educating girls in a different way: Teaching and learning in Chinese girls' schools. *Chinese Education and Society, 34,* 1–10.
Ross, H., & Lin, J. (2004). Schools of goodwill in China: Helping poor students succeed. *Journal of Thought, 39*(1), 131–146.
Subject Group of Higher Education Research Institute of Beijing Institute of Technology. (2005). *Opportunity to receive higher education: Narrowing gaps.* Report of the Subject Group of Research on Equity in China's Higher Education. Ford Foundation, Beijing, Beijing University.
UNDP. (2005). *Human Development Report, 2005. International cooperation at a crossroads: Aid, trade and security in an unequal world.* New York: UNDP.
Watkins, D., & Biggs, J. (1996). *The Chinese learner: Cultural, pedagogical, and contextual influences.* Hong Kong: CERC and ACER.
Weis, L., & Fine, M. (1993). *Beyond silenced voices: Class, race and gender in U.S. schools.* Albany: State University of New York Press.

GIRLS' SCHOOLING AND MARRIAGE IN RURAL BANGLADESH

Simeen Mahmud and Sajeda Amin

ABSTRACT

In Bangladesh, girls' ability to complete schooling is compromised by poverty and the practice of early marriage. Although most girls enroll in school, rates of dropping out are high around puberty. This paper uses a panel survey (2001 and 2003) of nearly 3,000 adolescent girls in rural Bangladesh to predict schooling outcomes. The analysis explores household and community factors to explain school enrollment, dropping out and marriage. Girls in poor households are more likely to drop out before reaching secondary school. Girls in wealthier households are more likely to drop out later, because of marriage, and having more siblings increases this possibility.

INTRODUCTION

Two of the most striking recent changes in Bangladesh are the near universalization of basic schooling, and the closing of the gender gap in school enrollment. Today, most primary school-age children and half of the secondary school-age children in Bangladesh are enrolled in school, with girls outnumbering boys. The gross enrollment ratio[1] at the primary level (grades 1–5) is close to 100% (the net enrollment ratio is 89%, UNESCO, 2003, p. 333). Female enrollment at the secondary level (grades 6–12) has also increased considerably. Female gross enrollment ratios have risen from 13.6% in the 1990s to 46.9% in 2000 (UNESCO, 2003, p. 349). By the year 2000, five million girls were enrolled, representing 49.7% of total enrollment (UNESCO, 2003).

Even 50 years ago, education was viewed as the prerogative of a negligible urban elite, and was not generally considered necessary or valuable by the majority of Bangladeshis. If school enrollments reveal demand for education, then up to the late 1970s, the demand for education was quite small, with attendance rising slowly and unsteadily during the 1980s (Hossain & Kabeer, 2004). Since the early 1990s, primary school attendance has begun to spread rapidly and consistently, with a closing of the gender gap and doubling of gross enrollment ratios in the last decade.[2] The demand for girls' secondary education rose even faster, as indicated by the rapid rise in female secondary gross enrollment ratios discussed in the preceding paragraph.

The rising demand for girls' secondary education is further supported by the fact that the transition ratio of girls from primary to secondary level – the number enrolled in grade 6 calculated as a percentage of the number completing grade 5 in the same year – increased steadily during this period. The transition ratio from primary to secondary was estimated at 79% in 1994, and rose to 83% in 1997, as calculated from national educational statistics (Bangladesh Bureau of Educational Information and Statistics, World Bank, 1999, p. 21). Moreover, with the exception of grades 11–12, girls' gross enrollment rates (children enrolled in grade as a percentage of all children in target age) exceeded that of boys for all grades in secondary school,[3] and the female advantage was seen in both poor and non-poor households (World Bank, 2003, p. 51).

Thus, the tremendous rise in school participation is a fairly recent phenomenon in Bangladesh. Within this context, the demand for girls' education has been rising faster than the demand for boys' education, and is evident among all socioeconomic classes. This is indeed remarkable in a society that has been characterized by extreme gender differentiation in economic roles, lower parental investments in daughters than in sons, and significant restrictions on girls' public mobility. It is even more remarkable that the demand for education increased the most during a period when poverty levels remained static or may even have worsened.[4] Clearly, the cost–benefit calculation made by parents about children's education has been changing, and the cost–benefit calculus surrounding girls' schooling has changed to a greater extent. Since in the past, girls have lagged behind boys in school enrollment, the more rapid increase in girls' school enrollment relative to boys' could simply represent a catching-up effect triggered by gender-specific financial incentives. On the other hand, it could also represent a genuine transformation in parental sex preferences for investing in children.

Our calculations based on national education statistics collected in 2000 indicate that despite girls' increased access to basic education, only two-thirds of all girls enrolled at the primary level finish grade 5 and are eligible for secondary school (BANBEIS, 2002). Among these, not all enter secondary school (BANBEIS, 2002). Gross enrollment ratios at the secondary level are not only much lower than at the primary level, but they also decline with rising grade.[5] A major reason for this phenomenon is that more than one-third of girls entering secondary school drop out before completing grade 10.[6] This means that, although nearly all parents are investing in girls' schooling at the younger ages (under 12), many are less inclined to do so for older adolescent girls. Thus, despite financial incentives for girls' secondary school attendance, schooling of adolescent girls continues to present a more difficult cost–benefit trade-off to parents, especially those under resource constraints.[7]

An important element of the cost–benefit trade-off for parents is the marriage market. Peculiarities of the marriage market in Bangladesh, of which early age at marriage for girls is one, mean that the costs of and returns to adolescent girls' schooling are mediated by many factors at the community, household, and individual levels that do not come into play for younger girls. Indeed, Lloyd's (2005) recent global review of marriage and education trends in contemporary developing societies identifies Bangladesh as the only country in which marriage is a significant reason for girls dropping out of school. Lloyd shows that in every other contemporary setting, there is a substantial period of waiting time between when children drop out of school and when they marry, averaging around three years. In most countries that have marriage ages comparable to Bangladesh's, schooling does not interfere with marriage, because typical school attainment rates are low.

This paper examines school attainment of adolescent girls in rural Bangladesh, within the context of programs that help to defray the costs of schooling. The competing roles of marriage and attributes of the natal household and community are explored in order to understand the factors that contribute to early marriage and high rates of dropping out of school.

A THEORETICAL FRAMEWORK

In situations of resource constraint, children's school attainment is usually conceptualized as being a product of parental decision making. For parents, investments in children's education form an integral part of household survival strategies. In economic explanations of rising school participation, investments in children's education are made on the basis of expected returns from education relative to returns from other household investments. In the case of developing countries, returns from and costs of schooling vary considerably by sex. For boys, returns to education are seen in terms of increased labor market opportunities. These sorts of returns are almost negligible for girls in societies characterized by extreme forms of sex-based labor market segmentation.

Importantly, however, there are significant returns to girls' education in terms of contributions to the household sector, specifically from the positive effects on the human capital of future generations (for a review, see Behrman, Foster, Rosenweig, & Vashishtha, 1999). Better-educated women are better mothers and home teachers, better caregivers, more responsive to emergencies and illnesses, and so on. Moreover, in contexts where women have a lower relative social status compared to men, educated women command more resources both within the household (greater say in household resource allocation) and outside (networks, micro credit, mobility into the public domain), and they choose to allocate these at higher levels than would men (Behrman et al., 1999). Parents are motivated to invest in their daughters' education even when they are not direct beneficiaries, as they would have been by investing in sons' education, because education increases their value as future wives and daughters-in-law. Parents may also think of returns to education in terms of costs averted. A bad marriage for a daughter entails costs for her parents because they are responsible for her welfare in the event that her husband does not fulfill his role. However, when girls' schooling has a high opportunity cost (domestic work responsibility), parents may not be equally motivated to educate all daughters. The "domestic sphere" determines returns to girls' education, even as the expansion of schooling takes place by reproducing gender inequality through the allocation of children's time in the home (Post, 2001). Since returns to children's education are undermined by the high opportunity cost of school, returns to girls' schooling will be perceived only in relation to their domestic work responsibility. Thus, when older daughters take on responsibility for domestic chores, the returns to education for younger daughters are perceived as more advantageous, and the chances of attending school increase for younger daughters.

There are cultural explanations for variations in parental perceptions about returns to education, based on the social and psychological costs and benefits of schooling, that have particular bearing upon gender differences in aspirations. Recent evidence of the highly context-specific nature of family decisions regarding education of sons and daughters indicates the importance of cultural norms in shaping educational aspirations (Buchmann & Hannum, 2001, p. 85). Returns to girls' schooling will be low in societies where girls' public mobility is restricted and women have major, even sole, responsibility for household production. Cultural norms and practices that portray men as breadwinners and women as homemakers are particularly rigid in non-poor households. Cultural norms of investing differently in sons and daughters can raise the social costs of girls' schooling, such as breaking norms of seclusion, and weaken returns (Sathar et al., 2005; Amin & Sedgh, 1998; Kabeer & Mahmud, 2004). Conversely, local norms and practices that support girls' schooling strengthen less tangible returns to school, such as a sense of inclusion and the expectation of a return from schooling, even if these are vague and not immediately apparent.

The nature or quality of education provided also influences the social and psychological benefits and costs of schooling. Returns to school, especially as perceived by the poor, will be low if the type of education provided and the process of teaching are insensitive to peoples' socioeconomic situation, needs, and constraints, and may even encourage self-exclusion and marginalization (Nambissan, 2003, p. 137). In contrast, even when benefits of girls' schooling are not well perceived, the creation of a more hospitable environment for girls, through motivational campaigns, establishment of girls' schools within villages, and special provisions such as female stipends, reduces costs and encourage the practice of sending girls to school (Hossain & Kabeer, 2004, p. 4095).

In Bangladesh the marriage market also significantly impacts the returns to girls' education, and the subsequent impact of girls' schooling on human capital of future generations. When labor market opportunities are curtailed for women, a woman's well-being and that of her children depend upon securing a good marriage. Better-educated women are able to attract better grooms, and their households are able to negotiate a more desirable marriage for them. Usually, this enables them to move up the income and social class scale, thereby increasing their chances of a better-endowed future generation (Behrman et al., 1999; Elder, 1969).

In addition, because marriage grants social status to women and reduces their economic insecurity,[8] securing a good marriage for a daughter is a smart and risk-averse strategy for parents. Parents may even be willing to bear some of the monetary and non-monetary costs of girls' schooling. This is especially true if the type of schooling provided is perceived to enhance the possibilities of securing a good marriage by improving a girl's appearance, personality, and social skills (White, 1991; Rozario, 2002). Because women's labor market opportunities are limited, an unsuccessful marriage can end up as an economic burden on parents. Thus, from the perspective of poor parents, securing a good marriage is not only an investment in their daughter's future, but eventually an investment in their own future well-being.

In this respect, the peculiarity of the marriage market plays an important role in the extent of investment in girls' schooling. In the Bangladesh marriage market, customs are such that grooms have greater say in determining the type and timing of a match. The bride and her family are relegated to a passive role. Grooms have to initiate a proposal that the bride can then accept or reject, but usually within a short period of time. Girls cannot deliberate over a proposal long, and often have to accept or reject within days. Rejections are not made or taken lightly, as they have implications both for the bride's and groom's reputation and future marriage prospects.

These rules of the marriage process create situations of information asymmetry. The families of brides are at a disadvantage, while the grooms (or those deciding on his behalf) have the advantage of more information and time in the decision-making process. The loss of reputation can have important implications for future marriage prospects and regarding the amount of the dowry that has to be paid. Since reputation can suffer from malicious gossip, anxiety about maintaining a good reputation can lead to early age at marriage (Huq & Amin, 2001).

Thus, in Bangladesh, investment in girls' schooling may actually be seen as a household investment in the future well-being of daughters, and that of future generations, through securing a good marriage (Arends-Kuenning & Amin, 2001). To that extent, the schooling decision and the marriage decision are seen as complementary, rather than competing, when households are making investment decisions. The trade-off faced by Bangladeshi parents is not so much between investing in their daughters' schooling and investing in their marriage, but between competing household investments and the actual monetary and non-monetary costs and benefits of different investments, including schooling.

For Bangladeshi parents, costs of schooling are real, readily identified, and immediately experienced. These include direct money costs for fees and books, and indirect money costs of better clothing, better food, and private tuition to improve classroom performance. For the poor, there are additional opportunity costs of girls' schooling that may not be of concern to non-poor households: long workdays for girls accompanied by increased family income (since if girls perform domestic chores this usually frees their mothers for market work), and the costs of delayed marriage for girls (higher dowry, greater insecurity) (Amin & Suran, 2004). Benefits of girl's schooling, on the other hand, are generally perceived rather than real, and, where real, are deferred. The expected positive impact on the well-being of future generations is at best uncertain (striking a good marriage is largely a matter of chance), and less likely to be realized by parents, unlike investments in sons' education. The psychological benefits for girls in receiving additional schooling are all vague. Girls may feel more included or less different, they may feel better equipped to get along in the world, or they may believe schooling provides them with a possible fallback against a lack of material resources. Returns to girls' education are also less visible and less concrete than returns to other types of household investment in human capital, such as investment in health, nutrition, housing, etc. These statements suggest that the poor experience relatively lower returns to girls' schooling because they discount future returns at a higher rate than the non-poor. It is well documented that government action to promote a favorable environment for girls' school participation has actually been quite successful in reducing the short-term costs of education, even among the poor (Amin & Sedgh, 1998; Khandker, Pitt, & Fuwa, 2001). Government actions include the use of slogans like "education for all" the reduction in traveling distance to school by expanding the number of schools, and the provision of subsidies (food/cash for education, free tuition, stipends for girls).

Strong private and state support for widespread public education and the education of girls, in particular, has been instrumental in getting more parents to consider providing their female children with a good education (Hossain & Kabeer, 2004). Unfortunately, while school provision may have equalized perceptions about returns to schooling, cost-mitigating interventions have not increased the preference for girls schooling uniformly (Hossain, 2005). Girls from poor households are still less able to take advantage of educational opportunities than girls from non-poor households.[9]

Thus, in Bangladesh, when the cost of schooling was high, school participation was limited to children, mostly sons, from wealthy households. When immediate money costs and some social and psychological costs of girls' schooling declined (due to an increase in the supply of schools), there was a rise in girls' enrollment across socioeconomic class, since girls' education was seen as enhancing the likelihood of a good marriage and the human capital of future generations. However, since the costs and benefits of girls' secondary school continue to be differentiated by socioeconomic class, there is considerable heterogeneity among girls who discontinue schooling. Some girls never enroll in secondary school. Among those who do, some drop out before completing grade 10 and are married, and some drop out for other reasons and may or may not be married. A smaller proportion continues to attend school but does not marry, and may go on to take the public certificate examination after grade 10.

To understand factors that affect school rates of dropping out we need to differentiate between the reasons for dropping out. In particular, girls who drop out for marriage may not be disadvantaged in the same way as girls who drop out for other reasons. Our framework provides the following explanations for the observed school/marriage outcomes in Bangladesh:

(1) Girls who attend school and drop out to be married tend to belong to households that view school as an investment for a good marriage, and can afford to keep daughters in school as long as it is necessary to arrange a good marriage.
(2) Girls who continue in school tend to belong to households that can afford to keep daughters in school as long as needed, but there are divergent reasons for this. For the majority, marriage negotiations take longer than usual, due to issues such as problems with a girl's complexion or reputation. For a small minority, getting an education is seen as important, beyond securing a good marriage, in order to increase labor market opportunities in terms of a salaried job. These girls are likely to perform better in school, and this is the only group for which additional schooling results in increased age at marriage.
(3) Girls who attend school and drop out for reasons other than marriage belong to households that can only pay for their daughters' education up to a certain point. Then, they have to discontinue it due to school costs, regardless of whether a good marriage is arranged or not. Among them, some are married after awhile (they will be older than those who drop out for marriage). The rest are not married, because marriage negotiations are taking longer than expected. This is usually due to high dowry demands made as compensation for some characteristic of the girl, such as complexion or reputation. For them, age at marriage will be higher than average, but not because of school attendance.
(4) Finally, girls who never enroll in secondary school belong to households that cannot pay any costs of girls' secondary education, even when they are aware of the returns to schooling in terms of a good marriage.

DATA AND METHODS

This paper models the joint household decision on schooling and marriage of adolescent girls in rural areas of Bangladesh in order to explain the observed outcomes outlined above. The study uses data from a panel survey of nearly 3,000 adolescent girls (between ages 13 and 22)[10] in three rural regions or districts of Bangladesh originally surveyed in 2001 and followed up in 2003: Chapainawabganj in the northwest, Sherpur in northcentral, and Chittagong in the southeast. The surveys were designed to inform policy and programing on a range of issues important for adolescents in the areas of education, health, work and livelihoods, and social life. They were also intended to illuminate the impact of an intervention program targeted at adolescent girls (the "Kishori Abhijan" program of the Ministry of Women Affairs; hereafter "the program").

The baseline survey was conducted between January and June 2001, among randomly selected adolescents residing in 90 villages. (For a description of the baseline survey experimental design, see Amin, Mahmud, & Huq, 2002.) In addition to the randomly selected sample, the original survey also included a second group of girls (15%) who were not randomly selected, to ensure adequate numbers in the intervention group. This sample was necessitated because one of the two implementing NGOs, the Bangladesh Rural Advancement Committee (BRAC), announced that girl children enrolled in BRAC schools would be given preference for inclusion in the program.

For budgetary reasons, the follow-up survey was limited to a randomly selected subset of 75 villages. It was conducted from January to June 2003, after the programs had been implemented in the intervention villages. Since the programs only included girls, 2,386 female respondents who had been successfully interviewed in the baseline survey were contacted for a follow-up interview, and 2,214 of these respondents were successfully interviewed.[11] A detailed community profile was also conducted at this time for each village in which the survey was undertaken. The community profile was based on interviews with at least three male and female key informants from the community, including program personnel involved in the particular intervention (see Amin & Suran, 2004).

Only respondents between the ages of 15 and 22 were included in the analysis, to avoid age-related outcomes that could potentially bias the results. Sample weights were constructed to adjust for over-sampling of girls considered eligible for the program. Weights were applied to make the sample representative of the adolescent girl population and to ensure that girls in BRAC schools were not overrepresented.

In addition, only those respondents who were successfully interviewed in both rounds of data collection were included in the analysis.[12] We were interested in examining the joint schooling and marriage outcomes for adolescent girls, and more specifically school attendance and discontinuation within the existing policy environment of free tuition and stipends to all girls residing in rural areas and enrolled in grades 6–10.

We distinguish between marriage-related reasons for school discontinuation and other reasons, since almost 60% of girls report other reasons than marriage for dropping out. Marriage-related reasons included girls who drop out because they are actually getting married and moving to their marital home, as well as those who drop out because marriage negotiations have begun. Other reasons included schooling being too costly, parents not allowing girls to continue their education, and girls' own apathy or lack of interest in school. The dependent variable of "girls' school/marriage outcome" is constructed from school attendance and marital status information in the baseline and follow-up surveys. Girls who dropped out before grade 5 and thus did not enter secondary school were ineligible for government stipends and therefore were included with the category of girls never enrolled.

There are five comparison categories for school/married outcome as follows:

- never enrolled or dropped out before grade 5,
- dropped out (after grade 5) for marriage, and married in 2001,
- dropped out (after grade 5) for other reasons, and married in 2001,
- dropped out (after grade 5) for other reasons, and not married in 2001, and
- continuous school attendance (enrolled in 2001 and 2003).

Factors that influence the household decision on schooling and marriage are identified at three levels: community, household, and individual. All explanatory variables are taken from the baseline survey. Since the baseline survey results showed that school attendance and marriage patterns varied significantly by girls' age and region of residence, these are treated as background variables whose effects have to be controlled in order to estimate net effects of other explanatory variables on girls' schooling/marriage outcomes.

There are three community-level factors: the proportion of literate villagers, which is a proxy for the value accorded to education by the community; the distance to high school from the village, which is an indicator of school access; and the distance to a main road or village remoteness, which is a measure of exposure to outside ideas and information. In addition, we have two village aggregate indicators of a favorable/secure social environment for girls: girls' safety on the road (proportion of girls in the village who report being teased or harassed by boys on their way to school), and girls' mobility (based on places girls usually visited in the past week).

Household factors included the following: household wealth, based on land and asset ownership; household food availability, which was considered an indicator of economic vulnerability; parents' education, as a proxy for parental aspirations; and female headship, which suggested both economic insecurity as well as greater female decision-making power. Household vulnerability or exposure to risk (from events such as a bad harvest, loss of investment, sudden illness, death, or flood) is considered an important determinant of schooling, because it increases the need to diversify investment in children (Amin & Arends-Kuenning, 2001). Finally, individual factors include the following: participation in productive work, which is a measure of the opportunity cost of school; aspiration for a salaried job, which reflects higher expected returns to schooling; and school performance and program membership.

Girls' schooling behavior is explained through multivariate regression techniques using multinomial logistic regressions[13] of school outcomes on the above community, household, and individual factors. The results are presented in Table 1, where the estimated parameters of the coefficients are converted into odds ratios by exponentiating them. They are also known as relative risk ratios (rrr). The rrr is the relative risk or odds of being in the dependent variable category of interest and not being in the base or reference category (never enrolled), for the dummy independent variable

Table 1. Distribution of Adolescents by Current School Status in Rural Bangladesh in 2001.

School Status 2001	Age Group			
	13–15	16–18	19–22	All ages
Girls				
Never attended school	8	20	37	27
Currently in school	71	25	7	35
Attended in past, discontinued	22	55	56	43
Total number	919	706	919	2,544
Boys				
Never attended school	19	25	32	24
Currently in school	57	37	21	43
Attended in past, discontinued	24	38	47	34
Total number	778	549	402	1,729

Source: Amin et al., 2002.

versus the omitted category of the independent variable. The magnitudes of the estimated odds ratios show the relative size of the effects of explanatory variables on school outcome. Only estimates significant at the 5% level or below are indicated with an asterisk.

RESULTS

School Attendance: 2001 Level and Trends

Table 1 presents the distribution of adolescents by current school status at the time of the baseline in 2001. Over a third of rural adolescent girls in the study population were enrolled in school, while more than one-fifth had never enrolled, and 43% had attended in the past and discontinued. A comparison of the proportions currently in school and never enrolled for ages 13–15 and 19–22 shows that school attendance by adolescent girls has become almost the norm, compared to quite low levels of educational attainment even a few years ago. This confirms that expansion in adolescent girls' school attendance is indeed a very recent change.

The majority of girls (83%) attended formal mainstream schools, while 12% were enrolled in religious schools (madrasahs) and 5% in NGO informal schools. Formal schools follow curricula designed by the government; NGO schools follow special curricula designed by each NGO; and madrasahs follow a standard nationalized curriculum with special emphasis on Islamic religious education. The vast majority of girls enrolled in school are beneficiaries of school financial incentives: 88% receive a stipend and all receive free tuition. While a tuition waiver is given to all girls, the criteria for receiving stipends are more stringent (minimum attendance and performance are required).

Fig. 1 compares change in overall levels of school participation in this sample between 2001 and 2003. There was an increase in the level of current school attendance and a decline in the level of those who never attended school. The increase in the proportion of past school attendance indicates an increase in the proportion of school drop outs. Thus, girls' school attendance increased during the two-year period for the study sample, either because girls who had never been enrolled had joined school, or because girls who had dropped out (not in school in 2001) had returned and were in school in 2003.

Marriage remained the most important reason for girls' school discontinuation in both surveys, and its importance did not decline (41% in 2001 and 42% in 2003). Other important reasons for discontinuation included schooling being too costly (16% in both surveys), girls not being interested in school (16% and 12%, respectively), and parents not allowing girls to

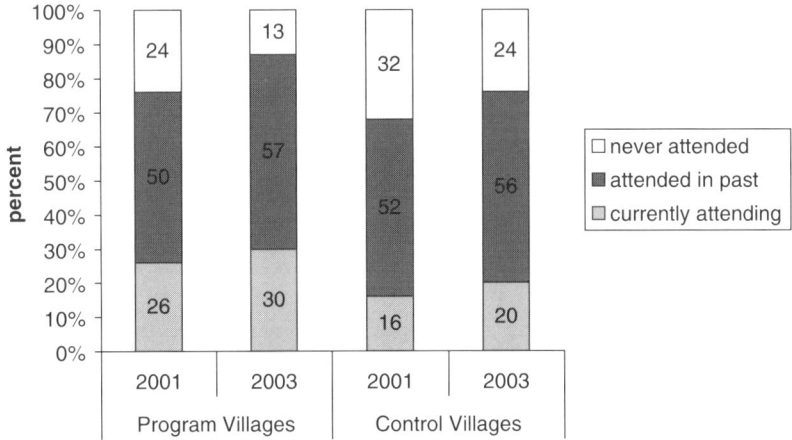

Fig. 1. Overall Schooling Rates among 15–22-Year-Old Female Respondents, by Residence Type. *Source:* Amin and Suran, 2004.

continue attending school (20% and 13%, respectively). It should be noted that one reason for discontinuation – a lack of interest in school – declined in importance both among parents and among adolescent girls. This may have been a response to government programs that mitigate some of the immediate costs of school (Amin & Suran, 2004).

Qualitative case studies showed that respondents for whom marriage discussions had been held were much more likely to have dropped out between the two surveys. The importance of marriage seems to take precedence over education, and the issue of dowry appears to be a significant factor in schooling decisions. Girls who expected to pay dowry dropped out of school at higher rates than those who did not expect to pay dowry at marriage.

Predicting School/Marriage Outcomes

Two samples are used to model school/marriage outcomes, as observed at the end of the observation period in 2003. The full sample (2,211) includes all girls for whom information on the explanatory variables was available and who participated in the baseline as well as the midline surveys. This sample is used to explore the influence of background, community, village environment, and household effects that are fixed and do not vary over time. The second subsample (917) is restricted to girls who were in school and not married in 2001 (baseline), when they were also asked about their educational aspirations and work status. We felt that by limiting the analysis to those who are in school and not married, this minimized the possibility of overestimating the effects of these variables on schooling outcomes because of issues related to reverse causality. Table 2 compares the weighted frequency distributions of the explanatory variables in the two samples.

The distribution of the dependent variable changes significantly in the subsample. Nearly two-thirds of the girls were still in school after two years (61%), the continued school category. Another 13% had dropped out to get married, and the remainder had dropped out for other reasons (25%). Girls from wealthier households and from Chittagong are overrepresented, while poor girls and those living in Sherpur are underrepresented in the more restricted subsample. This is not unexpected, given the school and marriage patterns observed in the baseline survey. This sample allows us to determine the direction of causality of a number of endogenous variables that we could not control for in the full sample, but that are likely to be strong predictors of the outcome variable.

Tables 3 and 5 present multinomial logistic regression results for school/marriage outcomes for the full sample and more restricted subsample, respectively. Table 3 (the full sample) shows that school/marriage outcomes for girls vary significantly by region or district. Relative to girls in Chapainawabganj, girls in Chittagong are considerably less likely to drop out because of marriage and more likely to drop out before marriage. Both categories are attributable to a generally later regime of marriage in that district. Sherpur has a distinctly different pattern in that girls are either more likely never to enroll or to drop out before completing grade 5. These effects remain even after controlling for village social environment effects and community effects. Girls' age has a strong positive effect on all school/marriage outcomes, relative to continued schooling.

Village literacy reduces the chance of never enrolling in school and of dropping out to get married or dropping out for other reasons. However, it does not affect these chances nearly as much as it increases the chance of continued school attendance. School distance and village remoteness have no effect on outcomes. Girls' safety in the village has a weak positive effect on girls dropping out for other reasons, compared to continued school attendance. Girls' mobility, on the other hand, lowers the chances of dropping out for getting married. This suggests that a favorable village environment, one that gives girls greater mobility, allows parents to keep girls in school instead of getting them married. Household wealth significantly reduced the chances of never being enrolled or dropping out before grade 6, as well as dropping out for other reasons, but did not affect dropping out to

Table 2. Weighted Frequency Distributions of Explanatory Variables According to Full Sample and Subsample.

	Percent, Full Sample	Percent, Subsample
Observations in sample	2,211	917
Dependent variable		
Continuing school	24.49	61.33
Dropped out after grade 5 and unmarried	8.75	13.05
Dropped out after grade 5 for marriage and married	17.21	13.48
Dropped out after grade 5 for other reasons and married	9.3	4.99
Never enrolled/dropped out before grade 5	40.25	7.16
District		
Chapainawabganj	39.4	38.2
Chittagong	27.6	36.3
Sherpur	33.0	25.5
Wealth		
Lowest quartile	27.0	14.0
Second quartile	24.0	21.5
Third quartile	23.5	26.9
Highest quartile	25.6	37.6
Proportion of village literate, by quartile		
Lowest quartile	24.7	18.1
Second quartile	38.7	37.8
Third quartile	19.8	20.1
Highest quartile	16.8	24.0
Household food shortage		
Deficit throughout the year	14.1	8.6
Deficit in some months	32.7	29.8
Neither shortage nor surplus	40.5	42.9
Surplus	12.7	18.7
Mother had any education	23.6	33.2
Father had any education	41.0	51.4
Participated in productive work	54.9	4.05
Aspiration for salaried work	33.2	60.5
Lives in a female-headed household	4.3	4.8
Program membership	11.9	24.4
Performed well in school	24.0	50.7

get married. In other words, girls who drop out for marriage would continue in school if no marriage were arranged. Thus, household wealth allows parents to keep a girl in school regardless of the time taken to arrange a marriage for her, while household poverty forces parents to withdraw a girl from school even when a marriage has not been arranged (see Fig. 2).

Table 3. Multinomial Logit Regression: Outcomes for Girls[a].

	Outcomes Base Category: Continued Enrollment			
	Dropped Out after Grade 5 and Unmarried	Dropped Out after Grade 5 for Marriage and Married	Dropped Out after Grade 5 for other Reasons and Married	Never Enrolled/ Dropped Out before Grade 5
District, omitted category Chapainawabganj				
Sherpur	1.09	1.22	1.17	2.16*
	(0.849)	(0.460)	(0.672)	(0.014)
Chittagong	2.07*	0.265*	0.58	0.40*
	(0.036)	(0.000)	(0.071)	(0.003)
Age	1.34*	1.69*	1.88*	1.73*
	(0.000)	(0.000)	(0.000)	(0.000)
Wealth, lowest quartile omitted				
Second wealth quartile	0.59	1.25	0.78	0.38*
	(0.096)	(0.477)	(0.406)	(0.000)
Third wealth quartile	0.66	1.50	0.69	0.27*
	(0.171)	(0.171)	(0.175)	(0.000)
Fourth wealth quartile	0.33	1.13	0.36*	0.11*
	(0.000)	(0.717)	(0.001)	(0.000)
Proportion of village literate quartile, lowest quartile omitted				
Second quartile	1.64	0.76	0.51*	0.40*
	(0.32)	(0.33)	(0.05)	(0.004)
Third quartile	0.98	0.76	0.27*	0.45*
	(0.971)	(0.471)	(0.003)	(0.048)
Fourth quartile	1.80	1.29	0.62	0.46
	(0.285)	(0.514)	(0.214)	(0.099)
Distance to high school	0.94	0.95	0.91	1.04
	(0.546)	(0.651)	(0.351)	(0.760)
Distance to main road	0.99	0.93*	0.96	0.98
	(0.760)	(0.040)	(0.202)	(0.601)
Father's education	0.90	0.50*	0.67	0.34*
	(0.669)	(0.001)	(0.072)	(0.000)
Mother's education	0.49*	0.54*	0.45*	0.23*
	(0.018)	(0.002)	(0.004)	(0.000)
Food shortages, deficit throughout the year omitted				
Food deficits in some months	0.81	1.09	0.530.103	0.89
	(0.581)	(0.819)		(0.751)
Neither shortage nor surplus	0.91	1.13	0.63	0.66
	(0.814)	(0.751)	(0.217)	(0.244)

Table 3. (*Continued*)

	Outcomes Base Category: Continued Enrollment			
	Dropped Out after Grade 5 and Unmarried	Dropped Out after Grade 5 for Marriage and Married	Dropped Out after Grade 5 for other Reasons and Married	Never Enrolled/ Dropped Out before Grade 5
Food surplus	0.49	1.14	0.38*	0.37*
	(0.151)	(0.739)	(0.043)	(0.006)
Female-headed household	0.74	0.64	0.51	0.57*
	(0.527)	(0.346)	(0.257)	(0.206)
Engaged in productive work	2.10*	1.48*	1.46	1.53*
	(0.000)	(0.045)	(0.072)	(0.013)
Program membership	1.57	0.60*	0.70	0.22*
	(0.065)	(0.020)	(0.403)	(0.000)
School performance	0.68	0.86	0.42*	0.31*
	(0.139)	(0.467)	(0.011)	(0.000)
Preference for wage work	0.77	0.56*	0.57*	0.16*
	(0.257)	(0.001)	(0.015)	(0.000)
Safety of girls in village	4.90	1.31	7.53	1.56
	(0.058)	(0.758)	(0.045)	(0.593)
Mobility of girls in village	0.22	0.12*	0.12	0.25
	(0.221)	(0.012)	(0.069)	(0.159)
Total number of siblings	1.07	1.28	1.10	1.29
	(0.336)	(0.000)	(0.239)	(0.000)
Number of elder sisters	0.95	0.64	0.94	0.75
	(0.667)	(0.000)	(0.575)	(0.003)

$N = 21.56$
[a] Relative risk ratios, with p-values in parentheses.
*Significant at 0.05 level.

Father's education lowers the chances of dropping out for marriage and of never enrolling, but has no effect on reasons other than marriage. Thus, father's education is positively associated with keeping girls in secondary school and unmarried, and helps to send girls to secondary school after primary (grade 5). These effects are clearly shown in the predicted probabilities in Fig. 3. Mother's education lowers the chances of dropping out for all reasons, so the effect is more consistent across household economic status. This effect fits in well with the hypothesis that, in many situations, returns to female education is in terms of improved human capital of future generations.

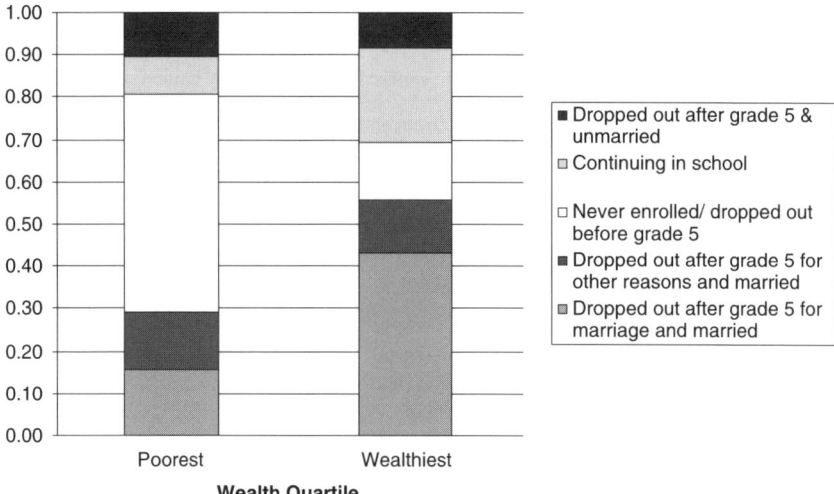

Fig. 2. Predicted Probabilities of Schooling/Marriage Outcomes by Wealth Quartile $N = 2156$. *Note:* Calculated from equation presented in Table 3. Based on panel data from Kishori Abhijan Project, Bangladesh 2001 and 2003, controlling for other individual or household level variables held at their mean/modal values.

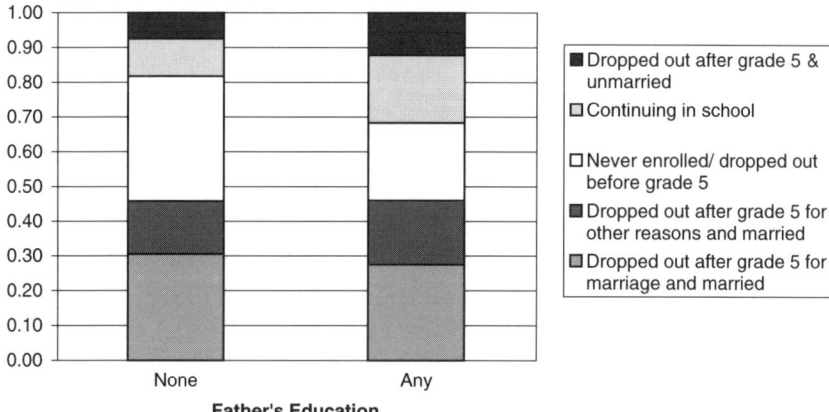

Fig. 3. Predicted Probabilities of Schooling/Marriage Outcomes by Father's Education $N = 2156$. *Note:* Calculated from equation presented in Table 3. Based on panel data from Kishori Abhijan Project, Bangladesh 2001 and 2003, controlling for other individual or household level variables held at their mean/modal values.

In general, food availability appears not to be a very good predictor of outcomes. It is only in food-surplus households that chances of never enrolling are lower. Thus, household economic vulnerability does not appear to have a very strong effect on girls' school/marriage outcomes. A similar effect is seen for female headship, which lowers the chances of never enrolling, but has no effect on dropping out of school to get married. Since female-headed households are, on average, poorer than male-headed households, the data suggests that the decision-making power of women with respect to investments in children and daughters is limited or constrained by structural factors like household poverty.

The total number of siblings has a generally negative effect on school continuation. Families with more siblings are significantly associated with a higher probability of girls dropping out of school to get married or for other reasons. However, the total number of elder sisters tempers these affects slightly.

Table 4 presents the distribution of the subsample of 917 adolescent girls who were in school and not married in 2001 and according to the five school outcome categories and selected explanatory variables at the time of the baseline survey. The effects of the explanatory variable estimated from the full model are clearly visible in the observed frequency distributions for the subsample of girls who were in school and unmarried in 2001.

It may be noted that girls who were in school continuously and those who had dropped out for marriage were of similar mean age (14 years). For girls who dropped out for other reasons, however, there was a waiting time of a little more than a year between when they dropped out of school and when they got married.

The impact of siblings and older sisters in the subsample is similar to the effects in the full model. The results presented in Table 5 (subsample) show that participation in productive work is associated with an increased chance of dropping out for other reasons and the chance of dropping before grade 6 but the latter relationship is weaker. Since both these categories are more likely to be in the poorest households and least likely to be in the wealthiest households (Table 3), participation in productive work may be due to a poverty effect (i.e., that girls in poor households are more likely to work).

Whether work causes girls in the poorest households to drop out of school is not immediately obvious. However, even if causality is not established, the strong relationship between participation in productive work and dropping out of school (highly significant odds ratio) is evidence that, in this case, girls' school attendance has a high opportunity cost in terms of inability to engage in productive work. More than half (55%) of the girls who drop out

Table 4. Distribution of Adolescent Girls 15- to 22 Years Old in School and Not Married in 2001, According to School Outcomes and Selected Explanatory Variables.

Outcome	Weighted Proportion	N (Weighted Frequency)	Mean Age	Percentage in Highest Household Wealth Quartile	Percentage in Lowest Household Wealth Quartile	Mother, any Education (Percentage)	Father, any Education (Percentage)	Any Food Shortage (Percentage)
Dropped out after grade 5, never married	13.05	119.62	15.16	29.19	19.54	26.58	57.40	36.66
Continued enrollment	61.33	562.42	14.42	41.75	11.37	40.46	59.15	35.73
Dropped out after grade 5 because of marriage and married	13.48	123.58	14.29	42.46	6.34	20.76	30.86	37.04
Dropped out after grade 5 for reasons other than marriage and married	4.99	45.76	15.64	31.75	12.67	37.84	55.16	33.60
Dropped out before grade 6	7.16	65.62	13.51	11.97	42.15	2.67	10.70	70.16

Table 5. Multinomial Logit Regression: Outcomes for Girls Enrolled and Unmarried in Baseline[a].

	Outcomes Base Category: Continued Enrollment			
	Dropped Out after Grade 5 and Unmarried	Dropped Out after Grade 5 for Marriage and Married	Dropped Out after Grade 5 for other Reasons and Married	Dropped Out before Grade 5
District, omitted category Chapainawabganj				
Sherpur	0.73	0.75	0.42	6.26*
	(0.57)	(0.424)	(0.166)	(0.001)
Chittagong	1.63	0.29*	0.25*	0.46
	(0.175)	(0.007)	(0.007)	(0.203)
Age	1.36*	1.05	1.43*	0.74
	(0.000)	(0.512)	(0.000)	(0.199)
Wealth, lowest quartile omitted				
Second wealth	0.60	1.99	1.29	0.39*
quartile	(0.171)	(0.208)	(0.669)	(0.053)
Third wealth	0.60	3.55*	0.92	0.26*
quartile	(0.148)	(0.020)	(0.892)	(0.041)
Fourth wealth	0.37*	3.86*	0.54	0.30
quartile	(0.001)	(0.029)	(0.312)	(0.061)
Proportion of village literate quartile, lowest quartile omitted				
Second quartile	1.74	0.98	0.80	0.42
	(0.348)	(0.95)	(0.710)	(0.082)
Third quartile	0.80	1.00	0.62	0.37
	(0.749)	(0.992)	(0.474)	(0.215)
Fourth quartile	1.61	1.91	0.79	1.23
	(0.503)	(0.114)	(0.759)	(0.750)
Distance to high school	0.93	1.03	0.90	1.24
	(0.538)	(0.747)	(0. 593)	(0.290)
Distance to main road	0.96	0.94	0.88*	1.02
	(0.508)	(0.167)	(0.041)	(0.692)
Father's education	1.09	0.35*	0.94	0.18*
	(0.773)	(0.001)	(0.909)	(0.009)
Mother's education	0.38*	0.49	0.8	0.18
	(0.022)	(0.059)	(0.799)	(0.121)
Food shortages, deficit throughout the year omitted				
Food deficits in	0.53	1.05	0.38	1.47
some months	(0.133)	(0.922)	(0.111)	(0.582)
	0.84	0.87	0.52	0.47

Table 5. (*Continued*)

	Outcomes Base Category: Continued Enrollment			
	Dropped Out after Grade 5 and Unmarried	Dropped Out after Grade 5 for Marriage and Married	Dropped Out after Grade 5 for other Reasons and Married	Dropped Out before Grade 5
Neither shortage nor surplus	(0.713)	(0.789)	(0.346)	(0.359)
Food surplus	0.39	1.08	0.41	0.06*
	(0.145)	(0.889)	(0.285)	(0.006)
Female-headed household	0.63	0.75	1.34	0.94
	(0.373)	(0.704)	(0.795)	(0.946)
Engaged in productive work	1.89*	1.05	0.84	2.12
	(0.011)	(0.842)	(0.644)	(0.059)
Program membership	1.87*	0.773	0.55	0.27*
	(0.038)	(0.334)	(0.247)	(0.014)
School performance	0.82	1.00	0.68	1.43
	(0.494)	(0.983)	(0.344)	(0.460)
Preference for wage work	1.61	0.854	1.04	0.37*
	(0.110)	(0.468)	(0.932)	(0.021)
Safety of girls in village	6.03	0.29	0.63	1.74
	(0.068)	(0.331)	(0.762)	(0.836)
Mobility of girls in village	0.46	0.17	0.90	0.02
	(0.556)	(0.140)	(0.315)	(0.098)
Total number of siblings	1.02	1.35*	1.23	1.44
	(0.842)	(0.009)	(0.133)	(0.084)
Number of elder sisters	0.93	0.53*	0.72	0.818
	(0.698)	(0.000)	(0.126)	(0.417)

$N = 917$
[a] Relative risk ratios, with *p*-values in parentheses.
*Significant at 0.05 level.

and are not married participate in work, compared to only one-third (37%) of the girls who are continuously in school or are dropouts and married.

Membership in the "Kishori Abhijan" skills development program is associated with an increased chance of dropping out of secondary school for girls who do not get married but leave for other reasons, and a reduced chance of dropping out before grade 6. Thus, membership promotes secondary school attendance by girls in relatively poor households, where the chance of dropping out before grade 6 is greatest. It could also be picking up a program effect on delaying marriage for girls who drop out in poor households.

School performance has no effect on school/marriage outcomes. In other words, returns to girls' education that are related to good performance (like getting stipends or increased labor market options) are not considered important when families decide if girls should continue in school or get married. In fact, school performance is also not correlated with continuing in school.

Aspiration for a salaried job is associated only with a reduced chance of dropping out after grade 5. In wealthy households, girls will stay in school or drop out to get married, regardless of job aspirations. It is only in the very poor households that girls who aspire to a salaried job will continue to secondary school in grade 6.

DISCUSSION

The choice of enrolling daughters in school and keeping them there is increasingly coming within the purview of parental decision making, so that socioeconomic differentials in school enrollment for girls are decreasing. In general, school attendance has become more common for rural Bangladeshi adolescent girls, and the majority of girls, other than those from very poor households, attend secondary school up to grades 7 or 8. However, because of the nearly unchanged practice of early marriage in Bangladesh, girls are withdrawn from secondary school to be married.

The dependent variable is a composite of two household investment decisions with distinct cost–benefit trade-offs: the decision to send daughters to school and the decision to get them married. In some households, these two decisions are complementary rather than competing: girls' schooling is viewed as an investment in their marriage, with some schooling perceived as increasing the likelihood of a good (early) marriage. In other households, school and marriage decisions for girls are only partly related, in that while some schooling is still seen to enhance prospects on the marriage market, cost of school is still the primary reason for girls to drop out of school. Finally, in some households the two decisions are made independently of each other, because the costs of secondary school outweigh returns, including any related to marriage.

Dropping out of school for marriage or continuing in school are driven by household economic conditions. That is, girls who continue in school are those who are waiting for a good (early) marriage to be arranged, which is most likely to occur in wealthy households. In such cases, the cost–benefit trade-off of schooling is not difficult to shoulder, since these households can afford the costs of schooling, and they expect returns in terms of securing a good marriage. It is evident that girls' schooling offers few other returns, given the fact that school performance and job aspirations do not affect whether girls continue in school or drop out to get married. However, educated parents in wealthy households who have higher educational aspirations for their daughters are more likely to keep girls in school.

When girls drop out of school for other reasons but do not get married, household wealth is usually the cause. While parents may be able to afford the costs of some secondary schooling, often they are unable to make adequate investments (a dowry) for an early marriage. Here, the return on parents' investment in schooling appears less certain regarding securing a good marriage for their daughters, while it remains relatively high in terms of the girls finding productive work.

Program membership and a favorable social environment allow some delay in marriage, but not a great deal. When the mother's education is higher, this tends to lower the chances of school withdrawal, but does not lead to delayed marriage. Neither are increased labor market opportunities seen as a return to schooling, since school performance and job aspirations were not important in predicting whether girls drop out of school for other reasons than marriage.

Poverty is an important factor as to whether girls complete primary school and enroll in secondary school or not. Girls from the poorest households do not enter secondary school, possibly because they are too poor to afford the costs of school. Whether these girls work or get married is a completely separate decision. Being engaged in productive work is not a significant factor in whether girls from poor families drop out of school early or never enroll in secondary school. This suggests that for this group, returns to schooling are not high either in terms of a good marriage or in terms of engaging in productive work. Program membership increases the chances of attending secondary school, as does job aspiration. So among poorer Bangladesh families, individual factors are important for continued school attendance.

It seems unlikely that government programs will significantly undermine the importance of marriage in the lives of the respondents until more time has passed and cultural values have changed.

CONCLUSIONS

The tremendous increase in girls' secondary school enrollment in Bangladesh has caught the attention of many, both inside and outside the country. Bangladesh is frequently cited as a trendsetter with respect to its educational policy, due in large part to its female secondary school stipend program, which has triggered this change. This policy is especially noteworthy in a country that is predominantly Muslim, and which is commonly believed to be extremely oppressive toward women and girls. In fact, the program has been hailed as a model that contains lessons for other countries.

The program's special provision for girls – which provides them with free tuition and stipends for secondary school enrollment in rural areas – has actually been quite successful in reducing short-term educational costs, even among the poor (Amin & Sedgh, 1998; Khandker et al., 2001). The program also appears to be promoting the view that in a highly stratified society such as Bangladesh, education can serve as an equalizer, and is now a necessity and a universal right, and no longer the sole prerogative of the wealthy. Notwithstanding the country's expansion in school enrollment among girls, however, this study points to the need to move beyond issues of availability and access that reduce short-term costs, yet have no effect on expected returns to girls' education in terms of labor market options. In fact, even the prime rationale for government action to promote girls secondary schooling, namely delaying marriage, has not occurred.

Certainly, enrollment expansion programs have been successful in expanding and even equalizing access, and many poor parents are benefiting from the reduction in school costs. But this has generated a unique demand to educate girls in a context where conventional returns to education, as measured by increased labor market options, do not operate. Returns are perceived more in terms of an investment for securing an early marriage for daughters by the relatively wealthy, minority and in terms of vague but similar expectations by the majority.

As a result, this has limited the potential for expanded girls' school attendance to influence the marriage market by raising the age at marriage. The fact that returns to girls' education are perceived more in terms of better marriage prospects is supported by the fact that school attendance is not driven by school performance or job aspirations, which also speaks to the poor quality of schools and the rigidity of labor market gender segregation. Both these are constraints to further expansion in girls' school secondary attendance and completion. Although aspirations for children's education are now almost universal, educational careers of children, particularly of girls, are irregular and repetitive, discontinued and incomplete, poorly monitored, and generally not related to performance. These features point to weak convictions on the part of employment providers about the long-term gains from girls' education. Getting girls to school was the first step; keeping them there and ensuring that they complete school are logical consequences that must follow. That this is not yet happening demonstrates the need for better service delivery and more responsive interventions. In Bangladesh today, education is seen as a tool for achieving gender equality in a society where girls and boys start from different positions of opportunity and are constrained differently. Boys are constrained by the need to earn incomes and girls are constrained by restricted mobility and lower investments in human capital. Since education is viewed as a right in itself, the first step needs to be to ensure equality of access. But there also need to be rights *within* the educational system to ensure that it promotes gender equality *outside*, in society. These rights have to do with providing equality of opportunity for school attendance and completion, and performance and learning, as well as returns from education by making learning more relevant. These are harder to guarantee, since they entail enacting school system reforms that are bound to be resisted.

Finally, there are rights through education, ensuring that education leads to equality of other rights (rights to voice, representation, security, participation). These have to do with bringing about broader social and economic change, to transform the initial positions of disadvantage and the structures that constrain boys and girls, rich and poor, differently. These rights are the hardest to provide, since they require changes outside the education system – changes that touch upon value systems and relationships of power.

NOTES

1. Gross enrollment ratios are calculated as children enrolled in a given level of schooling, regardless of age, expressed as a percentage of all children in target age group for that level of schooling. It thus can be biased toward high numbers, sometimes well over 100%, when there is a great deal of out-of-age enrollment. The net enrollment ratio includes only children in the target age range in the numerator, as well as in the denominator, and thus is a better estimate of actual enrollment rates.

2. Overall, primary school enrollment rates fluctuated but increased gradually until the 1980s. Then they rose rapidly and consistently in the 1990s from merely 46% in 1991 to 90% in 2000 (Hossain & Kabeer, 2004; Alam & Begum, 2003; UNICEF & BBS, 2004).

3. Estimates based on the 2000 Bangladesh Household Income and Expenditure Survey.

4. The incidence of rural poverty (head-count index) declined between 1983/1984 and 1988/1989, worsened between 1988/1989 and 1991/1992, and then showed a slight improvement by 1995/1996 to the level of the early 1980s (BIDS, 2001, p. 20).

5. The gross enrollment rate was 60% in grades 6–8, 51% in grades 9–10, and 48% in grades 11–12 in 2000 (World Bank, 2003, p. 51).

6. In 2001, the dropout rate for girls in grades 6–10 continued to be very high (38%) and higher relative to the average for boys and girls (37% total, BANBEIS, 2002).

7. Poor parents also continue to face difficult trade-offs with respect to boys' secondary school, which may be a reason for the closing of the enrollment gender gap, since costs of boys' schooling have not declined.

8. Married women have greater labor market opportunities, less restriction on mobility, access to non-kin resources like microcredit and networks.

9. Financial incentives unintentionally exclude the poorest girls because of fairly restrictive criteria that are difficult to meet without incurring additional expenditures, such as private tuition that requires maintaining a minimum score in examinations and passing public examinations.

10. The survey chose the age of 13 rather than the usual age of 10 as the starting point, because the planned intervention was to target girls 13 and older. The ending age range was deliberately chosen to be later than the usual cutoff age of 19 for adolescent surveys. This was because previous experience in adolescent research showed that age reporting is problematic, and many respondents who are younger or older report their age to be 20. This is particularly problematic when survey respondents do not know their age and the interviewer has to estimate it, as was the case with most of our respondents.

11. Of the 2,386 respondents with whom follow-up interviews had been attempted, 584 had migrated, mostly due to marriage. Interviewers asked about the new location of these migrated respondents, and as a result, 476 were found and successfully interviewed.

12. In order to ensure that respondents had been accurately identified in the follow-up survey, responses were matched between the two surveys to a number of variables, such as parents' education and number of siblings.

13. Multinomial logit/logistic models (MNLMs) involve response (outcome) variables with more than two categories. They are multi-equation models. A response variable (in this case school outcome) with k categories will generate $k-1$ equations. Each of these $k-1$ equations is a binary logistic regression comparing a group with the reference group (in this case never enrolled). MNLMs simultaneously estimate the $k-1$ logits.

ACKNOWLEDGMENTS

This paper was made possible through support provided by the Department for International Development, UK, the Mellon Foundation, UNICEF, Dhaka and the Office of Population and Reproductive Health, Bureau for Global Health, U.S. Agency for International Development, under the terms of Award No. HRN-A-00-99-00010. The opinions expressed herein are those of the author(s) and do not necessarily reflect the views of the U.S. Agency for International Development. We gratefully acknowledge the contribution of Laura Spess and Luciana Suran of the Population Council for their assistance in data analysis, and Kobita Chowdhury and Lopita Huq for their invaluable contribution in data collection.

REFERENCES

Alam, M., & Begum, H. (2003). Secondary education subsector in Bangladesh: Performance, challenges and way forward. Paper presented at the Unesco-Bafed Conference on Secondary Education in Bangladesh, Dhaka, December 2003.

Amin, S., & Arends-Kuenning, M. (2001). What does it mean to be a vulnerable child in Bangladesh? Paper presented at the General Conference of the International Union for the Scientific Study of Population, Salvador, Brazil, August 2001.

Amin, S., Mahmud, S., & Huq, L. (2002). *Baseline survey report on adolescents in Bangladesh (Kishori Abhijan)*. Dhaka: UNICEF and Ministry of Women and Children Affairs.

Amin, S., & Sedgh, G. (1998). *Incentive schemes for school attendance in rural Bangladesh*. Working Paper no. 106. New York: Population Council.

Amin, S., & Suran, L. (2004). *Bangladesh Adolescent Livelihoods Program: Midline Report*. New York: Draft, Population Council.

Arends-Kuenning, M., & Amin, S. (2001). Women's capabilities and the right to education in Bangladesh. *International Journal of Politics, Culture and Society, 15*(1), 125–142.

BANBEIS. (2002). *Statistical profile on education in Bangladesh*. Dhaka: Bangladesh Bureau of Educational Information and Statistics.

Behrman, J. R., Foster, A., Rosenzweig, M. R., & Vashishtha, P. (1999). Women's schooling, home teaching, and economic growth. *Journal of Political Economy, 107*(4), 682–714.

BIDS (2001). *Bangladesh Human Development Report 2000: Fighting Human Poverty*. Dhaka: Bangladesh Institute of Development Studies and Ministry of Planning, Government of the People's Republic of Bangladesh.

Buchmann, C., & Hannum, E. (2001). Education and stratification in developing countries: A review of theories and research. *Annual Review of Sociology, 27*, 77–102.

Elder, G. (1969). Appearance and education in marriage mobility. *American Sociological Review, 34*(4), 519–533.

Hossain, N. (2005). Role of community-level institutions on household practices relating to children. Paper presented at the Brac and Save the Children UK seminar on Inheriting Extreme Poverty, Dhaka, February 2005.

Hossain, N., & Kabeer, N. (2004). Achieving universal primary education and eliminating gender disparity. *Economic and Political Weekly, 39*(36), 4093–4100.

Huq, L., & Amin, S. (2001). Dowry negotiations and the process of union formation in Bangladesh: Implications of rising education. Paper presented at the Annual Meetings of the Population Association of America, Washington, DC.

Kabeer, N., & Mahmud, S. (2004). *Child labour, educational exclusion and household livelihoods in urban Bangladesh: Exploring the connections*. Research Report (forthcoming), Bangladesh Institute of Development Studies.

Khandker, S., Pitt, M., & Fuwa, N. (2001). *Subsidy to promote girls' secondary education: The female stipend program in Bangladesh*. Washington, DC: World Bank (Draft).

Lloyd, C. (2005). *Growing up global: The changing transitions to adulthood in developing countries*. Panel on Transitions to Adulthood in Developing Countries. Committee on Population, National Research Council and Institute of Medicine. Washington, DC: The National Academy Press.

Nambissan, G. (2003). Social exclusion, children's work and education: A view from the margins. In: N. Kabeer, G. Nambissan & R. Subrahmanian (Eds), *Child labour and the right to education in South Asia: Needs versus rights?* Dhaka: UPL.

Post, D. (2001). Region, poverty, sibship and gender inequality in Mexican education: Will targeted welfare policy make a difference for girls? *Gender and Society*, *15*(3), 468–489.

Rozario, S. (2002). Poor and 'Dark': what is my future? Identify construction and adolescent women. In: L. Manderson & P. Liamputtong (Eds), *Coming of age in South and Southeast Asia: Youth, courtship and sexuality*. Richmond, Surrey: Curzon Press.

Sathar, Z., Callum, C., & Haque, M. (2005). Effects of family and community on whether girls go to school, and stay on, in rural Pakistan. Paper presented at the Annual Meeting of the Population Association of America, March 29–April 2, Philadelphia, USA.

UNESCO (2003). *Gender and education for all: The leap to equality*. EFA Global Monitoring Report 2003/04. Paris: UNESCO.

Unicef and BBS (2004). *Pragatir Patha*y 2003. Unicef, Dhaka and Bangladesh Bureau of Statistics, Dhaka.

White, S. (1991). *Arguing with the crocodile: Gender and class in Bangladesh*. Dhaka: University Press Limited.

World Bank. (1999). *Bangladesh education sector review* (Vol. no. III Annexes). Dhaka.

World Bank. (2003). *Bangladesh public expenditure review*. World Bank and Asian Development Bank, Dhaka, May.

GENDERED HOMES AND CLASSROOMS: SCHOOLING IN RURAL NEPAL

Jennifer Rothchild

ABSTRACT

Development efforts in education have failed to conceive of gender as a socially constructed process that legitimizes gender inequality, and this article attempts to explain why gender inequality in schools should be problematized in this way. I argue that in developing countries like Nepal, promoting access to and participation in existing formal education programs is clearly necessary, but it is not, in itself, sufficient to transform gender power relations in the broader society. Reports of unequal distribution of girls' and boys' participation in school tell only part of the story; to fully understand gender inequality in schools and in societies as a whole, what is needed is an exploration of how gender is socially constructed and maintained in both the school and the home. This article examines the complexities of gender in a rural village of Nepal. Specifically, I interviewed community members, parents, teachers, and students and conducted observations in school and home settings. This article focuses on the educational experiences of girls and boys as they were affected and influenced by attitudes about gender.

INTRODUCTION

Around the world, efforts are being made to increase the enrollment of girls in schools. Developing countries, usually working with well-funded international non-governmental organizations (INGOs), have made significant attempts to promote girls' access to and participation in formal education systems. In Nepal, researchers, funding agencies, and various governmental offices have noted the substantially low enrollment of girls in its schools, and donor agencies such as USAID and the World Bank have spent millions of dollars on education initiatives aimed at girls.[1] This funding has been supported by a substantial body of literature that promotes educating girls and women for social and economic benefits.[2] In an effort to increase the numbers of girls enrolled in school, many national and international initiatives focus on the *obstacles* to girls' schooling. Researchers have generated a long list of factors that determine girls' enrollment and participation in school, including parents' socioeconomic status, religion, distance to schools, cultural attitudes, poverty, and parents' illiteracy.[3] But these analyses only tell part of the story.

Most research on girls in schools in developing countries has been insightful; however, the modes of analysis typically employed fail to apprehend the complexities of gender[4] in the cultures and societies where these educational inequalities exist. By looking at gender as a *process* rather than a demographic factor, we can begin to understand the obstacles and opportunities for girls and boys in school. Gender has long been used to legitimize inequality between girls and boys. This has negative effects on both girls' and boys' potential to succeed in school and subsequently to improve their standard of living through learning and, ultimately, opportunities gained through learning.

Educational funding initiatives aimed at girls tend to assume that girls and boys enter schools that are gender-neutral. I view the family and school as social institutions where established gender patterns are embedded within the organizational dynamics of those institutions. In other words, historically, the very institutions of family and school put girls at a disadvantage when it comes to maximizing opportunities for education and future opportunity.

Furthermore, the processes within schools and homes serve to maintain that social inequality. By failing to recognize this beforehand, research and initiatives to help girls in school risk missing the point. Embedded gender roles perpetuate inequalities, particularly in the context of Nepal's schools. Analyzing gender inequality in schools should be problematized with a careful exploration of how gender is socially constructed and maintained in both school and the home. Then, we can begin to understand and devise more effective ways to increase all students' enrollment, participation, and success in school. By doing this, INGOs, other donor agencies, and government programs will be able to formulate educational initiatives that anticipate and address attitudes and behaviors with regard to gender that, in the long run, will help girls enjoy longer, more meaningful school experiences. When this is accomplished, developing countries will benefit from the political and economic advantages of a more evenly educated population.

Nepal offers a particularly illuminating case study for examining the social construction of gender as it relates to education and opportunities for learning. The context for education in Nepal is influenced by gender inequality as reflected in the country's legal, political, economic, and family institutions. These institutions are founded upon cultural and religious beliefs that maintain similar attitudes about gender (Bennett, 1981; Acharya, 1981; Acharya & Bennett, 1981; Ashby, 1985; Subedi, 1993; Shtrii Shakti, 1995; Singh, 1995). To isolate and analyze the strains of thought that support gender inequality in Nepali schools, I will discuss the ways in which gender was socially constructed, reinforced, and maintained within a rural village.[5]

Specifically, my research (conducted in 1999–2000) examines families, the local education system, and the processes of gender (e.g., socialization patterns beginning at an early age, attitudes toward gender and education, and interactions with and control of youth) as exhibited in this particular village.[6] I conducted direct classroom observations; field observations of the daily lives of school-age children; and structured interviews with community members, parents/guardians, teachers, head teachers (school principals), and students. I also collected life narratives from older girls and boys, as well as adult women and men. With the data collected through these methods, this article focuses on the educational experiences of girls and boys as they were affected and influenced by gendered attitudes and actions.

THEORETICAL FRAMEWORK

Gender as a Social Construction

Gender has been conceived as a system in which biological females and biological males are classified, separated, and socialized into specific sex roles. Gender construction theorists (e.g., O'Brien, 1983; Mies, 1986;

Connell, 1987; Acker, 1990; Lorber, 1994; Risman, 1998; Kimmel, 2004) assert that gender, as a social system, is not natural, and that differences between women and men – aside from purely anatomical and reproductive ones – are socially constructed and maintained. Much effort goes into marking gender differences (Connell, 1987) by dividing people into contrasting social categories of "girls" and "boys," "women" and "men," and "feminine" and "masculine."

This study of students in Nepal draws heavily from this conceptualization of gender – that is, gender as a socially constructed identity and role, reinforced by processes and institutions that maintain similar attitudes and distinctions about gender. This results in a gendered social order that reflects those beliefs, even if they may be untrue (Lorber, 2000). Gender, then, is a process, rather than an attribute, and gender differences become ideas that are taught and reinforced by individuals through socialization, rather than tangible distinctions as determined by biology. In this light, gender is not what we are, but instead, something we do (West & Zimmerman, 1987), and each social interaction serves to create and reinforce these ideas.

At the macro level, it is often assumed that social institutions are gender-neutral, but this assumption ignores that most social institutions were contrived under circumstances of gender inequality. Jean Potuchek (1997) explains that social institutions formed within a context of unequal power and opportunity for women and men serve to institutionalize that inequality; to give it greater strength. Assumptions of male dominance render the inequality maintained by these institutions invisible and underscore the idea that everyone has equal potential to succeed in these institutions (Kimmel, 2000). Joan Acker (1990) states that the concept of gender neutrality "covers up, obscures the underlying gender structure, allowing practices that perpetuate it to continue even as efforts to reduce gender equality are underway" (p. 146).

So, instead of gender-neutral institutions, I argue that social institutions such as the family and school are *gendered institutions* in that they establish patterns of expectations for individuals according to their gender. These gendered institutions create normative standards and express an institutional logic that produces and promotes the differences many assume to be the inherent qualities of individuals. In this way, they determine the power, privileges, and economic resources available to a person based on her or his gender (Davison & Kanyuka, 1990; Lorber, 2000).

However, as gender is socially constructed, it is also dynamic: It can be reshaped and resisted by individuals through social interactions that flaunt existing assumptions about differences between women and men, and girls and boys (Lorber, 2000; Butler, 1990). Thus, the potential for people to make choices and have agency over their lives exists (Risman, 1998). I will later present examples of several students in this study to illustrate this point.

Understanding the false grounds that support gender differences within a society's institutions is a key first step for groups that seek to foster change in the school systems of developing countries. This understanding at once disassembles old assumptions about the abilities of girls and boys and identifies the potential to change these assumptions. However, it is also important to have a solid understanding of gender at the next level, as practiced and emphasized within the family and school.

Gender in the Home

A study sponsored by the United States Agency for International Development (USAID) determined that obstacles to girls' education in Nepal fall into five categories: economic barriers, labor issues, cultural attitudes, physical barriers, and national commitments (ABEL, 1996). Both Ashby (1985) and Jamison and Lockheed (1987) identify three factors that tend to lower incentives for investment in the education of daughters relative to sons: (1) daughters are expected to leave their natal households through marriage in their mid-teen years, while sons are expected to contribute to the welfare of parents in their old age; (2) non-agricultural employment is perceived as more appropriate and realistic for males than for females; and (3) the accepted gender-based division of agricultural work requires more routine work from females than from males. In a survey of rural farm households, Jamison and Lockheed (1987) showed that girls are discouraged from attending school in order to care for small children. Studies like these indicate that processes of gender outside school influence girls' participation in school, and the extent of that participation.

Many Nepali families favor sons, thereby giving them greater advantages than daughters (Reinhold, 1993), and parents typically define girls in terms of being good wives and housekeepers (ABEL, 1996). Sons often marry and live with their parents, whereas daughters go to "others' house," meaning they go to live with their husband's families once their marriages are arranged. Because daughters eventually "leave," their economic value to their natal families is greatest during the middle childhood and teen years when, as my observations and interviews demonstrate, they contribute significant amounts of labor. Sons, on the other hand, are expected to be of greatest economic value to their parents by providing security for them in their old age. In this sense, the way parents and guardians conceive of their children and education is rational, although inequitable.

During a study conducted in this particular village in 1996, I interviewed head teachers and parents. Though some parents emphasized the importance of educating sons and daughters, almost every parent gave priority to the education of their sons. In general, parents spoke of girls' education in terms of their presumed current and future roles as daughters, wives, mothers, and daughters-in-law, rather than as a source of individual opportunity and empowerment. Parents perceived girls' education as utilitarian rather than emancipatory. Daughters were educated to fit into a pre-existing gender structure, not to change it. The gendered social order, with its inherent gender inequality, is often rationalized with the stability it offers social arrangements.

Among high-caste Hindus in Nepal, purity of caste is considered very important.[7] Maintaining this purity is often used to justify restricting women's sexuality and reproductive powers so that the paternity of a child, especially of a son, is not in question. It is argued that only through such control can purity of lineage be maintained, a purity that is considered vital to maintain the caste system. Hindus are often so concerned with the purity of women that they require a bride to be a virgin and forbid widow marriage, as widows are regarded as polluted (Mathema, 1998). To ensure virginity, marriages are often arranged before the onset of puberty, a practice commonly known as *kanyadan* (gift of a virgin daughter).[8] Though Nepalese law forbids child marriage, many families in rural Nepal arrange their daughters' marriages when they are as young as 10 years of age (Subedi, 1993) and on average, at the age of 14 (ABEL, 1996). This sociocultural construction of gender limits girls' opportunities to further their education.

Women and men in Nepal tend to have gendered access to resources and opportunities. In rural households, women spend more hours doing productive and reproductive work than do men (Cameron, 1995). Women constitute an estimated 40.5% of the labor force, predominately in agriculture (Singh, 1995), yet much of this work, often unpaid, is not considered work per se, and is subsequently devalued (Subedi, 1993). Furthermore, the labor market in Nepal is gendered in that it offers limited opportunities for girls who complete school. Opportunity costs or indirect costs to education are often cited as a major obstacle to girls' participation in and completion of education.[9]

If sending a child to school is a burden for the family, either because of monetary costs or opportunity costs, many Nepali families choose to send boys rather than girls to school (Ashby, 1985; Shrestha et al., 1986). Nelly

Stromquist (1990), in her survey of research on girls' education, found that most studies demonstrated that opportunity costs of schooling for girls are greater than for boys. However, she asserts that what the literature fails to clarify is that these opportunity costs are greater by social definition; that is, because of the way societies construct gender roles and expectations, and not because of innate abilities of girls.

To summarize, while identifying the obstacles to girls' education is important (e.g., parents' socioeconomic status, religion, distance to school, cultural attitudes, poverty, availability of schools, parents' education, and unsuitable curriculum), analyzing these obstacles in a disconnected fashion without examining the significance of gender as a social construction "confuses immediate with ultimate causes and fails to understand gender as an institutionalized expression of power in society" (Stromquist, 1990, p. 108). In other words, perceived differences between the abilities of boys and girls form the basis for the aforementioned obstacles within a family context. Analyzing the obstacles without accounting for assumptions about gender may negate the potential for change.

Gendered Education

While schools, depending on the attitudes of staff as well as government policies, can be a source of social change, they can also act to maintain the existing system of norms. In countries such as Nepal, with a history of rigid social and political control, an educational system is often used to maintain existing gender constructions by transmitting representations and beliefs about a "natural" and "appropriate" gendered social order (Stromquist, 1992). School experiences often provide girls and boys with messages that reinforce rather than challenge the prevailing gendered division of labor (Stromquist, 1989a). As social institutions, schools most often reflect current gender norms rather than challenge them.

In Dorothy Smith's (2000) review of the literature on gender and schooling, she concludes that the research confirms a continuous reinforcement of existing gender relations through text materials and student–teacher interactions. Male voices and male activities are privileged in the classroom, on the playground and sports field, and in the hallways, even in highly industrialized, democratic countries such as the United States (Best, 1983; Thorne, 1993; Orenstein, 1994) and Australia (e.g., Lee, 1996). Girls receive a "gendered education" in schools: The gender they experience at home is reinforced in schools, as girls are encouraged to be docile, passive, and dependent (Staudt, 1998).

Gender bias in teaching, compounded with a gender-biased curriculum, only perpetuates the reproduction of gender inequality. Textbooks frequently impose stereotypical images of women and girls. Further, despite the vast diversity of race, ethnicity, language, and culture represented by students in schools, educational curricula and textbooks tend to offer homogenous images and expectations of women and girls (Staudt, 1998). Stromquist (1989b) cites several studies conducted in developing countries that demonstrate gender stereotypes in textbooks, including Harber (1988) for Kenya; Tembo (1984) for Zambia; Anderson and Herencia (1983) for Peru; Pinto (1982) for Brazil; and Silva (1979) for Columbia. Most studies cited reveal that women in textbooks are portrayed as passive, uncreative, and self-satisfied. Often, they are represented as functioning only within the home. If employed, they are represented only in subprofessional positions.

In this article, I argue that development efforts in education that fail to consider gender as a socially constructed process subsequently fail to see how these processes legitimize gender inequality among students. Specifically, assumptions about gender (by parents, students, and teachers) not only affect who goes to school, but also students' perceptions of their own abilities, educational achievement, particular areas of study, and career aspirations. I argue that socially constructed gender processes are institutionalized expressions of power and that these processes – enacted by community members, parents, guardians, teachers, and head teachers and observed in Nepali homes and schools during this study – constrained some students and enabled others.

Furthermore, students acting under the weight of these constraints consequently "did gender" within these socially constructed parameters. My findings, which were derived from interviews and observations, indicate that many students (both girls and boys), in forming attitudes toward education, had come to accept and embrace the different socially assigned roles and aspirations for women and men as adults in Nepali society. Thus, I argue that gender not only constrained girls' educational opportunities, but it also operated to benefit men and boys in Nepal's male-dominated society.

As pervasive as gender has been and continues to be in social institutions like the state, schools, and the family, gender constraints can be resisted and reshaped by "gender trouble-makers" (Butler, 1990). This study examines not only the constraints placed upon students, especially girl students, but also students' agency in resisting and negotiating those constraints.

RESEARCH DESIGN AND DATA

Three objectives served as touchstones for the field research: (1) to examine the socially constructed processes of gender within the institutions of family and school, through interviews eliciting attitudes and behavior of community members, parents and guardians, head teachers, and teachers in one particular village in Nepal[10]; (2) to investigate behavior and interaction in classroom and school settings through direct observations and interviews; and (3) to examine the consequences of socially constructed gender constraints through observations and interviews in school and home settings.

Using feminist theories as a guide, this study drew on case study research to address these objectives. Specific research techniques to collect data included direct classroom observations; field observations of the daily lives of school-age children; structured interviews with community members, parents and guardians, teachers, head teachers, and students; and life narratives from older girls and boys, as well as adult women and men. This article focuses on the gendered educational experiences of the girl and boy students interviewed and observed.[11]

For this study, interviewees from five separate subgroups were selected, including teachers, head teachers, community members, parents and guardians, and students (Table 1).

Student Profiles

Two sets of 10 students – five girls and five boys – were randomly selected from class 5 at the D School and class 9 at the J School for student home visits.[12] Of these students, eight were Jirel, the predominant ethnic group in the case study village (Tables 2 and 3).

Other ethnic groups represented in this student sample were Newar, Tamang, Sherpa, and Chhetri, Brahmin, and Biskokarma of the Hindu castes. In total, 11 students were Buddhist, and 9 were Hindu, which was not representative of Nepal's predominantly Hindu national religious profile, but was representative of the case study village. The average age of the class 5 (at the D School) boy students selected was 13 years old, and the average age of the girl students was 15 years old. The average age of the class 9 (J School) boy students was 17, and the average age for the girls was 16.

A variety of data collection methods were implemented more or less simultaneously. They included: direct observations of the focus school classrooms and content analysis of materials used in teaching class 5 and class

Table 1. Interviewees.

Type of Interview	Who was Sought for the Interviews	Number of Interviews
Teacher interviews	All the teachers from the two focus classes (classes 5 and 9) at the two focus schools (entire population)	$N = 12$ (Women = 2) (Men = 10)
Head teacher interviews	All the head teachers at each of the government schools (entire population)	$N = 10$ (W = 2) (M = 8)
Community member interviews	Community members from each of the nine wards in the village (purposive sampling)	Ward 1: $N = 12$ (W = 4) (M = 8) Ward 2: $N = 39$ (W = 21) (M = 18) Ward 3: $N = 41$ (W = 20) (M = 21) Ward 4: $N = 37$ (W = 21) (M = 16) Ward 5: $N = 41$ (W = 21) (M = 20) Ward 6: $N = 34$ (W = 16) (M = 18) Ward 7: $N = 43$ (W = 23) (M = 20) Ward 8: $N = 41$ (W = 21) (M = 20) Ward 9: $N = 40$ (W = 20) (M = 20) Total: $N = 328$ (W = 167) (M = 161)
Life history interviews	Selected women, older girls, men, and older boys from each of the nine wards (purposive sampling)	Ward 1: $N = 1$ (W = 1) (M = 0) Ward 2: $N = 1$ (W = 0) (M = 1) Ward 3: $N = 2$ (W = 1) (M = 1) Ward 4: $N = 2$ (W = 1) (M = 1) Ward 5: $N = 1$ (W = 1) (M = 0) Ward 6: $N = 1$ (W = 0) (M = 1) Ward 7: $N = 3$ (W = 2) (M = 1) Ward 8: $N = 4$ (W = 3) (M = 1) Ward 9: $N = 2$ (W = 1) (M = 1) Total: $N = 17$ (W = 10) (M = 7)

Table 1. (*Continued*)

Type of Interview	Who was Sought for the Interviews	Number of Interviews
Student home visit interviews	Randomly selected students from classes 5 and 9 at two focus schools and their parents and guardians (probability sampling)	Class 5 students: $N = 10$ (W = 5) (M = 5) Class 9 students: $N = 10$ (W = 5) (M = 5) Parent/guardian total: $N = 38$

Table 2. Selected Class Five Students by Gender, Ethnicity, and Religion (at the D School) ($N = 10$).

	Ethnicity	Religion/Caste
Girl students		
Sita	Jirel	Buddhist
Kamala	Newar	Hindu (non-caste)
Phul Maya	Tamang	Buddhist
Sagun	Tamang	Buddhist
Sanjita	Jirel	Buddhist
Boy students		
Kedar	Chhetri	Hindu (Chhetri)
Dal Bahadur	Chhetri	Hindu (Chhetri)
Ram Prasad	Newar	Hindu (non-caste)
Ritesh	Newar	Hindu (non-caste)
Ram Bahadur	Biskokarma (B.K.)	Hindu (Dalit)

9; observations of the daily lives of students; structured interviews with community members, parents and guardians, teachers, head teachers, and students; and life narratives of older girls and boys and adult women and men.

I interviewed all of the head teachers at each of the 10 government schools observed. In addition to collecting some data and making observations at these schools, I conducted ongoing observations of two classes, 5 and 9, at the two focus schools. Therefore, I also interviewed the class 5 and class 9 teachers ($N = 12$) at these focus schools. From these interviews, I hoped to glean teachers' and head teachers' attitudes and behavior toward girl students' and boy students' attendance, participation, and success in their classrooms.

In my interviews with students, I asked them questions pertaining to their attitudes toward gender as it related to a number of issues including general

Table 3. Selected Class Nine Students by Gender, Ethnicity, and Religion (at the J School) ($N = 10$).

	Ethnicity	Religion/Caste
Girl Students		
Monica	Chhetri	Hindu (Chhetri)
Minu	Jirel	Buddhist
Krishna Kumari	Jirel	Buddhist
Leela Maya	Brahmin	Hindu (Brahmin)
Nima	Sherpa	Buddhist
Boy Students		
Chhetra	Jirel	Buddhist
Dinesh	Newar	Hindu (non-caste)
Man Kumar	Jirel	Buddhist
Gopal	Jirel	Buddhist
Amrit	Jirel	Buddhist

intelligence, who should be educated, subject preferences, and subject aptitude. I also included questions to address their perceptions of educational and career aspirations, their use of time, and their thoughts regarding gender differences in attendance and persistence in school.

Using a set of predetermined questions for each type of interview, I elicited information about each respondent's thoughts, opinions, attitudes, and subsequent behavior regarding gender and education. I operated under the assumption that the respondents' thoughts were intricately related to their actions. Questions were designed to address the interviewees' meanings and interpretations of gender inequality.

FINDINGS: EFFECTS OF THE SOCIAL CONSTRUCTION OF GENDER

Analyzing the data from the adult samples (community members, parents and guardians, teachers, and head teachers) in this study revealed socially constructed gender processes within the context of two gendered institutions, family and school. The responses of interviewees from all four adult samples often included gender stereotypes, indicating the influence of gender processes in their own lives. Having been raised and continuing to live within a gendered society, the adults in this study had learned to divide girls and boys, and women and men, into socially constructed feminine and masculine categories.

Social Construction of Gender in the Home

Starting with examples from the family, I found that women and men both played an important role in the construction, reproduction, and maintenance of gender inequality within the home. Across religions and castes, many interviewees from both the community member and the parent/guardian samples talked of the following family arrangements: Sons married and lived with their parents, whereas daughters went to "others' house," meaning they went to live with their husband's family once their marriages were arranged. With these socially constructed arrangements, sons provided security for parents in their old age, and interviewees often mentioned this as a way of justifying why they had educated their sons more than (or instead of) their daughters.

In interviews with community members and parents and guardians, both women and men noted that girls did more domestic work than boys on a given day. The family, as a gendered institution, placed unequal constraints on the girls' and women's time as compared to that of the boys and men. Although girls were no more naturally inclined to do their assigned tasks than were boys, social constructions of gender had obliged girls to domestic responsibilities to a greater extent than boys. These gendered expectations were learned at a young age and reinforced over time within the family. Further, by assigning the women and girls in the family the majority of domestic responsibilities, this ensured that the household tasks would get done (Stromquist, 1990).

Subsequently, these socially constructed gender processes determined students' education. The division and organization of Nepali social life by gender influenced students' ability to attend, participate in, and succeed in school. Interviews with students illustrated this. For example, the students were asked to describe a typical day for them, and their responses were then compiled. The results (Table 4) demonstrated gender differences in the allocation of work. Among the 20 students interviewed, the girl students were obligated to do more chores at home than boy students. The gendered division of labor left the girl students with less time than boy students to do homework and to study. On average, because of their domestic responsibilities, girl students woke up earlier and went to bed later. Assuming girls would fulfill certain domestic roles was the everyday reality in the gendered context in which they lived. However, these assumptions had the effect of limiting the extent of girls' education in this particular Nepali village, and influenced what and how much girls could study, as well as girls' expectations for themselves.

Table 4. Composite of Typical Time Allocations for Students by Gender.

Time of Day	Girl in School ($N = 10$)	Boy in School ($N = 10$)
6 am–7 am	Wakes up, washes face	Sleeping
7 am–8 am	Washes dishes, makes tea for self and others, and does household work (e.g., cleaning, prepares meal, feeds animals)	Wakes up, washes face, and studies for a while
8 am–9 am	Dresses for school and has snacks	Eats morning meal, and then gets dressed for school
9 am–10 am	Walks to school	Walks to school
10 am–12 pm	Attends school	Attends school
12 pm–1 pm	"Tiffin" (snack) break	"Tiffin" (snack) break
1 pm–4 pm	School	School
4 pm–5 pm	Walks home from school	Walks home from school
5 pm–6 pm	Chores (e.g., brings fodder to the cattle, fetches water, and fuel wood, cleans)	Has snacks and tea and studies
6 pm–7 pm	Helps prepare evening meal/helps mother in kitchen	Studies
7 pm–8 pm	Eats "lunch" (light meal) Does dishes	Eats evening meal and watches television (if student has access to a television)
8 pm–9 pm	Does homework	Goes to bed
9 pm–10 pm	Goes to bed	Sleeping

This is exemplified by the story of Sanu Kumari. At the time of her life history narrative, Sanu Kumari was studying at the J School in class 9. She was from an impoverished Chhetri (Hindu) family. Her parents were farmers. She was the oldest child and had two sisters and one brother. At the time of her life history interview, one of her younger sisters was in Kathmandu, where she was learning stitching and knitting.

> ... In my childhood. I used to run away [from classes] and play with our friends. Sometimes we even went to the forest to hide ourselves to avoid the work at home. That's all I can remember ... [Thinks for a while ...] My father had gone away. [*Where?*] I don't know but some foreign land [out of Nepal] and there was nobody at home to help my mother since I was the eldest. So due to the household work, I had to stop going to school and I missed my studies for class 5. Now [at this time] I would have given my SLC [if she had continued with her schooling consistently], but later when my father returned he told me to go back to school and I started from where I had left [grade 5] ...
>
> ... I wake up early in the morning [and] wash my face. Tidy up my room. Have tea, then prepare lunch [morning meal of *daal bhaat* (rice and lentils)], serve it to my family, attend

class, then return home in the evening. Then have tea and snacks, and then do my homework or study for a while, then prepare dinner for the family. Then after dinner, I also study for a while, and go to bed. Then on holidays [days with no school like Saturdays] I go for herding, fetching grass and firewood. On school days I only go to fetch firewood and cut grass for the livestock. I don't have to go herding because it would make me late to go to school.

Similar to her girl classmates in the student sample, social constructions constrained Sanu Kumari to "do gender." She was expected to fulfill her gender obligations of household work, which limited the time available for studying. Although she started her homework and studied as soon as she returned home from school, her domestic responsibilities of preparing and serving meals, cleaning the house, collecting firewood, and cutting grass for livestock (in addition to the herding and collecting of grass and firewood she did when school was not in session) consumed the majority of her time at home. She was aware of these constraints as she spoke of "hiding in the forest to avoid work at home," and she knew she would be further along in her studies were it not for having to drop out of class 5 to help her mother with the household chores. She felt she was behind in her education because of it.

Girls in Nepal are more prone to repeat a grade than boys, and girls are also at a greater risk of dropping out of school than boys (Sibbons, 1999). Among the 10 girl students interviewed, 7 had to repeat at least one grade. Of the 10 boy students interviewed, only one boy student had repeated a grade: He had to repeat 2nd grade after breaking his leg. Having to shoulder a majority of the home chores was a significant gender difference for girls in Nepal, which negatively affected their achievement and hindered their finishing school.

For Sita, a class 5 student, domestic responsibilities were to blame when she had to repeat class 4. She explained, "I didn't have time to study and couldn't prepare well for the examination." Similarly, Minu failed class 8 because she didn't have time to study. Class 9 student Krishna Kumari had to repeat class 2 because she had to take care of a younger sister. With the internalization of gender processes, some students looked upon their repeating a grade as a reflection of their academic capability, rather than the result of constraints on their time. For example, class 5 girl student Kamala had to repeat kindergarten because "I didn't know much."

When asked why they thought girls in Nepal drop out of school, 60% of the students interviewed responded that it was due to the workload at home. More girl students than boy students cited this as a reason for girls' dropping out of school. Sita explained that, based on her own experience, there often was no time for girls to study because of household work. Man Kumar, a class 9 student, noted that girls and women in villages had so much work to do that "they don't have time to go to school." His classmate, Chhetra, observed that girls "give first priority to their housework, so they are always compromising work with school." Chhetra assumed that girls placed greater priority on housework themselves. Rather, it was the highest priority of girls' parents, who themselves were a product of a gendered society that valued women's domestic role as their greatest contribution to the family and Nepali society.

Among the students, there appeared to be an unconscious acceptance of the gendered division of labor without an understanding of how it came about. However, one class 9 student, Leela Maya, put it well when she observed, "They [parents] make the daughters do all the household work. They have the notion that girls shouldn't study and [want to] get them married [arrange daughters' marriage]."

In addition to the workload at home, 5 students (4 girls and 1 boy) cited marriage as a reason why girls drop out of school. Notably, 4 out of 10 girls cited early marriage as a constraint to completing education, which is comparable with their parents and guardians' perceptions.[13] Significantly, interviewees across samples noted the linkage between early marriage and girls' lack of persistence in school. This awareness is encouraging as a first step toward social change.[14]

Social Construction of Gender at School

Collecting data from both the home and the school helped uncover how pervasive the existing gendered social order in Nepal was. The students I interviewed reported varied educational experiences by gender. Interviews and observations also revealed the influence of parents' and teachers' gendered assumptions and actions. For example, I observed gendered teacher–student interactions. Teachers generally gave more attention to boys than they did to girls (e.g., calling on them, as well as giving them praise, criticism, remediation, and acceptance). As Sadker and Sadker (1994) argue, praising, probing, questioning, and correcting students sharpen their ideas, refine their thinking, and help them gain confidence. These gendered interactions reinforced what students had learned at home.

Similarly, although most of the head teachers wholeheartedly endorsed girls' education in their interviews, they did not appear to take action to make their schools "girl friendly" by hiring more women staff. I observed very few women teachers (and at some schools, none) employed at the schools these teachers headed. If such a situation is to be changed, the leaders of these schools must take active steps to assure gender equality in teaching staff.

With gender socially constructed in the home and then reinforced in school, classroom observations revealed both girls and boys "doing gender:" Girls chatted with each other and combed each other's hair, while boys fought and chased each other outside and inside the classroom, and tried to take charge. The social construction of gender in home and school, as reinforced by parents and teachers, not only influenced students' behavior, but also influenced students' attitudes toward education and their perceptions of their own educational and career aspirations, as well as their hopes and plans for the future.

While the majority of student interviewees stated that girls and boys were equally intelligent, five students responded that boys were more intelligent than girls. Of these, four were girls. This means that girls may have been more likely to view themselves as less intelligent than the boys, though the sample was small. Equal numbers of those four were from class 5 (2) and class 9 (2). Class 9 boy student Amrit explained,

> In my opinion, boys are more intelligent than girls. [*Why do you think so?*] Because girls cannot think as much as boys can. Even if they think they cannot bring into behavior [practice], so I think boys are more intelligent than girls.

Leela Maya, a class 9 student, rationalized that boys "are very active and good at games and other activities" and were therefore more intelligent than girls. She added that boys "are superior to girls in many ways." Her classmate, Nima, said that "sons are very brilliant and champions." Certainly, girls are not less capable than boys (as their statements imply), but rather, because boys have had more opportunities, their successes are more apparent. Boys having more opportunities and girls less was an aspect of the social order – opportunities were an everyday reality in the gendered context in which both the girls and boys lived.

Of the students who remarked that girls were more intelligent, gender was implicit in their explanations. Class 9 girl student Krishna Kumari explained that daughters were more intelligent than sons because "the daughter will understand the problems of the house and the mother." This defining of girls' intelligence in gendered terms (e.g., domestic responsibilities for girls) reflects the responses of many men and women interviewees from both the community member and parent/guardian samples.

Of the 20 students interviewed, 18 said it was important for both girls and boys to be educated. Specifically, all class 9 students interviewed said both girls and boys should be educated, and all but two of the class 5 students believed it was important for both girls and boys to attend school. The exceptions were Ram Prasad and Sanjita. Ram Prasad said that parents should give priority to boys because "they have to work to earn money and look after their family. They have to go for the war. So they have to know so many things."

Ram Prasad conceptualized men as the breadwinner and the protector – socially constructed conceptualizations of men that came from gender processes built into Nepali society. Sanjita, a girl, also said it was more important for boys to go to school. When asked why she felt this way, she became very shy and did not give a reason as to why. Through the gendered interactions and socialization that were part of her daily life, she most likely had come to presume boys were valued more and therefore should be educated ahead of girls.

Other than Ram Prasad and Sanjita, the student interviewees said children, regardless of their gender, should be educated equally. Dal Bahadur gave reasons why both boys and girls should attend school based on the existing Nepali gendered social order of which he was a part.

> It is important for both of them [boys and girls] to go to school. Because daughters also, if they study well, it will be good for their own future. Then, the sons also, if they study now, it will do them good in the future. They can do trekking [get into the trekking business]. Daughters, if they stay at home and their husband sends letter from foreign land, she will be able to read out the letter by herself.

Similar to so many interviewees from the parent and guardian, community member, and school staff samples, when Dal Bahadur spoke of sons, he couched his comments in job-related terms. Also, like many other interviewees, when he spoke of daughters, he described school as beneficial to them in domestic-related terms. Even though Dal Bahadur viewed education as important for girls and boys, the purpose for educating them differed in his mind. He had come to accept and embrace different social roles and aspirations for women and men in Nepali society.

Social constructions of gender also affected students' perceptions of educational achievement and particular areas of study. Some students explained that health was a suitable subject for girls because it was related to caring for a family, and it might help a girl to become a nurse. Two boy students and one girl student explained that if girls study health, they would then be able to look after their families if someone gets sick. Boy student Amrit further explained that, "After marriage, girls need to know how to raise their children." Linking girls with health care followed the general belief in Nepal that women were 'naturally' inclined to be caretakers and nurturers when, in actuality, these were socially constructed roles (Stromquist, 1990; Lorber, 2000). One boy, a class 9 student, did diverge from the stereotypes by suggesting that science, typically a male-dominated field in Nepal, might be good for girls. However, his reason for this choice was gendered: He explained that studying science was important so that girls "can be aware of their own health and will do good for their families."

Of the 10 students who chose math for boys, 7 explained their choice in terms of future careers that were socially defined as "masculine" in Nepal (e.g., engineer, businessman, pilot), pointing to the institutionalization of gender. Six students selected science. Similar to math, these students stated that boys who studied science could pursue future careers in male-dominated fields such as medicine. Class 5 girl student Phul Maya and class 5 boy student Ritesh explained that boys needed to study English in order to travel and get a trekking job with foreigners.

Socially constructed processes of gender also influenced this selected group of Nepali students' perceptions of their own ability to achieve in the educational system, and how gender affected their educational aspirations. For this sample, more boy students had higher aspirations than did the girl students who were interviewed. Five boy students but only two girl students hoped to achieve a bachelor's diploma or better. Socially constructed gender constraints appear to have influenced the educational aspirations of girl students more than the boy students.

None of the students aspired to achieve a master's degree, whereas their parents and guardians, teachers, and community members thought that students (both girls and boys) should aspire to this level. Notably, fewer girls (only 2) aspired to a bachelor's diploma than either their parents and guardians or community members (or their teachers) aspired for them. Only 2 of 10 girl students (20%) aspired to this level, whereas half of the boys did. Again, for this sample, the social construction of gender appears to have constrained the aspirations of girls more so than boys.

Linked to educational aspirations were students' career aspirations. As a result of the existing Nepali gendered order, students in the sample selected occupations that were aligned with socially approved, gendered occupations. Girl students' career aspirations reflected the gender processes that confined women to certain prescribed roles and occupations. For example, class 9 students Sanjita, Monica, Krishna Kumari, Leela Maya, and Nima all hoped to become nurses so that they could take care of sick people. They also wanted to be knowledgeable about hygiene and diseases in order to care for their families.

Boy students in the group had career aspirations that also reflected the existing gendered order. Ritesh hoped to join the military, Kedar and Chhetra aspired to become doctors, and Ram Bahadur hoped to be a pilot. Gopal wanted to go abroad for work. Two boy students aspired to become engineers, and another, an electronics expert, but none of the girl students chose these occupations.

Socially constructed gender, introduced in the home and reinforced in schools, also determined students' perceptions of their future. Tilak's life history interview illustrates this. At the time of his interview, Tilak was studying at the J School in class 9. He was 19 years old. A member of the Jirel ethnic group, he lived with 17 family members in one house, including 3 older brothers, 1 younger brother, 2 older sisters, a younger sister, 3 sisters-in-law, and a male cousin. Both his parents were farmers.

> When I was small, I used to play around, roam about, eat and sleep. Before I started my school, I only ate and played. But after I was put into school, I started going to school. I would be in school all day and return [home] in the evening. What to say? ... I have many friends. I have different group of friends in my village and different group of friends in school. Some of my friends work, some are studying, some go trekking with the foreigners, and some are working in a carpet factory. Our relatives are all farmers here. Sometimes the men go for labor work and sometimes for trekking and the women stay at home, either doing their fieldwork or housework ...
>
> ... I feel I am better off than the people who haven't been to school. I feel I have had a good chance in my life by being able to go to school. I can read and understand many things. I think now nobody will be able to cheat me like if I had been illiterate. I can speak and put forward my thoughts very easily in front of people whenever I have to. Now since I will be having my education certificates, I think it will be very easy for me to apply for jobs ...
>
> ... Yes, I am a member of our village club ... We are 20 to 30 people of the same village. We all gather and decide among ourselves on which game to play. And play accordingly ...
>
> ... [In the future] I will try to find a job. Then after I start earning money I will look after my parents. Try to help out the poor people in my village and neighbors. I will try to do all the works I can accomplish to help my family.

As was apparent in interviews with class 9 boy students, Tilak also appeared to know what was expected of him in the future as a man in Nepalese society – he recognized he would eventually become a breadwinner. However, for the time being, he concentrated on his studies and enjoyed time spent with friends. Tilak provides an example of how the gendered social order in Nepal typically constrained boys and their plans for the future to a much lesser extent than it did girls.

Yet, because gender constraints in any society are socially constructed, they can be challenged, contested, renegotiated, dismantled, and reconstructed (Potuchek, 1997). Some students in this study challenged existing gender constructs by changing their own aspirations and goals to those that more closely fit their needs, rather than what the prevailing gendered order dictated. Two class 5 girl students, Sagun and Phul Maya, are prime examples. Unlike her fellow girl students, class 5 student Sagun hoped to become a traffic controller with the Nepali police, a career choice that fell outside the small number of gendered occupations expected of Nepali women. She said she loved "everything about that job." In making such a choice, she pushed against the given gender constructs that privileged Nepali men in public security positions. Class 5 girl student Phul Maya hoped to run her own family business – a hotel/lodge. Phul Maya and Sagun not only challenged the norm that defined their job aspirations as "men's work," but by choosing alternative paths, these girls also became agents of change in modifying existing gendered expectations and assumptions.

Interviews yielded still other examples of girls whose career aspirations challenged Nepali gender constructs. Two class 9 students, Leela Maya and Monica, told me their favorite subjects were science and math, respectively. These two students refused to fit into any universal stereotype of math and science being too difficult for girls to comprehend. Monica selected math as her favorite subject because she was "interested" in math and it was also a subject she found easy. She did not link its usefulness to any future occupation. Leela Maya, in contrast, said that even though science was "not that easy," she figured it would help her to get a job.[15] Leela Maya appeared to be looking critically at course options and was cognizant of skills needed to succeed in a market economy. Even within the constraints of a gendered Nepali society and gendered educational system, these girls demonstrated independent thinking that pushed beyond the prevailing gendered norms of their culture.

Sita, a class 5 girl student, had high educational aspirations: She wanted to secure a bachelor's diploma and become a teacher. She explained that she wanted to become a teacher in order to "put forward some of my views regarding the environment." Sita's classmate Kamala also hoped to become a teacher because she had been impressed with her teachers at school.

Girl student Krishna Kumari and boy student Dal Bahadur both planned to pursue their studies as well. Class 9 student Krishna Kumari planned to study up to the campus level[16] so that she could get a job and make her own choices about her life. She said, "I'll go to places I wish to visit. I'll try to stand on my own feet [be independent]. Then only I'll marry ... later only." Krishna Kumari pushed gender constraints to reorder her priorities. For her, education came before marriage. With education, she would be independent and would make her own decisions as to when she would marry. Similarly, class 5 student Dal Bahadur wanted to study up to the School Leaving Certificate (SLC) level so he, too, would have more opportunities. He hoped to achieve a high enough position that would discourage anyone from cheating him. He elaborated, "We become wiser [with education]. People won't be able to mislead or deceive us." Dal Bahadur conceived of education as a tool to empower himself.

As expressed in her life history narrative, Sanu Kumari first and foremost aspired to finish her education. Afterwards, she intended to look for work and earn her own living. She only planned to marry later. Setting these priorities demonstrated her independence. As the eldest, she planned to help support her family. Although Sanu Kumari's position in her family obliged her to support her family and might have subsequently limited her future choices, envisioning herself as a breadwinner for the family demonstrated her resistance to the gender construct, which in Nepali society viewed men and boys as the providers of economic security for the family. She also resisted the gender norm that girls marry early. She was very committed to completing her education so that she could find a job to support herself.

Another example is Laxmi, a new teacher. At the time of her life history interview, she was 17 years old. She came from a poor Chhetri (Hindu) family. The fifth of eight children in her family, she had four sisters and three brothers. When she was interviewed, she was studying at the high school in the 10+2 program. She also taught at a primary school. She explained that after passing the SLC exam at the end of class 9 and joining the 10+2 program, she worried about whether or not she would be able to continue in her studies. She mentioned to a head teacher that she was thinking of one day becoming a teacher. "Come tomorrow and you'll be a Miss [woman teacher]," Laxmi said he replied. Thus began Laxmi's career as a teacher.

I went to observe Laxmi teach on several occasions. Laxmi had attended a series of teacher trainings offered by a British volunteer and a village community member in 1999–2000, and I observed Laxmi incorporating their suggestions for student-based learning in her teaching. She kept her students engaged with participatory activities and made sure she called on each student, at least once, regardless of their gender. In telling her story,

Laxmi began

> Our parents are not educated. I am heading [hoping] to study further and my uncle's daughter [cousin] is a diploma [bachelor's] graduate. So seeing her, I also want to study further ...
>
> ... I go to college from 6 am to 9:45 am. Then I hurry back home [rented room] and prepare food for myself very quickly [laughs]. Then I run down to the MS School. Then I reach the school at around 10:10 or 10:15. Then I take [teach] class until 3 pm. Then by the time I reach home, it [is] always getting dark. I reach home at 5 pm. Then I come and start preparing dinner. I sit down to study till 10 pm. Then after [that] I go to sleep. Besides studying, I teach. That's all ...
>
> ... There is a vast difference in my life because of school. As you might know, the girls in the village areas don't know about society and its whereabouts [aspects] and what would they become tomorrow. But that I have experienced [learned] after studying in school. Back in my house also, my parents are facing all the hardship, and those who did get married or not married are also trapped in hardship. Whereas since I have studied, I can make up my mind on what to become after I finish my studies. I might even be able to help my parents later. My family is very poor. So I will study very hard and after passing my 10 + 2, I'll join diploma and I'll continue my job as a teacher. That will help the children [her younger siblings], and they will also be able to think about their future ...
>
> ... Our village people are still backward [not developed]; what are the reasons for this? If [the problem is] because of no education, I would put forward the issues of schools and education. Then about women ... Why they are still behind, why haven't they been able to come out of their situation [of subordination]? ... Find out the reason behind these factors and ask them to solve the problems for the upliftment of womankind. The upliftment of womankind is most important.

Laxmi illustrates that she was very much a product of gender processes in Nepal, while at the same time wanting to change existing constructions of gender. In five years' time, at the age of 22, she predicted that she would already be married and "busy with domestic/household chores." At the same time, she wanted to continue her career in teaching. She also wanted to better the position of Nepali women and girls. To this end, she initiated a girls' club in the village as a beginning.[17]

Laxmi also demonstrates the fluidity of socially constructed gender constraints. Despite the gender expectations Nepali society obliged girls to fulfill, Laxmi shows how these constraints could be negotiated to achieve her goals. Laxmi's accomplishments – pursuing her education, working as a teacher, developing a club for girls – illustrate that gender does not dictate ability and agency. This village's schools and the chances of girls would be improved if there were more role models in them like Laxmi. But one teacher is not enough. It takes a critical mass to effect change in the ways schools construct, maintain, and reproduce gender.

CONCLUSIONS AND IMPLICATIONS

Gender is a socially constructed process embedded in social institutions. In this article, I argue that socially constructed gender processes are institutionalized expressions of power, and these processes – enacted by community members, parents, guardians, teachers, and head teachers in Nepali homes and schools – constrained or enabled students according to their gender. In essence, the expectations first learned in the home were reinforced in schools, and consequently these gender processes imposed constraints on students, particularly girl students, as revealed by student interviewees. However, gender is dynamic – continually constructed and reconstructed. And because gender is a socially constructed process, it can be reshaped and resisted by individuals (Lorber, 2000; Butler, 1990). Students who challenged gender processes, such as Laxmi or Sanu Kumari, illustrated individuals' capacity to negotiate the social construction and maintenance of gender.

Commonplace in much of the existing literature and in many of the existing national programs initiated to increase girls' enrollment in school are the presumptions that girls' access to school leads to equality between girls and boys, and that girls' enrollment in school guarantees their participation in school and equal participation in the broader society. These assumptions have significant implications for educational policy as well as for future education programs. Projects that assume schools are gender-neutral will only result in short-term gains, at best, and more often will fail in the long term.[18] Before spending money on initiatives that may be shortsighted – especially in an impoverished country like Nepal that is so dependent on international aid – those working for change need to understand the social forces at work that construct and maintain gender inequality.

Researchers can assist policymakers in implementing more effective programs by providing them with evidence that shows how and when society fails to conceive of gender as an institutionalization of power, it perpetuates gender inequality, particularly in education. While studies that examine girls' access to and participation in existing formal education programs are certainly valuable, they only tell part of the story. Research grounded in the assumption that girls and boys are enrolling in gender-neutral schools will not be sufficient to transform gender power relations in the wider society. Future research must analyze gender inequality in schools by examining how gender is socially constructed and maintained in *both* school and the home. Only then can we can begin to understand and devise more effective ways to increase all students' enrollment, participation, and success in school.

Government officials, policymakers, researchers, activists, and villagers need to work together to develop programs within the framework of gender as a socially constructed process. These programs should also address the intersections of class, caste, ethnicity, and religion with gender. Consideration should be given to the potential for change at the grassroots as well as the national levels. Future initiatives should examine villages where existing programs are in operation and consider how they can be restructured.

My research has led me to conclude that there are many different avenues that stakeholders might explore, both in this particular village and in Nepal as a whole. First, communities can increase awareness of gender through a range of activities and communication vehicles. A few examples include promoting gender equity by posting in key village locations posters of non-stereotypical images of women and men; creating a calendar of famous Nepali women and distributing it to all schools so it can be hung in every classroom; airing stories of women and men in non-stereotypical roles on the radio; promoting sporting events at schools for both girls and boys; and facilitating community discussions about gender relations.

Other possible activities include training school staff at every level about the social construction of gender; increasing the numbers of women teachers, who could serve as role models for both girls *and* boys; establishing mentoring programs and clubs for girls and boys; and critically examining the ways gender is constructed and reinforced in school programs, curriculum, and textbooks. Importantly, all efforts for change, on the macro and micro levels, must consider socially constructed gender processes within the context of gendered social institutions.

My findings also suggest various directions for future research. Students' viewpoints need to be examined further, as it is often the individuals most impacted by a problem who offer the best perspective on effecting social change. More research is also needed as to why some students challenge gender constraints while others do not. Research must also take a closer look at the intersections of race, class, caste, and ethnicity with gender, particularly in the context of family and education.

As a social construction, gender is fluid, rather than existing in a state of homogeneity, static in time. Because gender constraints in any society are socially constructed and can be challenged, contested, renegotiated, dismantled, and reconstructed (Potuchek, 1997), we must continue to examine people's individual lives and their varied, changing experiences of gender. By grounding our research and policy reforms in the lived gendered experiences and contexts of individuals, we will not only move toward providing girl and boy children in developing countries such as Nepal with meaningful educational experiences and improved life opportunities, but we also move toward transforming power relations within societies' social, educational, economic, and political institutions, resulting in a more equitable social order for all.

NOTES

1. Nepal has very few resources for improving its educational system. Financially and programmatically, Nepal depends heavily on international donors and loans for its public schools. This dependence enables Nepal to support a public school system, but also indicates that the country has inadequate means for making institutional-level changes.

2. See Floro and Wolf (1990); Cochrane, O'Hara, and Leslie (1980); Beenstock and Sturdy (1990); Pitt and Rosenzweig (1989); Schultz (1989); Behrman (1991); and King and Hill (1993). Many studies argue that educating girls yields outcomes such as increased female productivity; lowered infant, child, and maternal mortality rates; reduction in population growth; and healthier children, as well as better-reared and educated children. See Herz, Subbarao, Habib, and Raney (1991); Prather (1991); Cochrane (1979); Wolfe and Behrman (1984); Schultz (1989).

3. See Jamison and Lockheed (1987); Davison and Kanyuka (1990); Chernichovsky (1985); Behrman and Sussangkarn (1989); Mukhopadhyay (1994); Birdsall (1980); Kasaju and Manandhar (1985); and Csapo (1981).

4. The term "gender," as a noun, refers to the social distinctions between girls and boys, and women and men, including the roles that are deemed appropriate to each sex. When I use "gender" as an adjective ("gendered") or verb ("to gender"), it refers to any affect that reinforces gender roles, in other words, an affect that encourages a girl to "act like a girl," and a boy to "act like a boy." The "process of gender" then, is the means by which society pushes girls and boys into appropriate roles.

5. I am certain that the findings noted here are descriptive of the situation in that particular Nepali village at the particular time of this project. I will use the past tense throughout this article to illustrate that the social constructions of gender described existed in that place and time. I follow the lead of Skinner and Holland (1996), who also used past tense throughout their analysis as an effort not to freeze the people in their study in time and out of history.

6. It should be noted that this study was limited to a rural village community in the Himalayan foothills of Eastern Nepal; one cannot make broad generalizations about other populations from this research. However, documenting the processes of social interaction as they occur among different groups of people has a broad range of applications. The various meaning and interpretations individuals construct, value, and claim regarding gender and education have profound implications for educational systems, research, and reform.

7. As the world's only Hindu kingdom, a large percentage of the Nepalese population (86.5%) is Hindu.

8. Kanyadan also secures parents a place in heaven, as it is considered to be one of the greatest religious duties that parents can perform (Mathema, 1998).

9. "Opportunity costs" refers to the perceived, indirect costs incurred when a child, particularly a daughter, goes to school and is not available to conduct household chores, agricultural work, or income-generating labor.

10. The case study village is not referred to by name in order to preserve the anonymity of the study participants. Names of schools and research study participants have been given a pseudonym to preserve anonymity.

11. Because I define gender as socially constructed and different than biological sex (e.g., female, male), I purposely utilize gender terms and refer to students in this article as "girl students" and "boy students" (rather than "female students" and "male students"), even though many of the students in this study were teenagers.

12. My research design involved focusing on one class (grade) at two schools, while also collecting some data and making observations at each school in this village. I purposively selected class 5 (roughly the equivalent of 5th grade) to observe at the D School and class 9 to observe at the J School. I purposively selected the D School as one focus school because it was located in the village's bustling market area and the center of the most economically productive and populated area of the village. This school was one of only two schools with classes from pre-kindergarten through eighth grade. The other nine primary schools in the village were limited to pre-kindergarten (nursery) class through class 5. The D school had a higher enrollment of girls than boys. Further, at the time of this project, the D School enrolled students from a wide variety of Hindu castes and other religions, as well as socioeconomic backgrounds. I selected the J School as a focus school because it was located in a heavily populated area with equally wide diversity as the D School. This school was the only one in the village that offered classes up to the School Leaving Certificate (SLC) level. (The SLC is awarded after a student passes a set of national exams, externally administered at the end of the 10th year of the formal schooling cycle, with a $10+2$ program, or roughly the equivalent of 10th through 12th grade, after passing the SLC exam.) Some students walked for 2 hours everyday to go to this school. Other students came from distant villages and stayed in hostels in the village to attend the school.

13. Six parents/guardians (5 women and 1 man) acknowledged early marriage as an intervening factor. In the community member sample, 15% of the interviewees (28 women and 22 men) gave marriage-related reasons to explain why girls drop out of school. Further, 25% of teachers (1 woman and 2 men) and 40% of head teachers (all men) said girls getting married led to their dropping out of school.

14. Although students periodically mentioned economic constraints in their interviews (e.g., they often noted their educational aspirations were dependent upon their families' financial situations), none of the students gave poverty as an explanation for girls dropping out of school. Conversely, all four samples of community members, parents and guardians, teachers, and head teachers cited poverty as a reason. This suggests students were not yet as aware as their teachers and families of the economic constraints to education. For them, poverty had not yet interfered with their schooling. Or, they may have been more critical in their thinking than their parents and guardians, community members, and teachers: Perhaps they saw the underlying gendered implications of suggesting "poverty" as a reason for why girls drop out of school.

15. None of the class 5 girls selected math or science. Perhaps they had not yet seen the utility of either subject, or perhaps they had not been encouraged to excel in either subject by teachers or parents and guardians.

16. The campus level is also known as intermediate or "10+2." It is similar to 11th and 12th grade in the U.S. educational system. Students enter the campus level or 10+2 after passing the School Leaving Certificate (SLC) exam.

17. After I left the field, I heard that Laxmi had started a club for girls.

18. See Rothchild (2002) for specific examples of well-intended, but shortsighted programs designed to increase the enrollment numbers of girls in schools.

ACKNOWLEDGMENTS

This research project was made possible with funding from the Oxley Foundation in Tulsa, OK; Association for Women in Science (AWIS) in Washington, DC; and the American Association of University Women (AAUW) Educational Foundation in Washington, DC. Many individuals in Nepal, including Sworneem Tamang, Mala Rai, Robin Singh, Dinesh Rajbhandari, and Rekha Rajbhandari, played an extremely helpful role in facilitating this project. I must also add personal thanks to Christopher Butler, Jonathan Rothchild, Emily Hannum, and Bruce Fuller for their preliminary editorial work on this article.

REFERENCES

ABEL. (1996). *Exploring incentives: Promising strategies for improving girls' participation in school*. Washington, DC: Advancing Basic Education and Literacy Project (ABEL). Creative Associates International, Inc.

Acharya, M. (1981). *The Mathili women*. Philippines: Regional Service Center.

Acharya, M., & Bennett, L. (1981). *The rural women of Nepal: An aggregate analysis and summary of eight village studies*. Philippines: Regional Service Center.

Acker, J. (1990). Hierarchies, jobs, bodies: A theory of gendered organization. *Gender and Society*, *4*(2), 139–158.

Anderson, J., & Herencia, C. (1983). *L'image de la Femme et de l'homme dans les livres scolaires peruviens*. Paris, France: UNESCO.

Ashby, J. (1985). Equity and discrimination among children: Schooling decisions in rural Nepal. *Comparative Education Review*, *29*(1), 68–79.

Beenstock, M., & Sturdy, P. (1990). Determinants of infant mortality in regional India. *World Development*, *18*(March), 443–453.

Behrman, J. (1991). *Investing in female education for development: Women in development strategy for the 1990s in Asia and the Near East*. Mimeo, University of Pennsylvania, PA.

Behrman, J., & Sussangkarn, C. (1989). *Parental schooling and child outcomes: Mother versus father, schooling quality, and interactions*. Mimeo, University of Pennsylvania, PA.

Bennett, L. (1981). *The Parbatiya women of Bakundol.* Philippines: Regional Service Center.
Best, R. (1983). *We've all got scars: What boys and girls learn in elementary school.* Bloomington, IN: Indiana University Press.
Birdsall, N. (1980). A cost of siblings: Child schooling in urban Columbia. *Research in Population Economics, 2,* 115–150.
Butler, J. (1990). *Gender trouble: Feminism and the subversion of identity.* New York: Routledge.
Cameron, M. M. (1995). Transformations of gender and caste divisions of labor in rural Nepal: Land, hierarchy, and the case of untouchable women. *Journal of Anthropological Research, 51,* 215–246.
Chernichovsky, D. (1985). Socio-economic and demographic aspects of school enrollment and attendance in Botswana. *Economic Development and Social Change, 33,* 319–332.
Cochrane, S. (1979). *Fertility and education: What do we really know?* Baltimore, MD: Johns Hopkins University Press.
Cochrane, S., O'Hara, D., & Leslie, J. (1980). *The effects of education on health.* World Bank Staff Working Papers. No. 405. World Bank, Washington, DC.
Connell, R. W. (1987). *Gender and power.* Stanford, CA: Stanford University Press.
Csapo, M. (1981). Religious, social, and economic factors hindering the education of girls in northern Nigeria. *Comparative Education, 17*(3), 311–319.
Davison, J., & Kanyuka, M. (1990). *An ethnographic study of factors that affect the education of girls in southern Malawi.* A Report to the Ministry of Education and Culture and USAID Malawi. Lilongwe.
Floro, M., & Wolf, J. M. (1990). *The economic and social impact of girls' primary education in developing countries.* Washington, DC: Creative Associates International, Inc., USAID.
Harber, C. (1988). Schools and political socialization in Africa. *Education Review, 40*(2), 195–202.
Herz, B., Subbarao K., Habib M., & Raney, L. (1991). *Letting girls learn: Promising approaches in primary and secondary education.* World Bank Discussion Papers. No. 133. The World Bank, Washington, DC.
Jamison, D. T., & Lockheed, M. E. (1987). Participation in schooling: Determinants and learning outcomes in Nepal. *Economic Development and Cultural Change, 35*(2), 279–306.
Kasaju, P., & Manandhar, T. B. (1985). Impact of parents' literacy on school enrollments and retention of children: The case of Nepal. In: G. Carron & A. Bordia (Eds), *Issues in planning and implementing national literacy programs.* Paris: UNESCO and International Institute for Educational Planning.
Kimmel, M. (2000). *The gendered society.* New York: Oxford University Press.
Kimmel, M. (2004). *The gendered society.* New York: Oxford University Press.
King, E. M., & Hill, M. A. (1993). *Women's education in developing countries: Barriers, benefits, and policies.* Baltimore: The Johns Hopkins University Press.
Lee, A. (1996). *Gender, literacy, curriculum: Re-writing school geography.* London: Taylor and Francis.
Lorber, J. (1994). *The paradoxes of gender.* New Haven: Yale University Press.
Lorber, J. (2000). Using gender to undo gender: A feminist degendering movement. *Feminist Theory, 1*(1), 79–95.
Mathema, M. (1998). Women in South Asia: Pakistan, Bangladesh, and Nepal. In: N. P. Stromquist (Ed.), *Women in the Third World: An encyclopedia of contemporary issues* (pp. 583–592). New York, NY: Garland Publishing, Inc.

Mies, M. (1986). *Patriarchy and accumulation on a world scale: Women in the international division of labor*. Atlantic Heights, NJ: Zed Books.
Mukhopadhyay, S. (1994). Adapting household behavior to agricultural technology in West Bengal, India: Wage labor, fertility, and child schooling determinants. *Economic Development and Cultural Change*, 43(1), 91–115.
O'Brien, M. (1983). *The politics of reproduction*. Boston: Routledge and Kegan Paul.
Orenstein, P. (1994). *School girls: Young women, self-esteem, and the confidence gap*. New York: Doubleday, with the American Association of University Women.
Pinto, R. (1982). Imagem da Mulher atraves dos livros didaticos. *Boletim Bibliografico de Biblioteca Mario de Andrade*, 43(3–4), 126–131.
Pitt, M., & Rosenzweig, M. (1989). Estimating the intrafamily incidence of illness: Child health and gender inequality in the allocation of time in Indonesia. Paper presented at the conference on the family, gender differences, and development. Yale University, New Haven, CT, September 4–6.
Potuchek, J. L. (1997). *Who supports the family? Gender and breadwinning in dual-earner marriages*. Stanford, CA: Stanford University Press.
Prather, C. (1991). *Educating girls: Strategies to increase access, persistence, and achievement*. Washington, DC: Creative Associates International, Inc.
Reinhold, A. J. (1993). *Working with rural communities in Nepal: Some principles of non-formal education intervention: Action research in family and early childhood*. Westport, CT: Save the Children.
Risman, B. (1998). *Gender vertigo: American families in transition*. New Haven, CT: Yale University Press.
Rothchild, J. (2002). *Beyond enrollment numbers: An in-depth look at gender inequality in schools in rural Nepal*. Ph.D. dissertation, Department of Sociology, American University, Washington, DC.
Sadker, M., & Sadker, D. (1994). *Failing at fairness: How our schools cheat girls*. New York: Simon and Schuster.
Schultz, T. P. (1989). *Returns to women's education*. Washington, DC: The World Bank.
Shrestha, G. M., Lamichhane, S. R., Thapa, B. K., Chitrakar, R., Useem, M., & Comings, J. P. (1986). Determinants of educational participation in rural Nepal. *Comparative Education Review*, 30(4), 508–522.
Shtrii, S. (1995). *Women, development, and demography: A study of the socio-economic changes in the status of women in Nepal (1981–1993)*. Kathmandu: Shtrii Shakti.
Sibbons, M. (1999). From WID to GAD: Experiences of education in Nepal. In: C. Heward & S. Bunwaree (Eds), *Gender, education, and development: Beyond access to empowerment* (pp. 189–202). London: Zed Books Ltd.
Silva, R. (1979). Imagen de la mujer en los textos escolares. *Revista Columbiana de Educacion*, 4(II), 9–52.
Singh, Shakti (1995). *Statistical profile on women of Nepal*. Kathmandu: Shtrii Shakti.
Skinner, D., & Holland, D. (1996). Schools and the cultural production of the educated person in a Nepalese hill community. In: B. A. Levinson, D. E. Foley & D. C. Holland (Eds), *The cultural production of the educated person: Critical ethnographies of schooling and local practice* (pp. 273–299). Albany, NY: State University of New York Press.
Smith, D. E. (2000). Schooling for inequality. *Signs: Journal of Women in Culture and Society*, 25(4), 1147–1151.

Staudt, K. (1998). *Policy, politics, and gender: Women gaining ground.* West Hartford, CT: Kumarian Press.

Stromquist, N. P. (1989a). Determinants of educational participation and achievement of women in the Third World: A review of the evidence and a theoretical critique. *Review of Educational Research, 5*(2), 143–183.

Stromquist, N. P. (1989b). Recent developments in women's education: Closer to a better social order? In: R. S. Gallin, M. Aronoff, & A. Ferguson (Eds), *The Women and International Development Annual* (Vol. 1, pp. 103–130). Boulder, CO: Westview Press.

Stromquist, N. P. (1990). Women and education women and illiteracy: The interplay of gender subordination and poverty. *Comparative Education Review, 34*(February – special issue: Adult Literacy), 95–111.

Stromquist, N. P. (1992). *Women and education in Latin America: Knowledge, power, and change.* Boulder, CO: Lynne Rienner Publishers.

Subedi, P. (1993). *Nepali women rising.* Kathmandu: Sahayogi Press.

Tembo, L. P. (1984). *Men and women in school textbooks.* Paris, France: UNESCO.

Thorne, B. (1993). *Gender play: Girls and boys in school.* New Brunswick, NJ: Rutgers University Press.

West, C., & Zimmerman, D. H. (1987). Doing gender. *Gender and Society, 1*(2), 125–151.

Wolfe, B., & Behrman, J. (1984). Who is schooled in developing countries? The role of income, parental schooling, sex, residence, and family size. *Economics of Education Review, 3*(3), 231–245.

FAMILIES, SCHOOLS, AND READING IN ASIA AND LATIN AMERICA

Hyunjoon Park and Gary D. Sandefur

ABSTRACT

Using the data from PISA (Program for International Student Assessment), we compare the ways in which families and schools influence educational achievement among 15-year-olds between four Asian countries (Hong Kong, Korea, Indonesia, and Thailand) and four Latin American countries (Argentina, Chile, Mexico, and Peru). We find that family socioeconomic status (SES) affects student achievement considerably more in Latin America than in Asia. Compared to the relatively weak impacts of family SES in Asian countries, however, parental communication with children plays an important role in fostering achievement. The most evident difference between the two regions is the extent of school differentiation along family socioeconomic backgrounds. The extent to which students' individual and family characteristics account for between-school variance in student performance is substantially larger in Latin America than in Asia. Although the overall degree of students' sense of belonging at their school is significantly associated with increased student achievement in all eight countries, school climate factors are more relevant for student learning in Asian education than in Latin American education.

INTRODUCTION

In the development literature, high-performing Asian economies, particularly Japan and the four Tigers (Hong Kong, South Korea, Singapore, and Taiwan) have often been contrasted to Latin American economies (Birdsall & Jaspersen, 1997; World Bank, 1993). These Asian and Latin American countries had similar levels of economic development four decades ago, but they have followed very different paths since then, resulting in remarkable economic growth in the former set of countries but much slower growth in the latter. The changes in GDP per capita between 1960 and 2000 as seen in Table 1 clearly show much faster growth in Asia than in Latin America, although Indonesia and Thailand are distinguished from the other three Asian countries in their substantially lower levels of economic development.

Interestingly, Asian countries have managed to sustain rapid growth with relatively low economic inequality. The combination of high rates of economic growth and declining income inequality is one of the distinctive

Table 1. Economic and Educational Indicators in Asia and Latin America.

	GDP Per Capita (1996 $)		Gini Index[a]	Secondary School Enrollment (% Net)		Public Spending on Education
	1960	2000		1970	1999	(% of GDP)[b]
Asia						
Hong Kong	3,047	26,703	43.4	33	70	2.9
Japan	4,657	24,672	24.9	86	100	3.6
Korea	1,571	15,881	31.6	38	94	3.8
Indonesia	960	3,637	30.3	16[c]	48	1.5
Thailand	1,121	6,857	43.2	17[c]	55	5.4
Latin America						
Argentina	7,395	10,995	49.4	35	76	4.6
Brazil	2,395	7,185	59.1	18	67	3.8
Chile	3,818	9,920	57.5	28	72	3.9
Mexico	3,970	8,766	51.9	17	56	4.4
Peru	3,118	4,583	46.2	27	61	3.3

Sources: Perm Word Table Version 6.1 (GDP per capita), OECD (2003) and Székely (2001) (Gini). UNESCO Institute for Statistics, September 2004 (enrollment, spending on education).
[a]The reference years are 1996 for Hong Kong and Peru, 2000 for Indonesia and Thailand, 1993 for Japan, and 1998 for others.
[b]The reference years are 2000 except for Mexico and Peru (1999) and for Hong Kong (1995).
[c]Gross enrollment rates.

features of Asian economic development, which contributed to a drastic reduction in poverty in this region (World Bank, 1993). In contrast, substantial economic inequality has been notable in Latin America and continues to be so (World Bank, 2003). During the 1980s and 1990s, economic inequality has persisted or even increased in many Latin American countries, and substantial proportions of people remain impoverished despite a modest reduction in poverty in the 1990s (Székely, 2001). The Gini coefficients presented in Table 1 show significant gaps in the degree of economic inequality between Asia (particularly Indonesia, Japan, and Korea) and Latin America.

Along with considerable differences in economic performance, Asian and Latin American countries also exhibit contrasting patterns in educational development. High-quality educational systems in Asian countries, especially East Asian countries including Hong Kong, Japan, and Korea, have been appraised as a critical factor leading to their remarkable economic growth (Ratliff, 2003). The astonishing expansion of the educational system in these East Asian countries has been widely recognized (Park & Sandefur, 2005; Park, 2004). Furthermore, in various international comparisons of student achievement, students in Hong Kong, Japan, and Korea have demonstrated top levels of achievement by international standards. Meanwhile, there has been a much slower increase of educational attainment in Latin America, and students in the region consistently score at the bottom in international tests of student achievement (Ratliff, 2003; Wolff & Castro, 2000).

In this study, we compare the specific ways in which families and schools influence children's educational outcomes in four Asian countries (Hong Kong, Indonesia, Korea, and Thailand) and four Latin American countries (Argentina, Chile, Mexico, and Peru), taking into consideration the contrasting contexts of economic and educational development between the two regions. The effects of family and school factors on student achievement in individual countries in Asia and Latin America have been extensively examined in literature of school effectiveness in developing countries (see, for a review, Fuller, 1987; Fuller & Clarke, 1994). In addition, cross-national studies of student achievement have shown that, compared to family background, school factors had a stronger impact on student achievement in developing nations, whereas family background played a greater role in developed nations (Heyneman & Loxley, 1982, 1983).

However, our current study extends the previous literature in several ways. First, discussion of school effects in Asia and Latin America has been based primarily on findings from data collected in the 1970s and 1980s. Using data from 36 countries collected in the 1990s, Baker, Goesling, and Letendre (2002) show that the major conclusion derived from cross-national comparisons using 1970s data is no longer confirmed. Contrary to the 1970s findings of Heyneman and Loxley (1982, 1983), the analysis of the newer data indicates that, even in developing countries, the effect of school factors on educational achievement is no longer stronger than the effect of family background. The authors attribute the weakening effect of school factors in developing countries to increased state commitment to education since the late 1980s, which contributed to significant improvements in school quality in many developing countries. The study by Baker et al. (2002) suggests that we need to reexamine the effects of family and schools on educational achievement in Asia and Latin America in the context of increased school quality and overall educational expansion since the late 1980s. In the current study, we address this issue using data collected in 2000–2001.

Second, most of the previous studies that examined family and school effects among Asian and Latin American countries focused on students in primary or lower secondary education. For example, Heyneman and Loxley (1982, 1983) compared student achievement in primary schools. Numerous studies in developing countries have used the TIMSS (Third International Mathematics and Science Study) data to examine educational achievement among 13-year-olds, most of whom were in the eighth grade (Baker et al., 2002).

Our current study examines reading performance among 15-year-old students. In many Asian and Latin American countries (including Argentina, Chile, Peru, Korea, and Thailand), the first student selection into different types of schools does not occur until the age of 14 or 15 (OECD, 2005). After that age, students are selected into distinct types of schools that often differ significantly from each other in their curriculum and academic orientation. This implies that there are more significant institutional differences among upper secondary schools that most 15-year-olds attend than among primary schools or lower secondary schools. The larger school differences at the level of upper secondary education within countries suggest that the relative effects of school factors and family background found in previous research examining primary or lower secondary students may not be applicable to older students.

Finally, most of the studies examining family and school effects in developing countries utilized the production function approach, which tried to identify the specific educational inputs associated with educational outputs of student achievement (Fuller, 1987; Fuller & Clarke, 1994). This approach, which usually relied on ordinary least squares (OLS) regression and the R^2 measure to assess the relative importance of family and school effects, has been criticized with its methodological shortcomings, especially its neglect of the hierarchical structure of achievement data (Riddell, 1989; Bryk & Raudenbush, 1992; Buchmann, 2002).

Alternatively, since the late 1980s, multilevel modeling techniques have been increasingly applied to developing countries as well as to developed nations. They have allowed researchers to reassess the relative effects of family and school on student achievement by explicitly taking into account the nested structure of students within schools (Riddell, 1989; Lockheed & Longford, 1991). Another important feature of multilevel models used to measure school effectiveness is their ability to separate "contextual effects" associated with schools' socioeconomic composition from other school effects associated with specific pedagogical practices and other school factors. Contextual effects are effects of the aggregate of a person-level characteristic on the outcome, net of the effect associated with the person-level characteristics (Bryk & Raudenbush, 1992). A great deal of literature shows that a school's overall socioeconomic status (SES), which is the aggregate of individual students' family SES within the school, has an impact on student achievement over and above the effect of the individual students' family SES (Gamoran, 1992; Willms, 1986, 1992).

Because the contextual effect of schools' SES stems from the preexisting conditions of students attending the schools, individual schools or teachers cannot affect it. Therefore, the separation of the contextual effect from other school effects, caused by schools' specific policies on pedagogical practices, school organization, and other processes, results in better estimates of school effectiveness. As a review of school effect studies in developing countries showed, however, the advantages of multilevel analysis over traditional OLS regression models have not been fully utilized in studies of developing countries (Riddell, 1997). Consequently, our research extends earlier literature by examining the impacts of family and school on student achievement employing multilevel modeling techniques.

RESEARCH QUESTIONS

In this paper, we first look at the ways in which several components of family background are associated with student performance in Asia and Latin America. We are particularly interested in investigating the effects of family SES, represented by parental education and occupation. Another important aspect of family background considered in this study is parent–child communication, which indicates the extent to which parents communicate with their children at home about children's schooling and other general issues.

Representing the overall parent–child relationship, the frequency of parent–child communication has been found to be positively associated with children's educational outcomes in the United States (McNeal, 1999; Teachman, Paasch, & Carver, 1997; Ho Sui-Chu & Willms, 1996). This aspect of family environment has not received serious attention in previous studies of student achievement in developing countries, partially due to the lack of data.

We also look at the extent to which educational resources available in the home enhance children's educational achievement, independent of family SES. Tracking educational trajectories of American high school seniors, Teachman (1987) provided evidence of the significantly positive roles that home educational resources – such as a specific place to study in the home, reference books, a daily newspaper, or dictionary in the home – play in determining educational attainment.

In addition to the effects associated with family background, we examine how school factors affect student achievement. We first assess the extent of variation in student performance between schools in each country, and also the degree to which these between-school differences in student performance are explained by students' family characteristics. This analysis will indicate to what extent schools are segregated along the socioeconomic background of the students they serve in each country.

We then move to examine regional differences in the size of the achievement gap between students attending private and public schools. Next we assess the extent to which educational advantages associated with a specific type of school are attributable to the overall socioeconomic level of the school. This contextual effect associated with the overall SES of the school suggests that students from less-advantaged families do worse in schools, not only because of their lower socioeconomic background, but also because they attend schools with lower SES (Willms, 2003). The contextual effect of the average SES of the school may be considered as a peer-group effect resulting from peer interactions among more talented and motivated students in higher SES schools. The effect may also reflect other favorable school environments associated with the higher SES of the school (OECD, 2001).

Finally, we identify school characteristics that are related to student achievement in Asia and Latin America. A large number of studies of school effectiveness have identified several school-related factors that affect student learning (Mayer, Mullens, & Moore, 2001; Willms, 1992). Among them, we examine two groups of school factors: school material resources and school climate. The former indicates the levels of teacher shortage and educational resource shortage in schools, while the latter includes disciplinary climate, teacher's morale and commitment, student–teacher relations, and student's sense of belonging to the school (Lee & Bryk, 1989; Bryk, Lee, & Holland, 1993).

Although we highlight differences that Asian and Latin American education show as two distinct groups, we do not ignore the fact that significant differences as well as similarities exist within Asian countries (also within Latin American countries) in educational, economic, and other systems. As already seen in Table 1, for instance, in terms of the level of economic development, advanced economies of Hong Kong and two OECD (Organization for Economic Co-operation and Development) member countries, Japan and Korea, are contrasted to developing economies of Indonesia and Thailand. In addition, students from Hong Kong, Japan, and Korea have shown significantly higher performance on various international tests of academic achievement when compared to students from Western countries, while students from Indonesia and Thailand are often worse than average. Therefore, differences across countries within each region will also be discussed.

HYPOTHESES

Previous comparative studies of student achievement in the 1970s showed stronger effects of school factors than family background on student achievement in developing countries (Heyneman & Loxley, 1982, 1983). It might be expected, therefore, that family SES would be more strongly associated with student achievement in Hong Kong, Korea, and possibly Argentina, all of which have relatively advanced economic conditions compared to those in other developing countries in their regions (see Table 1). As described earlier, however, a recent study analyzing the 1994 data provides contradictory evidence. In addition, due to substantially high levels of economic inequality among Latin American countries, family SES may impact educational achievement in the region more than in Asia, and especially in Korea and Indonesia where economic inequality is much less pronounced (see Table 1).

On the other hand, we expect parent–child communication is impacting educational achievement more in Asian countries than in Latin America, and particularly in Hong Kong and Korea, where there is strong pressure for academic achievement. In societies with high levels of pressure to achieve academically, parent–child communication is more likely to be directed toward education-related issues. For example, parents in those societies may influence students not only by frequently discussing how students are doing in school, but also by trying to convey the importance of education for later life-chances.

In Latin America, students are more likely to be segregated along lines of SES, due to the region's greater economic inequality. Therefore, among Latin American countries, we should see more significant differences than in Asian countries in the overall socioeconomic condition of schools. Furthermore, the extent to which between-school variation in student achievement is explained by students' individual characteristics should be greater in Latin America than in Asia.

Studies of Latin American primary and secondary schools have shown substantially better educational outcomes, including achievement and retention, among students in private schools than their counterparts in public schools (Wolff & Castro, 2000). Private school students are more likely to come from families in which parents have greater educational attainment, higher income, and more engagement in their child's education than parents of students in public schools (Somers, McEwan, & Willms, 2004). In other words, the high degree of economic inequality in Latin America is likely to be linked to inequality of educational opportunity through differential accesses to private schools that have higher quality and greater educational resources than do public schools. We will show that the pattern of the achievement gap between private- and public-school students is strikingly different in Asia, where, in fact, students attending private schools do worse than those attending public schools.

As pointed out earlier, the stronger effect of school factors, especially school resources, found in studies using the 1970s data may not be replicated any longer. During the last three decades, even in developing countries, there have been widespread efforts to increase minimal levels of school resources and quality, which may help reduce the effects of school resources on student achievement (Baker et al., 2002). On the other hand, school climates are expected to be more strongly related to academic achievement in Asian education. The importance of academic and disciplinary climates in Asian education has been considered as a critical factor enhancing student achievement in the region (U.S. Department of Education, 1987).

DATA AND VARIABLES

Data

The data for this study comes from the Program for International Student Assessment (PISA). PISA was initially conducted in 2000 in 32 countries – 28 OECD countries and 4 non-OECD countries. In 2001, 11 additional non-OECD countries participated in the assessment using the same instrument. From the international data set of 43 countries, we extracted four Asian countries, Hong Kong, Indonesia, Korea, and Thailand, and four Latin American countries, Argentina, Chile, Mexico, and Peru.[1]

The primary focus of the first round of PISA data was to assess reading literacy of young people at age 15, although mathematical literacy and scientific literacy were also tested. The target population in PISA is defined as 15-year-olds enrolled in schools regardless of grade level, the type of institution (i.e., vocational or academic schools) in which they were enrolled, and whether they were full- or part-time students. A two-stage stratified sampling design was used to collect data. First, individual schools in which 15-year-old students were enrolled were selected systematically with probabilities proportionate to size, the size being a function of the estimated number of eligible (15-year-old) students enrolled. Then, students within sampled schools were selected with equal probability from a list of 15-year-old students in each selected school. Overall, PISA achieved a high quality of coverage of the national desired target population across all participating countries.[2]

In addition to students' self-reports on their individual and family characteristics, PISA asked students a series of questions to capture diverse dimensions of classroom practices such as teacher–student relations and disciplinary climates. Furthermore, the principals or head administrators completed a school questionnaire covering such things as composition and type of school, school staffing, principals' perceptions of teacher- and student-related factors affecting the school climate, and the degree of school and teacher autonomy for various aspects of school policy and management.

In studying the effects of family and school on student achievement, the PISA data offers researchers a number of advantages over other international surveys (Buchmann, 2002). First, the data contains a much broader range of information on family background, including measures of parental occupation and education, educational resources available at home, and family structure. Second, PISA is one of the rare data sets that includes comparable measures of the frequency of parent–child social communication across many different countries. These data allow us to examine the influence of parent–child communication in developing countries.

A major limitation of PISA should be noted as well. Since PISA includes 15-year-olds who are *in school*, sample selection bias associated with school attendance may affect the results for some countries, depending on the extent to which children drop out of school before the age of 15. In fact, secondary school enrollment rates presented in Table 1 show that only half of all 15-year-olds in Indonesia, Thailand, and Mexico enroll in secondary schools. In all other countries studied except for Korea, a quarter of all 15-year-olds are no longer in schools. Considering that children from lower SES families are more likely to stop their educational careers earlier than their counterparts from higher SES families, our results on the effects of family SES may be somewhat underestimated for those countries with low degrees of secondary enrollment.[3]

Reading Literacy

The main outcome variable in this study is students' performance on reading literacy. Although mathematical literacy and scientific literacy skills were also tested in PISA, in this study we focus on reading literacy in recognition of potential variations across the three literacy domains in the ways in which family background and schools affect students' literacy skills. Reading literacy was measured in a single composite scale having an average score of 500 and a standard deviation of 100 across students of the OECD countries participating in PISA.[4]

Reading literacy skills have been found to be closely related to a range of educational and occupational outcomes. Studies of Australian youth have documented that students' scores for admission to tertiary education and actual attendance at tertiary education are positively associated with earlier achievement in reading literacy (Marks, McMillan, & Hillman, 2001; Marks, Fleming, Long, & McMillan, 2000). The results from the International Adult Literacy Survey (IALS) have shown that adults with higher levels of reading literacy are more likely to be employed and to have higher incomes than those with lower levels, even after educational qualifications are taken into account (OECD and Statistics Canada, 2000). A study of adult literacy in the U.S. has also found that both educational attainment and literacy skills independently contribute to occupational status and earnings (Kerckhoff, Raudenbush, & Glennie, 2001).

Individual and Family Characteristics

Parental education and occupation are included as indicators of family SES. In our study, parental education is defined as father's highest level of education. If the information is missing, mother's highest level of education is used.[5] Similarly, father's occupation is used, but if unavailable, is substituted by mother's occupation. Data on occupation was scaled using the

International Socioeconomic Index of Occupational Status (ISEI). Developed by Ganzeboom and Treiman (1996), the index represents an internationally comparable measure of SES for the occupation. Higher values indicate higher SES of the occupation.[6]

In PISA, an index of home educational resources was constructed on the basis of students' reports on (1) the availability of a dictionary, a quiet place to study, a desk for study, and textbooks; and (2) the number of calculators at home. It was scaled to have a mean of 0 and a standard deviation of 1 across students in OECD countries.[7] Therefore, positive values indicate that students have home educational resources above the OECD average.

The PISA index of social communication was created using students' responses to questions about how often their parents do the following things: discuss with them how well they are doing at school; eat the main meal with them around a table; and spend time simply talking to them. A standardized summary index was created to have a mean of 0 and a standard deviation of 1 for the OECD student population. Higher values indicate more frequent parent–child communication. For multivariate analysis, we rescaled the index of social communication and the index of home educational resources to be standardized within each country.

We also include family structure (intact families versus other types of families) and the number of siblings as other aspects of family background. Among various individual characteristics, we include gender and grade.

School Characteristics

School principals were asked to indicate whether their schools were private or public. By linking principals' data with student data, we identified which types of schools students attended. To indicate the overall SES of the school, we used the average of parental occupational status among students attending the same school. Two indicators of school resources are included in the models. An index of teacher shortage and an index of the quality of the schools' educational resources were derived from principals' reports on the extent to which student learning in their language classes was hindered by the shortage or inadequacy of language teachers and by a lack of educational resources.

Note that these two measures are based on principals' subjective perceptions of the extent to which the lack of school resources hindered student learning. The two indices were scaled to have a mean of 0 and a standard deviation of 1 across students in OECD countries. High values indicate less of a teacher shortage problem and the presence of high-quality (plentiful) educational resources at the school (i.e., student learning is not being hindered by a lack of educational resources).

PISA provides three indices of school climate. The index of teacher morale was created on the basis of principals' reports on the extent of teachers' morale, enthusiasm, pride in school, and the value of academic achievement in their schools. The index of disciplinary climate was derived from *students'* reports on the extent of the disciplinary climate prevailing in their language class.[8] We averaged the index to create a school-level variable of *school* disciplinary climate. The index of sense of belonging to schools was derived from students' reports and intends to measure students' attitude toward school.[9] By averaging this index among students in each school, we created a *school-average* sense of belonging. These three indices were scaled to have a mean of 0 and a standard deviation of 1 across students in OECD countries. A higher value for each index indicates a more positive overall school climate.[10]

METHOD

To discern the effects of family and school variables on reading literacy, we estimate a set of two-level hierarchical linear models (HLMs) for each country separately. Compared to traditional OLS regression, hierarchical linear modeling (HLM) explicitly takes into account the hierarchical structure of data (i.e., students nested within schools) without assuming the independence of observations within the same unit. HLM facilitates a decomposition of the variation in student achievement within and between schools and allows explicitly testing the extent to which the effects of student-level characteristics vary across schools (Bryk & Raudenbush, 1992).

For each country, we estimate five different models. The first model (Model 1) is a null model that provides useful information about the proportions of total variation in reading literacy between and within schools. The second model (Model 2) predicts students' reading literacy by family SES, indicated by parental education and occupation, home educational resources, parent–child social communication, and other individual controls. This model does not include any school-level variables. The model produces estimates of the pooled within-school slopes of the student-level variables.[11] The main focus is on the size of the effects associated with family SES and the extent to which home educational resources and social communication influence student performance, after controlling for family SES. Moreover, comparing variance components between the null model and the second model establishes the proportions of total within- and between-school variances (estimated in the null model) that are explained by family characteristics and other student-level variables.

The third model (Model 3) predicts school mean achievement (β_{0j}) of reading literacy by a variable for the school sector (private versus public), keeping the specifications of student-level equation the same as the second model. The dummy variable for the school sector included in the school-level equation indicates the average achievement gap between students attending private schools and those attending public schools, after taking into account students' individual and family characteristics.

In the fourth model (Model 4) we add the overall SES of the school – as measured by the average occupational status of parents among students attending the school – and the two indicators of school resources (the indices of teacher shortage and the quality of educational resources) to the school-level equation predicting school mean achievement. Comparing the effect of the school sector between Model 3 and Model 4 shows the extent to which the achievement gap between private and public schools is accounted for by differences in the overall SES and school resources available between private and public schools.

Finally, the three indicators of school climate – the index of teacher morale, school disciplinary climate, and school-average sense of belonging to schools – are added in the fifth model (Model 5). The main purpose of Model 5 is to assess the extent to which school climate is related to improved student achievement, after controlling for school sector, schools' SES, and resources.

RESULTS

Descriptive Statistics

Table 2 provides descriptive statistics for some key student and school characteristics for each of the eight countries in the study. For comparison, results for the U.S. are also included. Note that reading literacy was scaled to have a mean of 500 points and a standard deviation of 100 points across students in OECD countries. Most apparent is significantly higher mean achievement among students in Hong Kong, and Korea, which is even far above the OECD average of 500 and the mean of the U.S. (504 points). In contrast, all six of the other countries show mean performance significantly below the OECD average. The average performance in Indonesia and Peru is particularly lower than the OECD average.

Table 2. Descriptive Statistics by Country.

	HKG	KOR	IDN	THA	ARG	CHL	MEX	PER	USA
Reading literacy									
Mean	526	526	376	432	423	412	425	337	504
SD	83	69	70	76	105	89	85	93	105
Variance between schools (%)	47.5	37.6	42.7	31.3	51.5	55.8	52.8	57.5	29.6
Family backgrounds									
Parental education (%)									
Primary or less	25.1	7.9	42.1	62.0	27.8	9.2	40.0	22.4	2.9
Lower secondary	35.7	18.6	19.6	14.1	17.7	17.3	20.6	14.8	5.6
Upper secondary	29.7	44.9	27.3	14.3	23.9	47.7	15.9	29.0	45.1
Tertiary	9.4	28.7	11.0	9.6	30.5	25.8	23.5	33.8	46.4
Family educational resources[a]	−0.19	−0.54	−1.70	−1.64	−0.84	−0.96	−0.70	−1.45	−0.23
Social communication[a]	−0.24	−0.18	−0.58	−0.26	0.18	0.38	−0.03	−0.24	0.08
School-related variables									
% of students in private schools (%)	4.9	52.3	45.9	19.6	36.1	45.8	16.0	16.4	6.4
Index of school resources									
Teacher shortage[a]	−0.22	0.33	−0.84	−1.19	−0.25	0.07	−0.52	−0.34	0.20
Educational resources[a]	0.66	0.00	−0.93	−0.81	−0.53	−0.28	−0.94	−1.26	0.40
Index of school climate									
Teacher's morale[a]	−0.31	−0.72	1.05	−0.38	−0.17	−0.40	0.40	−0.32	−0.04
Disciplinary climate[a]	0.01	0.20	0.39	0.18	−0.37	−0.32	0.17	−0.07	0.03
Sense of belonging[a]	−0.42	−0.39	−0.20	−0.30	0.19	0.21	0.10	−0.17	−0.06

[a]The index was standardized to have a mean of 0 and a standard deviation of 1 across students in OECD countries.

While mean performance provides useful information to assess the quality (or productivity) of educational systems, the distribution of student performance within a country is equally important, because it indicates the equality of educational outcomes (OECD, 2003). The significantly smaller standard deviations among students in Hong Kong and Korea, as compared to the OECD average standard deviation of 100 points, demonstrate that these two countries successfully *combine* higher mean achievement with substantial equality. Except for Argentina, the other Asian and Latin American countries also show distributions of student performance narrower than the OECD average, although their average performances are significantly lower than the OECD average. Argentina has a relatively wide distribution of student performance.

We partitioned the total variance in scores on reading literacy into variance between and within schools. The third row in Table 2 shows the proportion of the total variance between schools. In all four Latin American countries as well as in Hong Kong and Indonesia, about half of the total variance in reading literacy occurs between schools. Although between-school variance accounts for 37% and 31% of total variance in Korea and Thailand, respectively, this is still a considerable proportion compared to some Nordic countries such as Sweden and Norway, where between-school variance amounts to 10% or less of the total variance in student performance. However, the relative proportion of total variation due to school differences should be interpreted in the context of significantly smaller overall variation in student performance, particularly in East Asian countries. In other words, the absolute sizes of between-school variation in East Asia – where total variation in student performance is small overall – are still substantially less than those in many other countries.

Turning to the next set of family background variables, we observed significantly higher proportions of students in Latin America whose parents (mainly fathers) completed tertiary education than in Asia, except for Korea. If we compare results between Hong Kong and Argentina or between Indonesia and Mexico, these paired countries have similar proportions of students whose parents have only a primary education or less. However, they apparently differ in the proportions of students whose parents completed tertiary education (10% in Hong Kong and Thailand versus 31% and 24% respectively in Argentina and Mexico).

As noted earlier, both indices of home educational resources and social communication were standardized to have a mean of 0 and a standard deviation of 1 for OECD countries. The negative values of home educational resources in all eight countries indicate that families in these countries possess fewer home educational resources than the average OECD families. Fewer possessions were particularly evident in Indonesia, Thailand, and Peru. The negative values of social communication in all four of the Asian countries indicate that parents and children in the region are communicating less frequently with each other than on average in the OECD countries. However, students in Argentina and Chile communicate more frequently with their parents than do OECD students, on average.

The last set of statistics shows the mean of school-related variables in each of the countries. We found no systematic difference between Asia and Latin America in the proportion of students attending private schools, although the proportion varies substantially within each of the two regions. For instance, private schools accommodate relatively large proportions of students in Korea and Indonesia, while only 5% of students attend private schools in Hong Kong. The percentage of students enrolled in private schools in Korea and Indonesia is even higher than in most of Latin America, except for Chile.

On the basis of school principals' responses, the next two indices of school resources indicate the extent to which teacher shortages and the quality of schools' educational resources hinder student learning. Higher values indicate less negative impact on student learning. Again, we do not see a systematic pattern in the differences between the two regions. Instead, the lack of the two resources seems to hinder student learning more in Indonesia, Thailand, and Peru, all of which have a relatively lower level of economic development than the other countries.

Interestingly, there is some regional similarity on two of the three factors comprising school climate. All of the four Asian countries show ratings of disciplinary climate above the OECD average, whereas the degree of disciplinary climate seems to be relatively low in Latin America, except for Mexico. On the other hand, Asian students show a sense of belonging to schools significantly below the OECD average, while students in three of the four Latin American countries show a level of sense of belonging above the OECD average.

Effects of Family Background

Table 3 presents the results of the second model (Model 2) that includes only individual characteristics. The results of HLM presented in the table represent the average within-school effects. We focus our discussion on the variables of parental education and occupation, home educational resources, and social communication. Note that for comparison of the effects, the ISEI of parental occupation and the two indices of home educational resources and social communication were standardized within a country to have a mean of 0 and a standard deviation of 1. Therefore, the coefficients associated with the three variables indicate the change in reading literacy scores per one standard deviation increase in the variables.

The effects of family SES seem to be comparatively stronger in Latin America than in Asia, though Mexico shows relatively weaker impacts of family SES compared to other countries in Latin America. In Hong Kong, parental education and occupation are not significantly associated with student performance. The achievement gap associated with either parental occupation or education is not significant in Korea and Indonesia, respectively, once other individual and family characteristics are taken into account. In Latin America (except in Mexico), both parental education and occupation affect student achievement.

Table 3. The Effects of Family Background on Reading Literacy (HLMs).

	HKG	KOR	IDN	THA	ARG	CHL	MEX	PER
Intercept	525.271***	520.330***	357.089***	437.237***	419.902***	410.634***	423.596***	332.202***
Female	8.763**	18.940***	7.790***	32.400***	23.084***	6.635**	11.183***	−1.789
Grade	22.758***	N.I	20.806***	24.210***	40.142***	38.443***	19.032***	30.373
Intact family (Ref.: others)	−2.559	−2.540	−1.295	3.133	−2.201	1.401	−5.094*	−0.704
Number of siblings	−1.414	−3.082**	−0.800	−0.453	−4.027***	−0.779	−2.275***	−1.323*
Parental education								
Primary or less	−2.290	11.699***	1.111	−4.853†	−8.296*	−11.095***	−4.176	−10.704***
Lower secondary	−4.366†	−7.886***	2.329	−9.474**	−9.215*	−9.389***	−3.055	−7.668*
Upper secondary and tertiary (reference)								
Parental occupation (ISEI)	−0.151	0.315	5.793***	4.121***	6.221**	8.012***	4.474***	5.038***
Home educational resources	4.480***	2.569*	−0.337	10.826***	7.333***	3.652***	5.376***	5.325***
Social communication	6.369***	8.377***	4.423***	1.595	0.332	4.119***	1.415	3.812**
% of variance explained								
Within schools	13.9	4.0	5.3	10.7	9.4	10.0	2.5	21.7
Between schools	20.4	21.9	40.4	40.1	60.8	64.8	47.0	44.7

Note: N.I., Not Included.
*** $p<0.001$.
** $p<0.01$.
* $p<0.05$.
† $p<0.10$.

Interestingly, possessing home educational resources is significantly related to increased student performance in all the countries except Indonesia, even after controlling for family SES. The magnitude of the effect is also substantial compared to other family socioeconomic measures. For example, represented as changes in reading literacy per one standard deviation increase, the direct effect of home educational resources is similar or larger than the effect of parental occupation in all the countries except Indonesia and Chile. The significant association of home educational resources with student achievement is consistent with previous results in the U.S. (Teachman, 1987).

Another interesting finding from the table is the relatively strong association of social communication with student performance in Asian countries, although Thailand is an exception. Compared to other family background variables, the extent to which frequent communication with parents contributes to improvement in performance is particularly pronounced in Hong Kong and Korea.

At the bottom of the table, we show statistics on the proportions of within- and between-school variance that are explained by the student's individual and family characteristics. In Table 2, we already showed how total variation in student performance was partitioned into within- and between-school components. Thus, for example, we saw that in Korea, 37.9% of the variance in student achievement occurred between schools (therefore 62.1 (100–37.9) percent within schools). Table 3 shows that 22% of the total between-school variance and 4% of the total within-school variance were accounted for by students' individual and family characteristics.

Some of the differences between schools' average achievement are due to differences in student characteristics. Evident in Table 3 is the substantial difference between Asia (especially the two East Asian countries of Hong Kong and Korea) and Latin America in the extent to which those individual and family characteristics explain the between-school variance. In Hong Kong and Korea, only 20% of the between-school variance is accounted for by individual and family background variables, whereas the proportion is about 60% in Argentina and Chile. This comparison suggests that schools in Latin America tend to be differentiated more strongly along family socioeconomic background than schools particularly in the two East Asian countries.

Private and Public School Differences

Table 4 presents the results of HLMs that estimate the difference in mean achievement between private and public schools. The model predicts school

Table 4. The Effects of Private Schools Controlling for Individual Characteristics (HLMs).

	HKG	KOR	IDN	THA	ARG	CHL	MEX	PER
Student-level equation								
Intercept	525.257***	520.243***	357.282***	437.412***	419.741***	410.627***	423.763***	332.523***
Female	8.776**	18.875***	7.729***	32.525***	22.712***	6.799**	11.055***	−1.749
Grade	22.733***	N.I.	20.966***	24.713***	39.455***	38.377***	18.969***	30.216
Intact family (Ref.: others)	−2.552	−2.546	−1.348	3.103	−2.498	1.386	−5.139*	−0.535
Number of siblings	−1.413	−3.074	−0.818	−0.429	−3.853***	−0.764	−2.197***	−1.251†
Parental education								
Primary or less	−2.281	−11.670***	1.060	−5.014†	−7.980*	−10.892**	−3.585	−10.655***
Lower secondary	−4.344†	−7.888***	2.311	−9.558**	−8.964*	−9.255***	−2.518	−7.485*
Upper secondary and tertiary (reference)								
Parental occupation (ISEI)	−0.113	0.314	5.812***	4.154***	5.867**	7.863***	4.229***	4.675***
Home educational resources	4.469***	2.561*	−0.321	10.920***	7.157***	3.581***	5.243***	5.125***
Social communication	6.372***	8.368***	4.386***	1.581	0.376	4.152***	1.402	3.827**
School-level equation								
Effects on mean achievement								
School sector (Ref.: public)								
Private schools	−53.644**	−5.429	−21.817***	−21.799*	52.194***	31.128***	52.574***	85.816***
% of variance explained								
Within schools	13.9	4.0	5.3	10.7	9.4	10.1	2.5	21.7
Between schools	24.1	21.9	46.6	42.7	69.0	69.3	56.1	64.3

Note: N.I., Not Included.
***$p<0.001$.
**$p<0.01$.
*$p<0.05$.
†$p<0.10$.

mean achievement by a dummy variable that represents private or public schools in the school-level equation, while controlling for students' individual and family backgrounds in the student-level equation. Therefore, the mean achievement difference between private and public schools is the net difference after taking into account student compositions of the schools. Since the effects associated with students' individual and family background variables in this model are almost identical to those estimated from the earlier model in Table 3, we focus our discussion on the estimated differences between private and public schools.

There is an apparent difference between Asia and Latin America in the role that private schools play in affecting student learning. In all four of the Latin American countries, students who attend private schools on an average outperform their counterparts attending public schools, whereas the opposite is true in Asian countries. Although in this study we were not able to address the issue of the causal effect associated with students' self-selection into private schools (e.g., Morgan, 2001), the consistent pattern of the achievement gap between private and public schools in each region is striking.

Effects of School's Overall Socioeconomic Status and School Resources

In order to explore sources of private and public school differences in mean achievement, in the third model we include three additional school-level variables to predict school mean achievement, while continuing to use the same student-level equation as with the previous two models. The first school-level variable added is one considered to represent schools' overall SES – the school mean of the index of parental occupational status of students who attend the school (as measured by the ISEI). The other two school-level variables added indicate the extent to which student learning is hindered by teacher shortage and the lack of educational resources at the school. The effects associated with students' individual and family characteristics change very slightly compared to the two previous models, so that the general pattern remains the same. Therefore, we only present results of the school-level variables in Table 5.

Once the three school characteristics are added to the model, the private-school effects in Latin America are substantially reduced, and in Chile and Mexico the effects become insignificant. Stated differently, in Latin America, the private-school advantages result primarily from private schools' significantly higher socioeconomic conditions, due to selective attendance of students from families with higher socioeconomic backgrounds. In contrast, private-school disadvantages in Asian countries remain the same or become

Table 5. The Effects of School Resources (HLMs).

	HKG	KOR	IDN	THA	ARG	CHL	MEX	PER
School-level equation								
Effects on mean achievement								
School Sector (ref.: public)								
Private schools	−61.167***	3.694	−19.614***	−30.066***	15.723*	4.814	−7.876	19.921†
School mean of								
Socio-economic index of occupation	55.337***	48.613***	32.059***	27.271***	43.784***	49.665***	59.235***	58.731***
Teacher shortage	7.942†	1.005	2.114	0.376	−3.548	1.477	−2.607	8.035*
Educational resources	1.382	0.303	5.009**	3.807	10.359**	2.420	4.811*	4.193
% of variance explained								
Within schools	13.9	4.0	5.4	10.8	9.5	10.1	2.5	21.7
Between schools	40.3	46.6	60.6	53.0	81.0	84.6	76.9	76.7

Note: The results of the student-level effects are not presented (see the text).
*** $p < 0.001$.
** $p < 0.01$.
* $p < 0.05$.
† $p < 0.10$.

even larger when the school's overall socioeconomic conditions are taken into account.

In all eight countries, the school's overall SES is strongly associated with student achievement. Even for countries such as Hong Kong and Korea, where parental occupation does not significantly impact literacy performance at the student level, the effect of a school's SES is evident. As explained earlier, this effect associated with the school's SES can be interpreted as reflecting peer-group effects or effects of other unmeasured school-level variables correlated with the school's overall SES. In some countries, the higher quality of educational resources and fewer problems with teacher shortages contribute to improved student achievement. Once these three school-level characteristics are added, the model explains as much as 80% of the between-school variance in Latin America.

Effects of School Climate

In the final model, three additional school climate factors are added to predict school mean achievement (Table 6). As the table shows, all the countries' mean achievement is higher in schools in which students report higher levels of sense of belonging to schools. In addition, in most countries, the size of the effect associated with the school average of sense of belonging is similar to or even larger than the effect of school mean SES. Remember that for the purpose of multivariate analysis, the variable of parental occupational status and the index of sense of belonging were standardized to have a mean of 0 and a standard deviation of 1 within a country.

It may be argued that the school average of sense of belonging is the result, rather than the cause, of higher mean achievement. With the limitations of our data, it is difficult to discern which affected which. However, it is worth noting that the positive association of sense of belonging with student performance is evident for all countries analyzed, regardless of their students' overall levels of attachment to schools. As shown in the descriptive statistics, Asian students report levels of sense of belonging significantly below the OECD average, while the degree of attachment to schools among Latin American students is above the OECD average.

Another indicator of school climate is the school average of disciplinary climate, which is also significantly associated with improved student achievement in some countries, particularly in the two East Asian countries and Chile. Furthermore, the morale of the teachers in schools appears to contribute to improving student performance in Korea. The additional proportion of between-school variance accounted for by the three indicators

Table 6. The Effects of School Climate (HLMs).

	HKG	KOR	IDN	THA	ARG	CHL	MEX	PER
School-level equation								
Effects on mean achievement								
School sector (Ref.: public)								
Private schools	−38.407*	−6.864	−14.819***	−27.052**	16.091*	0.552	−9.123	17.527†
School mean of								
Socio-economic index of occupation	34.723***	34.756***	28.823***	19.764**	26.179***	46.635***	52.754***	42.728***
Teacher shortage	1.884	−0.433	1.232	1.326	−4.172	0.259	−2.437	7.718*
Educational resources	1.158	0.043	4.812**	1.922	8.614**	1.690	2.799	1.410
Teacher's morale	8.163	6.607*	2.055	3.573	3.049	0.788	2.708	−1.698
Disciplinary climate	31.082*	33.637***	10.394†	10.125	4.071	22.378***	11.602*	6.483
Sense of belonging	56.561***	44.698***	33.094***	33.932***	60.401***	35.441***	42.796***	56.073***
% of variance explained								
Within schools	13.9	4.0	5.5	10.8	9.6	10.1	2.6	21.7
Between schools	51.1	65.3	65.8	59.2	85.4	89.2	81.8	80.8

Note: The results of the student-level effects are not presented (see the text).
***$p<0.001$.
**$p<0.01$.
*$p<0.05$.
†$p<0.10$.

of school climate is substantial in Hong Kong, and Korea relative to the proportions in other countries. The model, together with these additional variables of school climate, explains 51% and 65% of between-school variance in Hong Kong and Korea, respectively, while the previous model in Table 4 accounts for 40% and 47% in each country.

CONCLUSIONS

Our comparisons of the ways in which family and school characteristics influence student performance in reading literacy have revealed some interesting differences between Asia and Latin America. First of all, family socioeconomic conditions seem to matter for student performance considerably less in Asia than in Latin America, though there are some exceptions in this pattern within each region (e.g., Thailand shows a relatively strong association compared to other countries within the region, while the opposite is true for Mexico). In particular, it is interesting to see relatively weaker impacts of family SES in Hong Kong and Korea despite their greater levels of economic development compared to other Asian and Latin American countries. The relatively stronger effects of family SES in Latin American countries may be understood in the context of significantly greater economic inequality in the region. It is notable, however, that despite its similarly high level of economic inequality, in Hong Kong, family SES does not appear to significantly affect children's educational achievement.

Compared to the relatively weak impacts of family socioeconomic conditions in the region, parental involvement in communication with their children plays a substantial role in enhancing children's achievement in Asian education. We hypothesized that the significance of parent–child communication on children's education is linked to strong academic pressure for higher achievement in Asian countries, which leads to education-focused communication between parents and children.

Another distinctive feature of Latin American education is the significant extent of school differentiation along with students' socioeconomic backgrounds. The proportion of variation between schools explained by students' individual and family characteristics in Latin America is two to three times that in Hong Kong and Korea. Evidence of the substantial school differences related to socioeconomic composition in Latin America is demonstrated by the significant achievement gap between students attending private and public schools. Because students from advantaged family backgrounds are more likely to attend private schools, the learning environment

– including school resources, peer-group emphasis on achievement, and parental supports for learning – is likely to be more favorable in private schools than in public schools. This accounts for why students who attend private schools enjoy additional advantages. In contrast, students attending private schools in Asia, on average, do worse than their counterparts attending public schools.

Once schools' overall socioeconomic conditions are taken into account, the private-school advantage is substantially reduced in Latin America. This is another indication that significant differences exist in socioeconomic conditions between private and public schools in the region. In contrast, controlling for the school average of parental occupational status and school resource variables does not affect higher achievement among public school students. In other words, the achievement gap between private and public schools in Asian education is not accounted for by the difference in socioeconomic conditions between the two school sectors.

It is not yet clear to us what causes public school advantages in Asian countries. Asian public schools tend to enroll students who have a high ability to pass the national entrance exams. Higher achievers in the national exams often go to prestigious public schools in Asian countries. More detailed information is needed on how public and private schools in Asia differ in various aspects of schooling including the selection process, school management, and school organization.

As mentioned earlier, PISA's sample selection of 15-year-olds enrolled in schools requires caution to interpret the findings from this study that examined countries, most of which have a significant portion of 15-year-olds out of schools.

However, there is evidence that despite their lower secondary enrollments, the population of 15-year-olds in schools does not considerably differ in their socioeconomic background from the population as a whole in those developing countries participating in PISA (OECD, 2003, p. 214). In other words, the effects of students' socioeconomic background may not be significantly biased, even in developing countries, despite the sample selection of 15-year-olds in schools. Moreover, if sample selection bias affected our results (given that students from disadvantaged socioeconomic backgrounds are more likely to drop out of schools before the age of 15), the unbiased estimates of the effects of family background would be larger than what we found in this study for those countries with relatively low secondary enrollment rates.

One interesting similarity observed between Asia and Latin America is that *schools* whose students report a strong sense of belonging tend to have higher mean performance. It is interesting to see this significant impact of school attachment in both Asia and Latin America, especially since the two differ considerably in their levels of sense of belonging. Although students in Hong Kong and Korea show considerably higher mean performance, they have substantially lower levels of sense of belonging than their counterparts in Latin America. This might reflect the considerable pressure on students to achieve academically, as well as the strong competition among students related to college entrance exams in the two countries. Despite overall poorer achievement among Latin American students, in contrast, they tend to show relatively higher levels of sense of belonging.

Although students' sense of belonging as an indicator of school climate is significantly associated with student performance in all the countries, school climate seems to matter more for student achievement in Asia than in Latin America. In addition to sense of belonging, school disciplinary climate contributes to increased student achievement in Hong Kong and Korea, and teacher morale is also a significant factor for fostering student performance in Korea. The proportion of between-school variance accounted for by the three indicators of school climate is considerably larger in the two East Asian countries than in the other countries.

If we consider school climate as a reflection of social relationships between students and teachers or among students themselves, it may be an indicator of social capital present in schools (Portes, 1998; Coleman, 1988). The significance of school climate in affecting student achievement in Hong Kong and Korea is consistent with the significant effect of parent–child communication in the two countries. Given that parent–child communication can also be considered as an aspect of social capital (McNeal, 1999), the results in general indicate the significant role of social capital in Asian education. Future research may want to investigate more closely how various forms of social capital affect student achievement in this region.

NOTES

1. Note that Japan and Brazil also participated in PISA. However, we excluded Japan from the analysis because of a high number of students who did not report parental education and occupation, which are two major measures of family SES in our study. Brazil was also excluded from our analysis. In the Brazilian data, a large number of schools enroll less than 10 students, so estimates from HLMs are considerably unreliable. Although we could have included the results using the OLS regression analysis rather than the HLM analysis, we excluded Brazil in order to maintain consistency with the results from other countries.

2. See OECD (2001) Annex A3 for a detailed introduction to PISA sampling procedures as well as to the target population coverage. Chromy (2002) provides an overview for comparing sampling design and target population across various international surveys of student achievement, including PISA.

3. Another limitation of PISA is that like previous international surveys of student achievement such as TIMSS, PISA does not have a pretest measure. Therefore, we were not able to control for prior achievement in our multivariate analyses.

4. Reading literacy was defined in PISA as "the ability to understand, use, and reflect on written texts in order to achieve one's goals, to develop one's knowledge and potential, and to participate effectively in society" (OECD, 2001, p. 21). Instead of a fixed value for the reading literacy scale, PISA provides five plausible values for each student, which should be used simultaneously to obtain the estimates of population parameters.

5. We classify parental education into four categories: completed primary education or less; completed lower secondary education; completed upper secondary education (including both academic and vocational programs); and completed tertiary education (including junior colleges and four-year universities).

6. In each country we substituted education-specific mean values of ISEI for those lacking information on parental occupation. In multivariate analyses, we included in the models a dummy variable indicating the cases with the substituted values. We also estimated the same models with the categorical classification of parental occupation, distinguishing professionals/managers, clerks/services/sales, agricultural workers, skilled and unskilled laborers, and a category of missing cases. The results were very similar to what we present here.

7. Using student responses to those items, the index was derived from weighted likelihood estimation by applying Item Response Theory (IRT) scaling methodology. For more information on the methodology used to create the index, see OECD (2002).

8. Specifically, the PISA index of disciplinary climate was created from students' reports on how often the following things happened in their language lessons: the teacher has to wait a long time for students to quiet down; students cannot work well; students do not listen to what the teacher says; students do not start working for a long time after the lesion begins; there is noise and disorder; and at the start of class, more than five minutes are spent doing nothing. For details about this index, see OECD (2002, p. 228).

9. Specifically, PISA used the following six items to create the index of sense of belonging: my school is a place where I feel like an outsider; I make friends easily; I feel like I belong; I feel awkward and out of place; other students seem to like me; and I feel lonely. For details about this index, see OECD (2002, p. 228).

10. It should be noted that the measures of disciplinary climate and sense of belonging to school are affected by cultural expectations on students' attitudes toward school. Therefore, comparability of such measures across cultures can be an important issue.

11. We tested whether the effects of parental education and occupation, home educational resources, and social communication vary across schools, and found that in most countries the effects did not vary significantly. Therefore, we fixed all the student-level effects in all the countries. All the explanatory variables were centered around grand means.

REFERENCES

Baker, D. P., Goesling, B., & Letendre, G. K. (2002). Socioeconomic status, school quality, and national economic development: A cross-national analysis of the "Heyneman–Loxley Effect" on mathematics and science achievement. *Comparative Review of Education, 46*, 291–312.

Birdsall, N., & Jaspersen, F. (Eds). (1997). *Pathways to growth*. Washington, DC: Inter-American Development Bank.

Bryk, A., Lee, V., & Holland, P. B. (1993). *Catholic schools and the common good*. Cambridge, MA: Harvard University Press.

Bryk, A. S., & Raudenbush, S. W. (1992). *Hierarchical linear models: Applications and data analysis methods*. Newbury, CA: Sage.

Buchmann, C. (2002). Measuring family background in international studies of education: Conceptual issues and methodological challenges. In: A. C. Porter & A. Gamoran (Eds), *Methodological advances in cross-national surveys of educational achievement* (pp. 150–197). Washington, DC: National Academy Press.

Chromy, J. R. (2002). Sampling issues in design, conduct, and interpretation of international comparative studies of school achievement. In: A. C. Porter & A. Gamoran (Eds), *Methodological advances in cross-national surveys of educational achievement* (pp. 80–114). Washington, DC: National Academy Press.

Coleman, J. C. (1988). Social capital in the creation of human capital. *American Journal of Sociology, 94*, S95–S121.

Fuller, B. (1987). What factors raise achievement in the Third World? *Review of Educational Research, 57*, 255–292.

Fuller, B., & Clarke, P. (1994). Raising school effects while ignoring culture? Local conditions and the influence of classroom tools, rules, and pedagogy. *Review of Educational Research, 64*, 119–157.

Gamoran, A. (1992). Social factors in education. In: M. Alkin (Ed.), *Encyclopedia of educational research*, (6th ed., pp. 1222–1229). New York: Macmillan.

Ganzeboom, H. B. G., & Treiman, D. J. (1996). Internationally comparable measures of occupation status for the 1988 international standard classification of occupations. *Social Science Research, 25*, 201–239.

Heyneman, S. P., & Loxley, W. A. (1982). Influences on academic achievement across high and low income countries: A re-analysis of IEA data. *Sociology of Education, 55*, 13–21.

Heyneman, S. P., & Loxley, W. A. (1983). The effect of primary-school quality on academic achievement across twenty-nine high- and low-income countries. *American Journal of Sociology, 88*, 1162–1194.

Ho Sui-Chu, E., & Willms, J. D. (1996). Effects of parental involvement on eighth-grade achievement. *Sociology of Education, 69*, 126–141.

Kerckhoff, A. C., Raudenbush, S. W., & Glennie, E. (2001). Education, cognitive skill, and labor force outcomes. *Sociology of Education, 74*, 1–24.

Lee, V. E., & Bryk, A. S. (1989). A multilevel model of the social distribution of high school achievement. *Sociology of Education, 62*, 172–192.

Lockheed, M. E., & Longford, N. T. (1991). School effects on mathematics achievement gain in Thailand. In: S. W. Raudenbush & J. D. Willms (Eds), *Schools, classroom, and pupils: International studies of schooling from a multi-level perspective* (pp. 131–148). San Diego, CA: Academic.

Marks, G., Fleming, N., Long, M., & McMillan, J. (2000). *Patterns of participation in year 12 and higher education in Australia: Trends and issues.* LSAY Research Report 17. Australian Council for Educational Research, Melbourne.

Marks, G., McMillan, J., & Hillman, K. (2001). *Tertiary entrance performance: The role of student background and school factors.* LSAY Research Report 22. Australian Council for Educational Research, Melbourne.

Mayer, D. P., Mullens, J. E., & Moore, M. T. (2001). *Monitoring school quality: An indicators report.* Statistical Analysis Report. National Center for Educational Statistics, Washington, DC.

McNeal, R. B., Jr. (1999). Parental involvement as social capital: Differential effectiveness on science achievement, truancy, and dropping out. *Social Forces, 78,* 117–144.

Morgan, S. L. (2001). Counterfactuals, causal effect, heterogeneity, and the Catholic school effect on learning. *Sociology of Education, 74,* 341–373.

OECD. (2002). *PISA 2000 technical report.* Paris: OECD.

OECD. (2003). *Literacy skills for the world of tomorrow.* Paris: OECD.

OECD. (2005). *School factors related to quality and equity.* Paris: OECD.

OECD and Statistics Canada. (2000). *Literacy in the information age.* Paris and Ottawa.

Organization for Economic Development and Cooperation (OECD). (2001). *Knowledge and skills for life: First results from PISA 2000.* Paris: OECD.

Park, H. (2004). Educational expansion and inequality in Korea. *Research in Sociology of Education, 14,* 33–58.

Park, H., & Sandefur, G. (2005). Transition to adulthood in Japan and Korea: An overview. *Sociological Studies of Children and Youth, 10,* 43–76.

Portes, A. (1998). Social capital: It's origins and applications in modern sociology. *Annual Review of Sociology, 24,* 1–24.

Ratliff, W. (2003). *Doing it wrong and doing it right.* Essays in Public Policy no. 110. The Hoover Institution, Stanford University.

Riddell, A. R. (1989). An alternative approach to the study of school effectiveness in Third Word countries. *Comparative Education Review, 33,* 481–497.

Riddell, A. R. (1997). Assessing designs for school effectiveness research and school improvement in developing countries. *Comparative Education Review, 41,* 178–204.

Somers, M.-A., McEwan, P. J., & Willms, J. D. (2004). How effective are private schools in Latin America. *Comparative Education Review, 22,* 131–141.

Székely, M. (2001). *The 1990s in Latin America: Another decade of persistent inequality, but with somewhat lower poverty.* Research Department Working Paper Series #454. Inter-American Development Bank, Washington, DC.

Teachman, J. D. (1987). Family background, educational resources, and educational attainment. *American Sociological Review, 52,* 548–557.

Teachman, J. D., Paasch, K., & Carver, K. (1997). Social capital and the generation of human capital. *Social Forces, 75,* 1343–1359.

U.S. Department of Education. (1987). *Japanese education today.* Washington, DC: Government Printing Office.

Willms, J. D. (1986). Social class segregation and its relationship to pupil's examination results in Scotland. *American Sociological Review, 51,* 224–241.

Willms, J. D. (1992). *Monitoring school performance: A guide for educators.* Washington, DC: The Falmer Press.

Willms, J. D. (2003). *Ten hypotheses about socioeconomic gradients and community differences in children's developmental outcomes*. Working Paper Series. Human Resources Development, Canada.

Wolff, L., & Castro, C. (2000). *Secondary education in Latin America and the Caribbean: The challenge of growth and reform*. Sustainable Development Department Technical Papers Series. Inter-American Development Bank, Washington, DC.

World Bank. (1993). *The East Asian miracle: Economic growth and public policy*. New York: Oxford University Press.

World Bank. (2003). *Inequality in the Latin America and Caribbean: Breaking with history?* Washington, DC: World Bank.

THE CONTEXTS OF CHILDREN'S LIVES IN ASIA: FAMILIES, SCHOOLS, AND COMMUNITIES

COMMENTARY ON ADAMS, ROSS AND LIN, MAHMUD AND AMIN, ROTHCHILD, AND PARK AND SANDEFUR

Emily Hannum

In a recent article about female education and global social change, Levine, Levine, and Schnell (2001, p. 1) critique the state of comparative research on schooling as follows:

> [This research] rarely includes direct data on what skills, attitudes, or other tendencies boys and girls acquire in school. The "black box" of imputed links between school attendance and its socially beneficial "outcomes" remains large and murky, as do the institutional and cultural contexts that selectively facilitate or block the processes of individual development.

Collectively, the Asia-related articles in this volume contribute significantly to filling these gaps by exploring questions about the nature and quality of learning at school, the ways that schools link children to beneficial outcomes, and the contexts that shape children's opportunities as they progress through the school system. These articles address two topics that have been mainstays of comparative sociological research on education, namely gender inequality and determinants of achievement, and a third that is gaining visibility: community disparities.

The first two papers in this section, one by Jennifer Adams and the other by Heidi Ross and Jing Lin, consider how communities in China shape the learning outcomes and broader educational experiences of children within their boundaries. The next two are set in rural South Asia: a study in Bangladesh by Simeen Mahmud and Sajeda Amin, and another in Nepal by Jennifer Rothchild. These papers illuminate important institutional and cultural contexts – the family, the labor market, and schools themselves – that shape girls' access to education, their experiences in school, and their future life trajectories. A final paper, by Hyunjoon Park and Gary Sandefur, considers how much children are learning, and the factors at home and at school that influence learning, in Asian countries as compared to Latin American countries.

COMMUNITIES AND SCHOOLING IN CHINA

As Jennifer Adams notes in her paper, a number of studies within the U.S., as well as some studies in China and other low- and middle-income countries, have begun to address the ways that communities impact schooling outcomes. The potential role played by communities in local education has strengthened with the shift toward administrative and fiscal decentralization in many developed and developing countries. Often, fiscal decentralization results in a greater reliance on community financing of schooling, which, in turn, strengthens the association between where students live and the quality of educational services they receive (Bray, 1996a, 1996b).

In China, educational decentralization has been part of larger initiatives to reform the government's fiscal system (Wong, 2002). Market competition has eroded the profitability of state-owned enterprises, and the government has struggled to establish an effective taxation system to replace the lost revenues previously provided by those enterprises (Hannum & Park, 2002). To provide stronger incentives for local government leaders to generate more revenue and to shed their own expenditure responsibilities, government at all administrative levels has decentralized its expenditure responsibilities as well as claims on revenue (Park, Rozelle, Wong, & Ren, 1996).

This change has reduced resource transfers from richer to poorer regions, increasing inequities in public spending, including educational spending (Piazza & Liang, 1998; Tsang, 1996), and ultimately, transferring costs to families and communities. Decentralization shifts have coincided with dramatic increases in regional inequality. Interprovincial income inequality increased markedly from the late 1980s to at least the mid-1990s, and the urban–rural gap in income and living standards remained large (Carter, 1997; Khan & Riskin, 1998). These differences have translated to great variation in educational spending across regions, and even within provinces and counties (see Li, Park, & Wang, 2006).

Research has also shown that community resources significantly impact children's educational enrollment and speed of progress through school in China (Adams & Hannum, 2005). However, we know little about how communities affect the learning that goes on in schools, or about the broader differences in the climates of schools serving different communities. The papers by Adams and by Ross and Lin address these limitations. These articles illustrate ways that schools in advantaged communities pass advantages on to children – including, but not only, by promoting academic achievement.

Adams' paper, based on an analysis of a survey of rural children in northwest China conducted in the year 2000, finds that community resources matter for student math achievement. Even with a sample limited to rural communities in one of China's poorest provinces, she shows that residence in villages with higher levels of economic and social resources is associated with better mathematics achievement, regardless of family socioeconomic status.

Children in villages with higher per pupil expenditures from non-governmental resources – communities with greater capacity for and commitment to investing in education – have higher mathematics scores. Adams suggests that the economic resources available to spend on schooling in a particular village may influence educational outcomes by shaping school quality. Villages with more economic resources may have more qualified teachers working at their schools, and a higher proportion of students with sufficient resources and materials for learning. She suggests that economic resources may also affect the quality of after-school activities available for children in the community, which may, in turn, shape student aspirations, effort, and attitudes about schooling.

Adams also finds evidence that community social relationships matter. Regardless of child background and other village characteristics, children living in communities where a greater number of parents knew the parents of their children's friends had higher math scores, on average. She indicates that it is probably not the actual friendships between parents that affect student achievement, but rather that communities characterized by close friendship ties may benefit from the support, guidance, and common values created by relationships among parents.

Adams' work shows how communities condition student outcomes that are consequential for children's futures, because achievement heavily influences children's capacity to continue in school, especially for poor children. Moreover, it seems likely that disparities across communities would be even more pronounced if wealthier urban and coastal communities were included in the analysis.

Ross and Lin's essay work complements that of Adams by providing snapshots of the different environments that characterize schools serving poorer and wealthier communities. Ross and Lin draw on field visits to schools in China conducted over many years. Through case studies of a diverse selection of private and girls' schools, Ross and Lin discuss how some poor but entrepreneurial communities are managing to build schools that can serve the needs of their own children, and sometimes fighting great political and economic barriers in order to do so.

Ross and Lin also provide concrete examples of how the climates in schools serving wealthier, more powerful communities differ from those in poorer, less powerful communities. These differences emerge in terms of the values, social resources, and expectations that schools and communities provide to children. Ross and Lin's interviews provide concrete examples of how the social climate at school can shape children's and parents' ideas about children's capacities, and possibilities for children's future lives.

GIRLS' SCHOOLING IN RURAL SOUTH ASIA

The educational paths of boys and girls connect deeply to their own and others' expectations about how they should live their daily lives, and what their future lives should be like. In many parts of the world, major changes in families, in the world of work, and in educational opportunities have reduced the degree to which girls' schooling is at risk. For some time, evidence from countries around the world has indicated that girls' access to schooling is catching up with boys' (King & Hill, 1993; Knodel & Jones, 1996; Schultz, 1993; Shavit & Blossfeld, 1993). Indeed, in recent years, a new phenomenon of a reverse gender gap has emerged in many settings, including the West and Latin America.[1] Even in some countries in Asia such as Mongolia, Malaysia, and the Philippines, there is now evidence of a female educational advantage.[2] This development calls for new ways of thinking about the sources and implications of gender gaps in education.

Still, the old gender gaps have not yet disappeared, and South Asia is often cited as a region where girls' educational disadvantages are particularly persistent. For example, girls' gross enrollment ratios (GERs) divided by boys' for India, Nepal, and Pakistan show rising trends between 1990 and 2000,[3] but remain well below parity, especially at higher levels (see Fig. 1). Bangladesh is a significant outlier: whereas Bangladesh figures for 1990 showed significant gender disparities at all levels – girls' GERs were 86% of boys' at the primary level, 52% at the secondary level, and just 20% at the tertiary level – by 2000, the picture was quite different: girls' GERs *exceeded* boys' by a small margin in primary and secondary levels, and girls' GERs at the tertiary level reached 54% of boys'.

In Nepal and Bangladesh, the focus of studies in this volume, girls' absolute access to schooling has generally improved in recent years, but remains limited. For example, in Bangladesh during the 2002–2003 academic year, about 86% of primary school-aged girls were in school, and just 47% of secondary

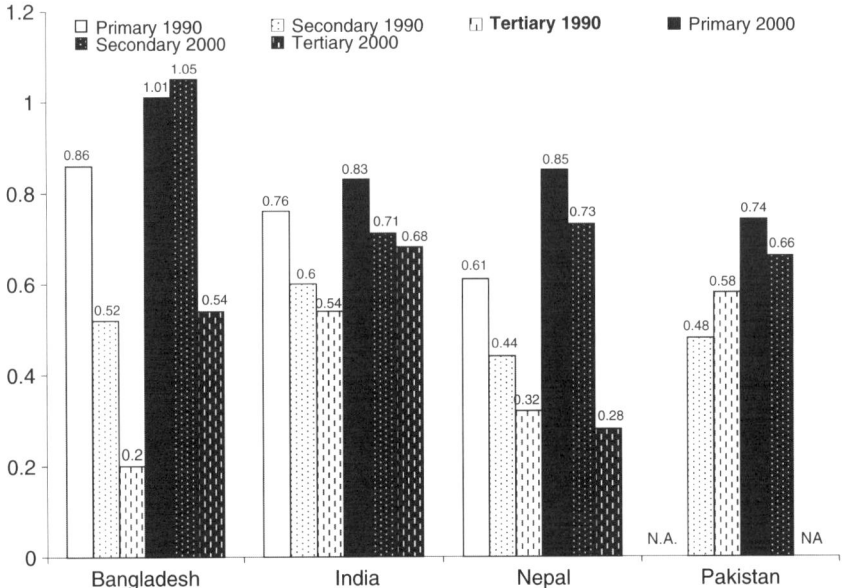

Fig. 1. Female/Male Gross Enrollment Ratios by Level, Country, and Year, Selected South Asian Countries. *Source:* Asian Development Bank (2005).

school-aged girls (UNESCO Institute for Statistics, 2005). In Nepal, where data is only available for the primary level and only for 2000–2001, just 66% of girls were in school (UNESCO Institute for Statistics, 2005).[4]

Written using different theoretical paradigms and methodological approaches, the Bangladesh and Nepal articles provide complementary perspectives on the education of girls in a time of rapid educational change. Girls in both countries, and especially Bangladesh, enjoy increasing access to education,[5] yet, few mechanisms are in place for girls to make use of their education outside of the home. The papers address two questions: First, how should parental calculations about educational investments be conceptualized, in these circumstances? Second, how do schools and families socialize girls, in light of the social realities that girls face as students and later on in life?

Mahmud and Amin investigate girls' educational opportunities in rural Bangladesh, where girls have few formal employment prospects, marry young, and join their husbands' families upon marriage. Analyzing a new panel survey of girls implemented in 2001 and 2003, the authors investigate household and community factors that explain why girls remain in school or drop out, either to get married or for other reasons. Not surprisingly, they show that girls in poor households are more likely to drop out before reaching secondary school. In particular, when girls drop out of school for other reasons but do not get married, economic constraints are usually the cause. Girls in wealthier households are more likely to drop out later, because of marriage. In fact, Mahmud and Amin suggest that girls who continue in school are often those who are waiting for a good marriage to be arranged, which is most likely to occur in wealthy households.

Mahmud and Amin also find that school performance has no effect on subsequent enrollment. This is consistent with the notion that "signals" of future economic prospects are not considered in decisions about whether girls continue in school or get married. Moreover, in wealthy households, girls' likelihood of staying in school or dropping out to get married is unrelated to their job aspirations. It is only in the very poor households, where marriage prospects are worst, that girls who aspire to a salaried job are significantly more likely to continue to secondary school.

On a more theoretical level, Mahmud and Amin's chapter addresses a question that holds broad interest for researchers studying education in South Asia: What is the motivation for increased educational investments in girls in settings characterized by strong patriarchal families and labor markets strictly segmented by sex? In the past, researchers have employed cost–benefit analyses to explain educational decisions in developing countries. From this perspective, expected earnings and parents' prospects of enjoying access to those earnings are seen as the primary factors motivating educational investments. However, as Mahmud and Amin point out, this analytical framework cannot explain the rise in girls' schooling in rural Bangladesh, where girls have poor prospects in the labor market and parents have little right to daughters' earnings after marriage, because wives are part of their husbands' households.

In other words, girls' education is increasing in Bangladesh, even though conventionally defined returns to investments in daughters' schooling are almost non-existent. Girls realize economic benefits from schooling primarily through favorable marriages, but there is no clear economic benefit to the natal family from favorable marriage arrangements. This situation suggests the need to modify the conventional household economy framework. Whether parents receive tangible economic benefits from arranging a better marriage for their daughters or only psychological benefits, considerations of marriage are an important part of household decisions about educational trajectories.

Rothchild's complementary study in Nepal considers the socialization processes that occur when girls' schooling expands while both family roles and employment opportunities remain stratified by sex. Like rural Bangladesh, rural Nepal is characterized by extreme labor segregation, and a marriage system that has detracted from incentives for investing in girls. Rothchild highlights three factors that reduce incentives for investing in the education of Nepalese girls. First, daughters are expected to leave their natal households through marriage in their mid-teen years, while sons are expected to coreside and contribute to the welfare of parents in their old age. Second, non-farm employment is perceived as more appropriate and realistic for males than for females. Third, the traditional gender-based division of farm work requires more routine household work from girls than from boys.

Rothchild's extensive fieldwork in a rural Nepalese village looks at what is happening as girls increasingly attend school despite persisting disincentives imposed by marriage patterns, labor segregation, and the gender-based division of child labor. Rothchild interviewed community members, parents, teachers, and students, and conducted observations in school and home settings. She found that the messages given to female students – at home and at school – often serve to socialize them into traditional female roles.

Just as Mahmud and Amin argue in the case of rural Bangladesh, Rothchild's article suggests that schooling is not seen by rural Nepalese parents, teachers, or girls primarily as a way to prepare girls for new lives in the labor market. This insight is consistent with the lines of thinking evident much of the existing research on women's education in Nepal. Little of this work has investigated labor outcomes, while much has focused on women's empowerment within the home, and on child rearing and home health skills (LeVine, LeVine, Rowe, & Schnell-Anzola, 2004, p. 863; LeVine et al., 2001; Rowe, Thapa, Levine, LeVine, & Tuladhar, 2005).

In this context, Rothchild's study of socialization makes an important contribution by investigating the messages schools give girls about their current and future lives. Rothchild suggests that providing girls with access to formal schooling is necessary but not sufficient to transform family systems and labor segregation that place women in a vulnerable position. Messages given in schools may reinforce norms about women being suited to family roles, rather than work roles. This finding may partly explain how it is that increases in the education of girls can occur without major changes in gender norms about family or work.

Yet, Rothchild's interviews also show that some girls' horizons are moving demonstrably beyond the household realm, most likely as a consequence of their expanding educational opportunities and of seeing other educated females who, by default, become role models. Given the very recent increases in education in rural Nepal, girls today see few examples of educated adult women, and even fewer in non-traditional roles. As education continues to expand and at least some women are able to parlay their education into formal jobs, there will be more and more role models for girls. It is likely that at least this aspect of gender socialization will encourage girls to aspire to non-traditional roles.

In summary, Mahmud and Amin suggest that marriage – as much as or more than a good job – is the desired outcome of educational investments in daughters in rural Bangladesh. Rothchild emphasizes how the education extended to girls in rural Nepal can serve to reinforce the importance of family roles for girls and women, even as it exposes girls to a broader swathe of educated role models and non-family networks. These papers offer insights into how family lives and the gender-based division of both child and adult labor impact the extension of schooling to girls, and shape the likely impact of education on these girls' futures in ways that do not pertain to boys, nor to girls in other cultural settings.

SCHOOL AND FAMILY EFFECTS ON LITERACY: ASIA AND LATIN AMERICA COMPARED

Studies seeking to assess the relative importance of school and family effects on achievement have been a mainstay of U.S. and global sociology of education research for decades.[6] The paper by Hyunjoon Park and Gary Sandefur updates this literature with new data and a sophisticated modeling strategy that makes it possible to separate school context factors that are within a school's control from those that are not.

The authors analyze reading literacy among 15-year-old secondary students with a multi-level modeling approach. They use Program for International Student Assessment (PISA) data from four countries in Asia (Hong Kong, Korea, Indonesia, and Thailand), and compare it to data from four Latin American countries (Argentina, Chile, Mexico, and Peru). Park and Sandefur offer a wealth of empirical evidence on sources of educational stratification in these countries. I focus here on two sets of findings that are particularly important, and linked to the themes of the other Asia papers in this volume.

One key finding among Park and Sandefur's results is that family socioeconomic status affects student reading literacy least in some of the most developed Asian countries – in this case Korea and Hong Kong. This finding is a provocative one, as it contradicts a well-known and widely cited finding – the so-called "Heyneman–Loxley effect". Based on analyses of data from the 1970s, the Heyneman–Loxley effect hypothesized that the importance of family effects on school outcomes increased, with economic development, while school effects declined (Heyneman & Loxley, 1983). Park and Sandefur's findings for Korea and Hong Kong also diverge from more recent tests of the Heyneman–Loxley effect that used data from the 1990s. This newer research showed that family effects swamped school effects on achievement in most countries (Baker, Goesling, & Letendre, 2002).

Park and Sandefur's paper also offers illustrations of particular ways in which family and school effects in Korea and Hong Kong are unusual. One example is the finding that communication with parents was closely tied to student learning outcomes in Korea and Hong Kong. A second example is children's experiences of school climate. While students' sense of belonging was significantly associated with student performance in all countries, it mattered more for student achievement in Asia than in Latin America. In addition to sense of belonging, the researchers found that school disciplinary climate contributed to increased student achievement in Hong Kong and Korea.

The results of Park and Sandefur's study raise interesting questions for ongoing reevaluations of the Heyneman–Loxley effect – questions that could be addressed with further global comparative analyses. Are these highly developed East Asian countries exceptional in providing educational systems in which family background matters less for achievement than in other societies? Is this finding attributable to the fact that literacy was used to measure student achievement, and not math or science, the outcomes in many earlier studies?[7] Park and Sandefur's findings also make clear that where nations fall on a simple scale of economic development can no longer be viewed as the dominant determinant of patterns of educational stratification. Rather, more sophisticated explanations for these patterns are needed – explanations that focus on differences in cultures, social institutions, or educational and family processes that condition children's progress through school in different societies.

DISCUSSION

Collectively, what do these papers contribute to the main goal of this volume, namely to offer examples of how children's diverse lives around the world intersect with their educational opportunities and experiences? And how does this research address the limitations in comparative research on schooling identified by LeVine et al. (2001), namely lack of attention to the links between school attendance and socially beneficial outcomes, and to the socio-cultural institutions that shape life-trajectories?

One set of insights is provided by the South Asia papers. These papers show that local gender norms regarding family and work roles condition access to schooling, experiences at school, and strategies for capitalizing on schooling as adults for girls and boys. Rothchild's analysis of school socialization in rural Nepal, and Mahmud and Amin's study of dropping out in rural Bangladesh, illustrate how the marriage system and a gender-based division of labor shape educational choices and experiences. The Nepal paper also suggests that the school system reflects, and can reinforce, traditional norms about women's roles. Thus, schooling may impact girls' and boys' lives differently depending on local cultural norms, and the impact of educational expansion on women's status, at least in the short run, may be lessened, if traditional gender norms are communicated at school.

A second way that these papers address the gaps highlighted by LeVine et al. (2001) is by pointing to the importance of local contexts in shaping educational access, experience, and consequences. This collection of papers suggests that local community contexts affect the economic and social resources of schools, and the aspirations and achievement of children. Adams shows that student achievement varies significantly across communities, with some of this variability linked to social and economic resources available in communities. Ross and Lin's discussion of school climate differences in China shows that children in richer and poorer communities experience schools that provide varying degrees of social capital for children to utilize in the future. These suggestive findings call for additional conceptual work to develop strategies for measuring community resources and contexts in comparative sociological research on schooling. The growing importance of local communities in educational finance and administration in many parts of the world makes this line of research even more pressing.

Finally, school environments themselves are highlighted as potentially crucial elements of educational opportunity and outcomes in these papers. Park and Sandefur's cross-cultural analysis points out that school climates might be particularly important predictors of student performance in Asia; the China papers offer examples of just how disparate school climates can be. Moreover, Rothchild's fieldwork in Nepal suggests that even in the same schools, climates experienced by girls and boys may be very different. These findings point to an important future direction for comparative research. Despite the seemingly obvious point that children's experiences at school matter for their school achievement and outcomes, there is no consensus in the research community about how to measure school climate in a systematic way.

At the broadest level, these papers serve to elaborate Park and Sandefur's finding that countries differ substantially in the factors that matter for children's school achievement, and in ways that cannot be explained solely in simple terms such as level of economic development. The papers underscore the need for careful theoretical and empirical attention to how family systems, school systems, and labor markets shape individual trajectories differently across countries, within communities, and among children from different social groups.

NOTES

1. For recent evidence, see sources in Hannum and Buchmann (2005).

2. For example, a substantial gender gap favoring girls is evident in Mongolia, where girls' combined gross enrollment ratios (GERs) for primary and secondary levels of education were 1.10 times those of boys, and at the tertiary level were 1.69 times those of boys in the 2002–2003 academic year. By official estimates for the same year, girls were more likely than boys to be enrolled in Malaysia (ratio of 1.05 for primary–secondary GERs and 1.28 for tertiary GERs) and the Philippines (1.02 for primary–secondary and 1.28 for tertiary) (UNESCO Institute for Statistics, 2005).

3. Data for Pakistan only allows a comparison at the secondary level (Asian Development Bank, 2005).

4. For example, for the 1998–1999 year in Bangladesh, the corresponding primary figure was 84%, and the corresponding secondary figure was 38%. For Nepal, the 1998–1999 primary net enrollment ratio was 60% (UNESCO Institute for Statistics, 2005).

5. In Nepal, older data show that as entrance and completion rates rose for girls, rates for boys also rose such that gender gaps did not substantially narrow (Stash & Hannum, 2001). More recent data, cited in the text, shows some relative progress for girls, but also that the gap has not closed.

6. For a recent review of research on the Heyneman–Loxley effect, see Baker et al. (2002).

7. In fact, Park and Sandefur's results for Hong Kong are consistent with Baker et al. (2002). In the earlier study, Hong Kong was one of the countries with the smallest effect of family socio-economic status on achievement. Interestingly, results using math and science achievement suggested a very different finding for Korea, with the vast majority of explained variation in math and science achievement attributable to family background. The inconsistent results for Korea raise the question of whether there are systematic differences in factors that matter for achievement in literacy, compared to math and science, or in the effects of each of these types of achievement on subsequent life outcomes.

REFERENCES

Adams, J., & Hannum, E. (2005). Children's social welfare in China, 1989–1997: Access to health insurance and education. *China Quarterly, 181*, 100–121.

Asian Development Bank. (2005). *Key indicators 2005: Labor markets in Asia: Promoting full, productive, and decent employment (on-line edition)*. URL: http://www.adb.org/Documents/Books/Key_Indicators/2005/xls/MDG03.xls. Manila, Philippines: Asian Development Bank.

Baker, D. P., Goesling, B., & Letendre, G. K. (2002). Socioeconomic status, school quality, and national economic development: A cross-national analysis of the "Heyneman–Loxley Effect" on mathematics and science achievement. *Comparative Education Review, 46*(3), 291–312.

Bray, M. (1996a). *Counting the full cost: Parental and community financing of education in East Asia*. Washington, DC: World Bank.

Bray, M. (1996b). *Decentralization of education: Community financing*. Washington, DC: World Bank.

Carter, C. A. (1997). The urban–rural income gap in China: Implications for global food market. *American Journal of Agricultural Economics, 79*, 1410–1418.

Hannum, E., & Buchmann, C. (2005). Global educational expansion and socio-economic development: An assessment of findings from the social sciences. *World Development, 33*(3), 333–354.

Hannum, E., & Park, A. (2002). Educating China's rural children in the 21st century. *Harvard China Review, 3*(2), 8–14.

Heyneman, S. P., & Loxley, W. A. (1983). The effect of primary-school quality on academic-achievement across 29 high-income and low-income countries. *American Journal of Sociology, 88*(6), 1162–1194.

Khan, A. R., & Riskin, C. (1998). Income inequality in China: Composition, distribution and growth of household income, 1988 to 1995. *The China Quarterly, 154*, 221–253.

King, E. M., & Hill, M. A. (1993). *Women's education in developing countries: Barriers, benefits, and policies.* Baltimore, MD: The Johns Hopkins University Press.

Knodel, J., & Jones, G. (1996). Post-Cairo population policy: Does promoting girls' schooling miss the mark? *Population and Development Review, 22*, 683–702.

LeVine, R. A., LeVine, S. E., Rowe, M. L., & Schnell-Anzola, B. (2004). Maternal literacy and health behavior: A Nepalese case study. *Social Science and Medicine, 58*(4), 863–877.

LeVine, R. A., LeVine, S. E., & Schnell, B. (2001). Improve the women: Mass schooling, female literacy, and worldwide social change. *Harvard Educational Review, 71*(1), 1–50.

Li, W., Park, A., & Wang, S. (2006). Fiscal decentralization and school equity in rural china. In: E. Hannum & A. Park (Eds), *Education and reform in China.* London: Routledge. (Forthcoming).

Park, A., Rozelle, S., Wong, C., & Ren, C. (1996). Distributional consequences of reforming local public finance in China. *The China Quarterly, 147*, 751–778.

Piazza, A., & Liang, E. H. (1998). Reducing absolute poverty in China: Current status and issues. *Journal of International Affairs, 52*, 253–264.

Rowe, M. L., Thapa, B. K., Levine, R. A., LeVine, S. E., & Tuladhar, S. K. (2005). How does schooling influence maternal health practices? Evidence from Nepal. *Comparative Education Review, 49*(4), 512–533.

Schultz, T. P. (1993). Investments in the schooling and health of women and men: Quantities and returns. *Journal of Human Resources, 28*(4), 694–734.

Shavit, Y., & Blossfeld, H. P. (1993). *Persistent inequality: Changing educational attainment in thirteen countries.* Boulder, CO: Westview.

Stash, S., & Hannum, E. (2001). Who goes to school? Educational stratification by gender, caste, and ethnicity in Nepal. *Comparative Education Review, 45*(3), 354–378.

Tsang, M. C. (1996). Financial reform of basic education in China. *Economics of Education Review, 15*(4), 423–444.

UNESCO Institute for Statistics. (2005). Education statistics (on-line database) in UNESCO institute for statistics [database online]. Montreal. [Accessed on October]. Available from http://stats.uis.unesco.org/

Wong, C. (2002). *China national development and sub-national finance: A review of provincial expenditures* (World Bank poverty reduction and economic management unit, east Asia and pacific region, Report no. 22951-CHA, April 9). Washington, DC: World Bank.

CHILDREN'S WORK AND SCHOOL ATTENDANCE IN GHANA

Niels-Hugo Blunch

ABSTRACT

Most of the empirical literature on child labor considers work per se, independent of the nature or extent of work. This study fills this void by examining child work that directly conflicts with the schooling of children in Ghana. It finds evidence of a cultural bias in the way questions regarding working status are perceived. Additionally, the study addresses shortcomings of the empirical analyses of previous studies related to collapsibility, spatial heterogeneity and specification testing. While a substantial share of children who work rather than attend school are forced away from schooling by poverty, an alarmingly high share report that school is "useless" or "uninteresting." This should be of concern to policymakers. Eradicating poverty is not enough to "send children back to school" – norms, traditions, and perceptions must be changed, as well.

INTRODUCTION

Child work is a widespread phenomenon. The ILO estimates that there are more than 250 million child workers between the ages of 7 and 14 worldwide, of whom at least 120 million are involved in work full-time (ILO, 1997).

UNICEF (1999) estimates that as many as 400 million children are working.[1] Disregarding the different methodologies and definitions underlying these estimates, child work is a pervasive phenomenon. This is especially true for developing countries, where parents face a very real trade-off between sending their children to school and (possibly) receiving part of the child's future labor earnings, or having them work now to help sustain the household. In the face of extreme poverty, parents often do not really have any choice.[2]

Partly as a result of the large numbers and sharp sentiments over the notion of child work, the issue of child work has received widespread attention in recent years. This has resulted in a growing academic literature on the subject in the social sciences, spanning, among others, the fields of anthropology (Nieuwenhuys, 1996), economics (Jensen & Nielsen, 1997; Basu & Van, 1998; Blunch et al., 2005), and sociology (Buchmann, 2000; Bass, 2004).

This study focuses on five issues that have received little attention in past studies. First, while the topic of child work is certainly an emotional one and the number of children involved in it are massive – is child work necessarily harmful? I will argue that it is not unless it affects children's health, their educational attainment, or both. This is the case if one (or both) of the following conditions exists: either the children are working under hazardous conditions, which affect the children's health and then subsequently possibly also their school enrollment or achievement – or they are working such long hours that the work directly conflicts with school enrollment or achievement. These are the types of child work that should be of primary interest to academicians and policymakers. For the most part, however, the empirical literature considers all child work in its analyses, and in doing so disregards the nature or extent of that work.[3] I revisit the issue of children's work in light of this notion of harmful child work, in particular to establish whether previous findings on "generic" child work are robust.

The second focus of this study is whether past studies may have contained cultural bias in the way that questions were understood and subsequently answered by the respondents. For example, the typical question in such studies is, "Did [name] work during the past 7 days?" While this may seem to be a straightforward question, it fails to define exactly what "work" is. For example, are household chores considered work? Is being an unpaid family worker? If there is indeed a cultural bias to what really constitutes work, then researchers may not have been examining the determinants of child work but rather something else.

Examining the issue of possible cultural bias in practice requires a dataset that contains information both on the "standard" measure of child work, and also on some other alternative work measure – that is based on a more transparent work status question – so that the standard measure may be cross-validated. This survey design does exactly that – it incorporates both the standard work status question and an alternative question, as well.

Third, the implicit assumption that the alternative to work is schooling – potentially a quite West-centric view – seems to be quite widespread in the research on child work. The presence of poverty or credit constraints, however, may cause the alternative to be idleness, and not schooling. Whether or not this view holds, then, seems to require a closer examination.

Fourth, it would be useful to examine in more detail under what circumstances child work and schooling are compatible: if engaging in child work activities is necessary to ensure one's own or ones family's livelihood, we – meaning researchers and policymakers alike – must try to understand the conditions under which these two activities may be combined. In this case, simply banning child work does not seem a viable strategy.

Lastly, while child work has been established as a research area in most of the social sciences, little interdisciplinary work has occurred on this topic. Integrating this research would likely provide a deeper understanding of the nature and dynamics involved in this complex concept. More specifically, it might offer further insights into conceptual issues, such as what the underlying determinants of child work status really are, whether economic, sociological, or due to other factors. Doing so will also likely strengthen the empirical analysis by paying more attention to statistical issues such as acknowledging the possible presence of endogeneity and spatial heterogeneity, as well as performing specification tests after estimation.

This study addresses these five issues from the perspective of harmful child work through five specific research questions (described in the next section) by examining the second type of harmful child work as suggested above for the case of Ghana.[4] By "harmful," it is therefore here meant that child work conflicts with a child's schooling. Specifically, I define a child of school age as engaging in harmful child work if her reported main activity during the past seven days is work rather than schooling. If this is the case, work can be expected to affect schooling negatively in terms of enrollment, achievement, or both.

This paper is structured as follows. The next section discusses the methodology of this study, including its conceptual framework and empirical strategies and issues, and also presents the five research questions to be examined. I then present the data and descriptive analyses and the multivariate results. The final section offers conclusions and a direction for further research.

METHODOLOGY AND RESEARCH QUESTIONS

This section discusses study methodology and the research questions to be examined. First the conceptual framework is presented. This is followed by a discussion of empirical strategies and issues. Lastly, the research questions are presented in light of the issues discussed in the introduction and the study methodology.

Theoretical Framework

The theoretical framework for this paper is standard human capital theory, according to which an individual builds up knowledge and skills through education, experience, and training (Becker, 1964; Mincer, 1974). At the same time, however, rather than – or in addition to – attending school, the individual may engage in work activities. In developing countries – especially for children, which are the object for the analysis here – this decision would involve not just the individual child (as postulated in the "classic" version of the human capital model), but also the adult household members. It would also be affected by multiple economic and non-economic factors.[5] This leads to the following simple model of child work determinants at the household level:

$$W = W(I, H, C) \qquad (1)$$

where W is a measure of child work status; I a vector of individual child characteristics, including gender, disability status, and age – also, since not all children necessarily are biologically related to the household head, the relationship to the household head is included here, as well; H a vector of household characteristics, including age, gender, and education of household head[6] and socioeconomic status of the household; C a vector of community characteristics, including distance to nearest school, rural–urban location, region of residence, and socioeconomic status of the community. These variables are chosen based on the previous literature (see Canagarajah & Nielsen, 2001 for a review of the evidence for Africa).

In this model, child work is expected to be positively affected by a child's age since older children are both more productive and more likely to be out of school. Similarly, gender is expected to affect child work with more girls than boys working, especially doing household chores. Socioeconomic status of the household is expected to affect child work negatively, so that children from poorer households or households with less educated household heads are more likely to work than children from non-poor households. Transport costs are expected to increase child work since schooling then becomes relatively more expensive, so that children living far away from the nearest school will be more likely to engage in harmful child work.

Empirical Strategy and Issues

The empirical strategy for estimating Eq. (1) proceeds as follows. First, the estimation method is by means of a univariate probit model. The reason why I do not model the work and schooling decision simultaneously in a bivariate probit or multinomial logit model is that for this application, the decision mainly boils down to a decision of *either* working *or* attending school: very few (about 0.3%) work *and* attend school, while almost 80% attend school but do not work. It therefore seems more worthwhile to focus on the work decision.

At the outset, Eq. (1) is estimated for the full sample by pooling, on one hand, girls and boys and, on the other, children from rural and urban areas. To allow the possibility of omitted individual heterogeneity due to norms and traditions and economic conditions and opportunities to affect girls and boys and children from rural and urban areas differently, however, Eq. (1) is also estimated separately for these four groups.

Additionally, due to endogeneity concerns for several variables, the empirical analyses include sensitivity analyses with different sets of explanatory variables. In particular, when examining the possible impact from economic factors, for example, previous studies have mostly included per capita household expenditures or household income, while frequently stating something like "the parameter estimates of the other explanatory variables were mostly unaffected" – typically without formally testing for whether this was the case. The same is true for other potentially endogenous variables, such as land or livestock ownership. Lacking valid instruments for potentially endogenous variables – which is frequently an issue in applied research – formally applying instrumental variables estimation to account for the endogeneity is not possible.

Even so, it is still possible to examine the relative importance of potentially endogenous variables on the parameter estimates of the other explanatory variables by means of a Wu–Hausman-type test for collapsibility (Wu, 1973; Hausman, 1978; Clogg, Petkova, & Shihadeh, 1992; Clogg, Petkova, & Haritou, 1995). This amounts to asking, do inclusion of the potentially endogenous variables matter? in terms of the stability of the parameter estimates of the other explanatory variables and is a minimum requirement when dealing with potentially endogenous variables and no valid instruments are readily available. Coupled with a test for the joint statistical significance of the potentially endogenous explanatory variables – that is, testing whether the reduced model encompasses the full model (Mizon & Marcellino, 2002) – this together helps determine whether the potentially endogenous variables belong in the set of explanatory variables.

Another issue that many studies have not considered is the possibility of spatial heterogeneity above and beyond that is captured by an inclusion of a rural–urban dummy. For instance, in Ghana there are 10 regions, each of which is likely to be "different" in more ways than simply local economic conditions or schooling infrastructure. Local norms and traditions may influence or even prescribe whether a child works and if so, how much. In addition, the economic conditions of the local community may influence child work, so that children in wealthier communities would tend to work less. I examine this by also controlling for region of residence and average per capita household expenditures in the community.

Lastly, I examine the possibility of more complex dynamics between sociological, economic, and geographic factors. For example, does the impact of poverty depend on the gender of the child, or does the impact of gender depend on the geographical location? Similarly, there may be modifying effects within the factors themselves such that, for example, the relationship to the household head might depend on other sociological factors such as gender.

Throughout the analysis, adjustments are made for the survey design by incorporating clustering and sample weights in the estimations. The analyses also employ robust Huber–White standard errors to correct for heteroskedasticity of unknown form (Huber, 1967; White, 1980).

Research Questions

In the light of the issues raised in the introduction and the methodology discussed above, the following five research questions will be addressed:

RQ1. Is there potentially a cultural bias in the way questions are understood and subsequently answered? In particular, it may not be transparent exactly what "work" means. Is being an unpaid family worker, for example, considered work?

RQ2. Does the – possibly quite Western-centric – view that "the" alternative to work is schooling, which is implicit in most of the research on child work, hold? In other words, will a child who formerly engaged in work-related activities but now for whatever reason stops working, more or less automatically enter school?

RQ3. Is child work sometimes compatible with schooling, and if so, when? In particular, what are the types of work-related activities that allow children to simultaneously attend school?[7]

RQ4. Are previous findings on child work robust to changing the child work measure to harmful child work – where harmful child work here refers to pursuing work activities to an extent that they cut into a child's enrollment or achievement?[8] These findings mainly regard – especially in an African context (Canagarajah & Nielsen, 2001) – the presence of a gender bias in child work (with girls working more than boys), the sensitivity of child work to economic conditions (with children from poorer households being more likely to work) and school costs, especially transportation costs (so that children facing a longer distance to school or higher direct schooling cost are more likely to work).

RQ 5. Does inclusion of potentially endogenous variables such as household expenditures, land, and cattle ownership affect the parameter estimates of the other explanatory variables? Lacking valid instruments, a Wu–Hausman-type test for collapsibility coupled with a joint test for their relevance provides an alternative way to assess whether the potentially endogenous variables "belong" in the estimations.

DATA AND DESCRIPTIVE ANALYSES

This section describes the data and then provides an analysis of the main correlates of child work status. It attempts to answer the following questions: Is there potentially a cultural bias in the way questions are asked and subsequently answered? What are the main correlates of child work status and what is the relative strength of the various associations? What type of work are children doing? Is the alternative to work schooling, or something else? When is child work compatible with schooling?

The Data and Choice of Child Work Status and Explanatory Variables

The data examined here originates from the Core Welfare Indicators Questionnaire (CWIQ) for Ghana, which was given between September and

November of 1997 by the Ghana Statistical Service in collaboration with the World Bank. The CWIQ is a nationally representative multi-purpose household survey and includes approximately 15,000 households. The survey contains information on labor force status and educational attainment of household members as well as on background variables such as age, gender, and rural–urban location and region of residence, which are also important factors in analyses of human capital processes. This information was given by the household head or, if not present, by other person(s) presently in charge of the household. For this study, the unit of analysis is the individual child, and household- and community-level information is then merged with the information of the individual child.

The estimation sample is children from 8 to 14 years of age (both included). This range seems to be consistent with the age when most children should be attending primary school.[9] The initial sample consists of 12,025 children; due to missing observations on one or more variables, the effective estimation sample is reduced to 11,968, that is, by 57 observations or less than 0.5%. Therefore, there do not appear to be any serious problems with sample selection.

The definition of the dependent variable, work status of the child, is not straightforward and so requires some explanation. There are two possibilities for defining this variable. The first is to use the question on whether the child was working (full-time, part-time, or not at all) during the past four weeks.[10] This resembles the question on which the working measure typically is based for these types of analyses – often the question is framed as, "Did [name] work during the past seven days?" The other possibility is to use the question on the child's main work status during the past four weeks, where work status is given as one of the 10 different categories, including regular employee, casual employee, unpaid family worker, student, and so on. It is not a priori clear that these questions contain the same information.

First, as discussed previously, academicians and policymakers really should be concerned mainly with child work that affects the human capital accumulation of the child, either in terms of directly affecting the child's health or in terms of cutting into the child's time available for school attendance or study time. While neither of these questions has anything to say about the hazardous type of harmful child work, the question on main work status addresses the non-hazardous variant of it. If a child answers "regular employee," "casual employee," or other work-related category rather than "student/apprentice" to the question, "What was [name's] main work status during the past 4 weeks?," then I assume that child work was undertaken at the expense of schooling.

Second, a question may not be interpreted by the respondent as intended. For example, when answering the question on whether the child has been working full-time, part-time, or not at all during the past four weeks, what exactly is meant by "work?" Is being a housekeeper or an unpaid family worker considered work? In other words, there may be a cultural bias in the way certain questions are understood and subsequently answered by the respondent. To shed light on whether this is the case here, I tabulate the responses to the two questions against each other in Table 1.[11]

The most striking findings in Table 1 are that more than 30% of unpaid family workers and almost 70% of housekeepers do not consider themselves working. Though less striking, the same is true for about 7% of the casual employees and about 2% of the self-employed workers. So, yes, there seems to be a cultural bias in the way questions on work status are asked and subsequently answered. Is this a problem? Since the share of unpaid family

Table 1. Contrasting and Comparing the Two Child Work Measures (Percent).

	Full-Time	Part-Time	Not Working	Total
Unemployed/child not in school	0.5	0.2	99.3	100.0
	0.4	2.2	7.5	6.8
Self-employed	94.2	3.5	2.4	100.0
	4.0	1.7	0.0	0.4
Regular employee	100.0	0.0	0.0	100.0
	0.4	0.0	0.0	0.0
Casual employee	64.8	28.7	6.6	100.0
	0.4	2.1	0.0	0.1
Unpaid family worker	64.3	5.1	30.7	100.0
	86.2	80.2	4.1	12.1
Housekeeper	28.8	2.2	69.0	100.0
	1.5	1.4	0.4	0.5
Student/apprentice	0.8	0.1	99.1	100.0
	7.0	12.4	88.0	80.1
Total	9.1	0.8	90.2	100.0
	100.0	100.0	100.0	100.0

Note: The number of observations is 11,941, with 27 missing observations as compared to the main analysis sample: this is due to these children not answering the "part-time–full-time" work question. Estimations incorporate sampling design (weights and clustering).

workers comprises about 12% of the entire analysis sample, the answer must be "yes": using the "full-time–part-time" question as the basis for the child work measure is not valid when so many in the sample are engaged in work activities in the household, while at the same time do not consider themselves working.

These two issues taken together lead me to consider a binary child work measure, which is one if the main work status of the child during the past four weeks was "regular employee," "casual employee," or other work-related category rather than "student."

The explanatory variables were chosen in accordance with the previous literature, and so include age, age squared, and gender of the child, along with the child's relationship to the household head,[12] age, age squared, gender, education of head, and (the log of) per capita household expenditures, where the latter captures the welfare level or economic conditions of the household.[13] This is included both at the household and the community level, where the latter is calculated as the average (the log of) per capita expenditures in the community.

The rationale for including both is that while presumably there may be a direct relationship between the welfare or poverty level of the household and individual child work status, the economic conditions as measured by the community average of per capita household expenditures may also affect child work status. For example, if a poor household resides in a relatively wealthy community, it may receive transfers from friends and family in the community. In turn, this may mitigate somewhat the work demands on the child. The full list of explanatory variables and their definitions are given in Appendix A.

Incidence and Main Correlates of Child Work Status

To better understand the patterns in the data, the first thing to note is that the incidence of harmful child work, while not earth shattering, is still considerable. About 13% of the full sample engages in harmful child work activities, with girls at 14.5%, and boys at 12% (Appendix B, Table B1). The association between harmful child work and its possible determinants, including the partial correlation of child work status and various child, household, and community characteristics, is depicted in Table 2. While all of the partial correlations (except for disability) are statistically significant at 1% or higher, their magnitudes vary widely. For example, while being female is associated with a higher likelihood of engaging in harmful child

Table 2. Partial Correlation of Child Work Status and Child, Household and Community Characteristics, and Geographical Location.

Child Characteristics						
Female	Age	Child of head	Disabled			
0.036	0.068	0.027	−0.010			

Household Characteristics						
Female head	Age head	Primary and above	Secondary school	Log (per capita expenditures)	Owns land	Owns cattle
−0.097	0.070	−0.250	0.099	−0.148	0.060	0.316

Community Characteristics			
Water source	Primary school	Secondary school	Log (mean per capita expenditure in community)
0.068	0.165	0.099	−0.219

Geographical Location

Urban	Western	Central	Greater Accra
−0.143	−0.066	−0.062	−0.083

Region

Volta	Eastern	Ashanti	Brong Ahafo	Northern	Upper East	Upper West
−0.072	−0.110	−0.101	−0.084	0.303	0.214	0.170

Note: The number of observations is 11,968. The partial correlations are all statistically significant at 1% or higher, except that between child work status and disability (the p-value of the latter is 0.264). Definitions of variables can be found in Appendix A. Estimations incorporate sampling design (weights and clustering).

work (positive partial correlation of 0.036), this is more than mitigated if living in an urban area (negative partial correlation of 0.143).

The main conclusion that can be drawn from Table 2 is that child workers tend to be older, female, from rural areas, and live relatively further away from water sources and primary and secondary schools than non-working children. Perhaps surprisingly, the partial correlation between work status and mean per capita household expenditures in the community is greater than that between work status and per capita household expenditures. Again, this may reflect the possibility of the extended family system successfully mitigating work demands on poor families. Since the results in Table 2 only reflect the partial association between work status and its various characteristics, these results are, of course, very preliminary. In particular, some of the characteristics may be substitutes for others, or there may be mediating effects. For example, the relationship between work status and gender may be conditional on economic conditions or location of residence. To incorporate such considerations, one must apply a multivariate framework, simultaneously controlling for all of these factors; this is the object of the next section.

What Type of Work are the Children Doing?

Having examined the main correlates with child work and the relative strength of the various associations, I next describe what kind of work the children in the sample are actually doing. In particular, some types of work appear more compatible with schooling than others. Being an unpaid family worker or casual employee, for example, seem to be more compatible with schooling than being a regular employee.

Based on 1,300 observations in this study, the overwhelming majority of the working children (almost 93%) are engaged as unpaid family workers. Only 3.6% are working as housekeepers, about 3% as self-employed workers, and just over 0.5% as regular and casual employees.

Is the Alternative to Work Schooling – or Something Else?

As discussed previously, the approach taken here – and in most other studies on child work – implicitly assumes that the alternative to work is schooling. This approach can be seen as containing a strong Western bias, however, since poverty and credit constraints may cause the alternative to be idleness,

Table 3. Reasons Why Not Currently in School.

Not of school age/completed school	13.9
Too far away	3.2
Too expensive/can't afford	23.9
Working	10.3
School is useless/uninteresting	40.9
Illness	8.6
Pregnancy	0.7
Failed exam	2.5
Got married	2.8
Other	12.0

Note: The number of observations is 481. The total exceeds 100% since multiple responses are allowed. Estimations incorporate sampling design (weights and clustering).

and not schooling. Fortunately, the survey includes a question on why school-age children who previously had attended school are not currently enrolled.[14] The responses may provide insights into the major constraints of school attendance for Ghanaian children.

As Table 3 shows, in response to the question, "If [name] is not currently in school, explain why," for a sizeable portion of the sample of children currently not in school (about 24%) "Too expensive/Cannot afford" is given as a reason. This lends support to the hypothesis that poverty and credit constraints may account for some of the children not enrolled in school. Even if these children did not work, the alternative would not be schooling but rather idleness. So there is some evidence that contradicts the Western view, which assumes schooling is the natural alternative to engaging in child work.

At the same time, however, nearly twice as many children (about 41%) are not attending school because "school is useless/uninteresting." This is clearly a view based more on norms and traditions or simply lack of knowledge of the potential benefits of education. It is likely that if the parents of these children could be convinced of the value of education, they might make sure their children were enrolled, if not full-time then at least part-time.

Is Child Work Compatible with Schooling?

So far the data has provided some evidence that contradicts the Western view that schooling is more or less "the" alternative to work, with poverty and credit constraints being important factors for non-enrollment. Having pointed out the even greater importance of attitudes, norms, and traditions on schooling, I now look at whether child work in practice is compatible with schooling, and if so, under what conditions. The results of the data reveal that work and schooling are generally *not* compatible, and that most children are either working *or* attending school, but not doing both.[15] In only a few cases, however (about 0.4%) are the two activities compatible. Next I attempt to find out under what conditions certain types of work activities *are* compatible with schooling.

What was found is that there are two types of work frequently undertaken by children who are currently attending school. They are either self-employed or are unpaid family workers. Since the number of observations upon which this result is based is quite low, however – only 38 children, or about 0.3% of the total sample – the results should be interpreted with caution.

While illuminating and providing a good first look at child work and its main correlates, all of the analyses and observations in this section were based on partial correlations. To better assess the joint impact of all these factors, multivariate regression analysis is required. This is the focus of the next section.

MULTIVARIATE RESULTS

I start by presenting the pooled results and then goes on to present the results for the models disaggregated by gender and rural–urban location. Lastly, it presents several specification tests for the estimated models.

Starting with the results for the full sample, many of the partial correlations from the previous section "survive" the inclusion of other factors, while a few do not (Table 4). One of the main sociological factors, gender, exerts a strong, positive, and statistically significant influence on harmful child work status, with girls being about 3.6% age points more likely to engage in such activities than boys. This gender gap, while presumably reflecting primarily social norms and customs – including "traditional" gender roles that still dominate in Ghana (Chao et al., 1999) – may also reflect the fact that females in Ghana, as in most other countries, receive lower wages than males for a given level of education and experience (Blunch, 2005b).

Another important sociological factor, the relationship to the household head, also exerts a strong influence on child work, though not quite as

Table 4. Results from Child Work Probit Regressions for Full Sample, Girls and Boys.

	Full Sample	Girls	Boys	Rural Sample	Urban Sample
Individual child characteristics					
Female	0.036***			0.035***	0.035***
	[0.006]			[0.009]	[0.006]
Age	0.072***	0.116***	0.044**	0.104***	0.006
	[0.022]	[0.035]	[0.023]	[0.029]	[0.019]
Age squared/100	−0.253***	−0.424***	−0.155	−0.383***	0.006
	[0.095]	[0.157]	[0.100]	[0.128]	[0.083]
Child of HH head	−0.026**	−0.062***	0.009	−0.018	−0.039***
	[0.012]	[0.017]	[0.010]	[0.015]	[0.013]
Disabled	−0.032	−0.037	−0.023	−0.036	−0.014
	[0.028]	[0.046]	[0.026]	[0.038]	[0.029]
Household characteristics					
Female HH head	−0.006	−0.01	−0.002	0.0001	−0.002
	[0.010]	[0.012]	[0.011]	[0.013]	[0.010]
Age, HH head	−0.002	0.0001	−0.002	−0.003	−0.001
	[0.002]	[0.002]	[0.002]	[0.003]	[0.002]
Age squared/100, HH head	0.001	−0.001	0.002	0.002	0.0001
	[0.002]	[0.002]	[0.002]	[0.002]	[0.002]
Some primary, HH head	−0.026**	−0.032**	−0.017	−0.023	−0.01
	[0.010]	[0.016]	[0.011]	[0.015]	[0.012]
Primary, HH head	−0.035***	−0.047***	−0.021**	−0.044***	−0.01
	[0.010]	[0.013]	[0.010]	[0.013]	[0.014]
Middle/junior secondary, HH head	−0.053***	−0.063***	−0.040***	−0.065***	−0.021**
	[0.008]	[0.011]	[0.010]	[0.011]	[0.010]
Secondary or above, HH head	−0.061***	−0.071***	−0.055***	−0.079***	−0.032***
	[0.009]	[0.011]	[0.008]	[0.013]	[0.008]
Voc/tech or other, HH head	−0.044***	−0.051***	−0.036***	−0.055***	−0.017
	[0.011]	[0.014]	[0.012]	[0.016]	[0.010]
Log (per capita HH expenditures)	−0.030***	−0.019	−0.042***	−0.053***	−0.001
	[0.010]	[0.014]	[0.013]	[0.014]	[0.010]
HH owns land	−0.005	−0.002	−0.005	−0.011	0.011
	[0.009]	[0.011]	[0.011]	[0.012]	[0.010]
HH owns cattle	0.061***	0.084**	0.039**	0.057***	0.052
	[0.018]	[0.034]	[0.018]	[0.020]	[0.032]
Community characteristics					
Water, 30 min or more	−0.004	0.02	−0.018**	−0.009	−0.012
	[0.009]	[0.014]	[0.008]	[0.011]	[0.015]
Primary school, 30 min or more	0.021**	0.018	0.019*	0.035***	−0.017*
	[0.010]	[0.014]	[0.010]	[0.012]	[0.009]
Secondary school, 30 min or more	0.023*	0.023	0.023*	0.050***	0.007
	[0.014]	[0.017]	[0.013]	[0.018]	[0.009]

Table 4. (*Continued*)

	Full Sample	Girls	Boys	Rural Sample	Urban Sample
Log (per capita HH expenditures) cluster mean	−0.049*	−0.04	−0.050*	−0.061*	−0.033
	[0.027]	[0.035]	[0.029]	[0.035]	[0.031]
Urban	−0.032**	−0.026	−0.040***		
	[0.015]	[0.018]	[0.014]		
Pseudo-R^2	0.271	0.251	0.310	0.295	0.117
Number of observations	11,968	5,854	6,114	8,163	3,805

Note: "HH" denotes "household." Robust Huber–White (Huber, 1967; White, 1980) standard errors in brackets under parameter estimates. The estimations also include regional dummies. To conserve space, the results for these have been omitted; they are available upon request. Test results for their joint significance are given in Table 5. Estimations incorporate sampling design (weights and clustering).
*Statistically significant at 10%.
**Statistically significant at 5%.
***Statistically significant at 1%.

strong as gender, with an impact estimate of 2.6% age points. These results accord with previous results (Jensen & Nielsen, 1997; Bass, 2004).

Turning to economic factors, average per capita household expenditures in the cluster have a larger positive impact on child work than household per capita expenditures (about 5% age points versus 3% age points), although the community-level estimate is somewhat less precisely measured than the household-level estimate. Land ownership does not affect child work, neither in substantive nor statistical terms. This may be due to land ownership capturing both economic status and the labor demand of the household, so the two factors cancel out in the aggregate. Owning cattle affects child work positively significantly and with a large magnitude: controlling for other factors, children from households owning cattle are about 6% age points more likely to work than children from households who do not own cattle. These results are also consistent with previous findings, which find child work increasing with poverty, both at the household level (Jensen & Nielsen, 1997) and national level (Bass, 2004).

Moving next to the gray zone between sociological and economic factors, the education of the household head captures both. Through education, norms and attitudes are influenced (Bass, 2004), while at the same time education also positively affects the ability to create a better livelihood for oneself and one's family. This expectation of a negative impact from education on child work is supported by the results in Table 4, with all levels of education exerting statistically significantly negative impacts on child work for the full sample relative to "no education" (the reference category), as high as minus 6.1% age points for household heads, who completed secondary education or higher.

In line with the partial correlations of Table 2, school supply and geographic factors remain important in the multivariate framework. Living 30 min or more away from the nearest primary or secondary school increases the probability of engaging in harmful child work, with about 2% age points in both the cases. In turn, this provides evidence favoring Lavy's (1996) supply constraint hypothesis, namely that supply constraints on secondary schooling may affect the demand for primary schooling because primary school may be a "ticket" to secondary school.

The multivariate analysis revealed a couple of other interesting findings. Surprisingly, the distance to the nearest water source appears to have no effect on child work. Also, children from urban areas are less likely to engage in harmful child work (about 3% age points), indicating that child work is mainly a rural phenomenon. Additionally, the results indicate the presence of spatial heterogeneity of child work above and beyond that related to rural–urban location. Most significantly, children from the Northern, Upper Eastern, and Upper Western regions are much more likely to engage in harmful child work relative to Greater Accra (the reference region), with marginal probabilities of about −11%, −13%, and −18%.[16] While these three regions are among the poorest and least developed of the 10 regions in Ghana, it is possible to rule out poverty as the reason why children from these regions are more likely to work. The reason for this is that both local- and household-level economic conditions are controlled for in the regressions. The main other "candidates," then, are local norms and traditions, possibly related to religion, in these three regions. The dataset examined here does not include information on these issues, however, so that further examination of what exactly it is about these three regions that causes more children to be working is not possible with the current dataset.

So far, the analysis has implicitly assumed that the correlates affect the probability of engaging in child work identically for girls and boys. However, in a society with traditional gender roles such as Ghana (Chao et al., 1999), this is likely not to be the case. I therefore next divide the sample by gender and estimate the model separately for girls and boys. The results from this reveal strong asymmetries in the impacts for several key variables.

Being a child of the household head, for example, matters much more for girls (a difference of almost 6% age points), while the effect for boys is practically negligible.

When it comes to the impact from per capita household expenditures, however, the picture is reversed, with the working status of boys being more responsive to household expenditures – with higher household expenditures leading to a lower probability of working – while that of girls is not. For cattle ownership, however, the working status of girls is much more responsive than that of boys, with increased probabilities of working from cattle ownership of about 8% and 4% age points, respectively. In turn, this last result indicates that girls are the ones responsible for taking care of the household's cattle.

Geographic factors also influence child work quite differently for girls and boys. While proximity to the nearest water source did not matter in the aggregate, it does when considering the impact separately for girls and boys. The impacts are practically mirror images of each other, being around 2% age points and positive for girls while negative for boys. Although the impact for girls is somewhat imprecisely measured and therefore statistically insignificant, this indicates that girls are the ones responsible for fetching water in Ghana.

Similarly, to allow for the possibility that child work determinants differ between rural and urban locations, I estimate separate regression models for rural and urban areas, as well. Table 4 reveals that the gender gap is identical across rural and urban areas, with girls being 3.5% age points more likely to engage in harmful child work. Older children are more likely to work in rural areas, possibly because the older children are more useful for the physically demanding work at the family farm. Being a child of the household head, on the other hand, has a larger effect in urban than in rural areas – about −2% and −4% age points, respectively – and is only statistically significant in urban areas.

The education of the household head is much more important in rural than in urban areas – possibly due to the fact that rural heads are generally less educated. Children from a household where the household head has completed primary education, for example, are about 4.5% age points (statistically significant) less likely to engage in human capital detrimental child work in rural areas, whereas the estimate for urban areas is 1% age point (not statistically significant). The supply of schooling, on the other hand, is much more important for engaging in harmful child work in rural than in urban areas, which should not come as a surprise, since access to schooling in urban areas is generally quite good in Ghana.

Surprisingly, economic conditions as measured by household expenditures matter much less in urban areas than in rural areas. This is the case for both the household-level measure and the community-level measure. At the household level, the impact estimate is virtually nil for urban areas. However, poverty impacts child work markedly in rural areas.

Owning cattle is associated with a higher likelihood of engaging in harmful child work in rural areas than in urban ones, with 5.7% versus 5.5% age points. The estimate is also only statistically significant for rural areas. These two findings seem plausible, since raising livestock is more relevant in rural areas, which thus gives rise to both a higher and a more precisely measured estimate in rural areas.

Lastly, I perform a few robustness checks and specification tests. A major concern is the possibility of some of the explanatory variables being jointly determined with the work status of the child, potentially causing endogeneity bias in the estimated parameters of the other (i.e. predetermined) variables, as well. The main "candidates" here are household expenditures per capita, land and cattle ownership. I therefore estimate the models in two flavors, the first of which includes all explanatory variables except these three possibly endogenous explanatory variables. This is the "reduced" model. The second adds the three possibly endogenous explanatory variables to the reduced model to create the "full" model. The results from this exercise indicate that the parameter estimates are roughly similar across the two specifications, for the full sample as well as across gender and rural–urban location.[17]

This is confirmed by formally testing for parameter constancy across the two model specifications by means of a Wu–Hausman-type test for collapsibility (Wu, 1973; Hausman, 1978; Clogg et al., 1992, 1995). The test results imply that inclusion of the potentially endogenous variables do not greatly alter the parameter estimates of the other explanatory variables overall, although the test statistic for the rural subsample is weakly statistically significant (Table 5). Again, while this is not a test for endogeneity, it does provide some evidence that there are no serious consequences associated with inclusion of these potentially endogenous explanatory variables in the analysis. In contrast, previous studies on child work in Ghana and elsewhere have often merely included household expenditures or income and implicitly treated these as exogenous or at least predetermined (Blunch & Verner, 2000; Maitra & Ray, 2002), while frequently stating something like "inclusion of these variables did not affect the results" – without formally testing for whether this was the case.

Table 5. Results from Specification Tests.

	Full Sample	Girls	Boys	Rural	Urban
(1) Wu–Hausman-type test for collapsibility					
Full versus reduced model	$F(27, 561) = 1.34$ [0.121]	$F(26, 561) = 0.75$ [0.812]	$F(26, 562) = 0.94$ [0.553]	$F(26, 345) = 1.44^*$ [0.078]	$F(26, 191) = 0.61$ [0.931]
(2) Test for joint significance of added variables in Model 2/encompassing between Model 1 and 2					
Full model	$\chi^2(3) = 80962.15^{***}$ [0.000]	$\chi^2(3) = 43713.82^{***}$ [0.000]	$\chi^2(3) = 47674.48^{***}$ [0.000]	$\chi^2(3) = 70517.46^{***}$ [0.000]	$\chi^2(3) = 12394.89^{***}$ [0.000]
(3) Test for sample splits – across gender and rural/urban location:					
Full model		$\chi^2(29) = 56.34^{***}$ [0.002]		$\chi^2(29) = 74.44^{***}$ [0.000]	
(4) Test for joint significance of regional dummies:					
Full model	$\chi^2(9) = 167.49^{***}$ [0.000]	$\chi^2(9) = 106.19^{***}$ [0.000]	$\chi^2(9) = 118.08^{***}$ [0.000]	$\chi^2(9) = 203.30^{***}$ [0.000]	$\chi^2(9) = 13.35$ [0.148]
Number of observations	11,968	5,854	6,114	8,163	3,805

Note: P-values in brackets under t-statistics. "Reduced Model" refers to the initial model (all variables shown in Appendix A, except log (per capita HH expenditures) and variables for land and cattle ownership); "Full Model" adds log (per capita HH expenditures) and variables for land and cattle ownership to "Reduced Model." The tests apply robust Huber–White (Huber, 1967; White, 1980) standard errors. Estimations incorporate sampling design (weights and clustering).
*Statistically significant at 10%.
***Statistically significant at 1%.

Additional specification tests presented in Table 5 include first, another test of the two model specifications mentioned above against each other, this time in terms of their relative explanatory power – a so-called test for "encompassing" (Mizon & Marcellino, 2002). This complements the previous test for collapsibility – whether the potentially endogenous variables have an effect on the coefficients of the other explanatory variables – by additionally testing for their relevance in the estimations. The results imply that these variables are indeed relevant and hence that the full model (where the potentially endogenous variables are included) is preferable to the reduced model.

I also test for whether the two sample splits – across gender and across rural–urban location – are formally valid in terms of a Chow-type test for sample split. The results here imply that both of the sample splits are valid, indicating that there are structural differences in the correlates of harmful child work across gender and across rural–urban location.

The last specification test measures the joint significance of the regional variables. The test strongly rejects that these variables – as a whole – may be excluded from the estimations. Again, this indicates structural differences in the likelihood of engaging in human capital detrimental across regions in Ghana as discussed above.

CONCLUSION

This study has examined harmful child labor in Ghana and arrived at a number of new contributions on this subject. First, I offered a new definition for child work, one that is more relevant conceptually and academically, as well as for public policy purposes. The new definition says that child work should only be a concern – to academicians, policymakers and, ultimately, parents – if it negatively affects children's health, educational attainment, or both. This may occur either by the work being directly hazardous, hence possibly additionally affecting school enrollment or achievement through its impact on child health, or by requiring work hours of a duration that would conflict with school enrollment or achievement, or both. Due to data limitations, this study examined only one of these two types of harmful child work – work that directly interfere with school enrollment or achievement.

Second, the study corroborated previous findings on the linkages between child work and sociological, economic, and geographic factors for the proposed measure of harmful child work, while at the same time also pointing out the importance of further allowing for modifying effects either between the three main groups of factors – economic, sociological, and geographic – or within a given group.

Third, the study pointed out the possibility of a cultural bias in past research in regard to what "work" actually means. This holds implications for data collection in future research efforts, and particularly in conducting household surveys that pertain to children's work activities.

Fourth, this study questioned a Western viewpoint that is often inherent in research on child work – namely that if we could simply stop children from having to work, they would automatically switch to schooling. In particular, it was found that a major reason why almost one-fourth of all children who were currently not attending school, were not enrolled was due to poverty. The alternative to working for these children, therefore, would seem to be idleness, not schooling. However, the study also found that almost twice as many were out of school for a different reason – due to a belief that school was "useless or uninteresting" – thus indicating that norms, traditions, and beliefs are even more important than poverty in causing non-enrollment.

Fifth, the study examined the possibility of child work being compatible with schooling, and the conditions under which this was possible. Sixth, it addressed potential methodological issues in previous research related to endogeneity, spatial heterogeneity, and specification tests.

Additionally, I pointed out the possibility that more complex dynamics were operating between sociological, economic, and geographic factors. For instance, the impact of poverty on child labor may depend on the gender of the child or whether the child lives in a rural or urban setting. Similarly, there may be modifying effects within the factors themselves, so that the relationship to the household head, for example, may depend on other sociological factors, such as gender. This study found evidence for both of types of effects.

To be sure, additional research is required to better understand the complex dynamics between harmful child work and sociological, economic, and geographical factors. First, research that explicitly examines the determinants of human-capital detrimental child work needs to be carried out for other countries to see if previous findings hold up. Second, the current dataset did not permit examining the other type of harmful child work proposed here, namely the hazardous kind. Third, the current dataset also did not permit examining the possible impact of ethnicity and religion, both of which may be important determinants of child work (Bass, 2004). To the extent that this information is not already available, researchers and national statistical offices should attempt to collect it.

NOTES

1. Some studies talk about "child labor," others about "child work." It has been argued that "child work" concerns school-aged children engaged in lighter work, such as household chores, whereas "child labor" concerns the participation of school-aged children in the labor force on a regular basis, for the purpose of either supporting themselves or to supplement household income (Canagarajah & Coulombe, 1997, p. 3). Since both types potentially can be detrimental to a child's human capital (as discussed later), I use the more inclusive term "child work."
2. There is of course also the possibility that children may be able to combine school and work; for now, for the sake of the argument, I focus on the two extreme cases of either school or work.
3. See, however, O'Donnel, Van Doorslaer, and Rosati (2002); Beegle, Dehejia, and Gatti (2004); Rogers and Swinnerton (2002); and Dessy and Pallage (2005).
4. The dataset examined here does not include information on the first type of harmful child work.
5. The choice may also be affected by the supply of schooling and the complex factors associated therewith. This issue will be disregarded here, however, except for the possibility of the distance to the nearest primary and secondary school affecting the work choice. See Fuller and Rubinson (1992) for a review of the empirical evidence on how the state, competing economic interests, family, churches, and the schools themselves play independent roles in spurring or constraining the growth of mass schooling. Although their research focuses on economies in developed countries, much of the discussion is also applicable to economies in the developing world.
6. This obviously disregards possible intra-household bargaining over resources for children, which is beyond the scope of the analysis here, however. See the seminal work of Manser and Brown (1980) and McElroy and Horney (1981) on issues related to marriage and household decision making. For a review of family economics more generally, see also Bergstrom (1996).
7. There is, of course, still a possibility that these types of work-related activities will affect school achievement, even though they allow for school enrollment.
8. Again, I propose that there are two types of harmful child work: the one examined here and the type involving hazardous child work, which affects children's human capital through the impact on child health. This latter type, however, cannot be examined with the present dataset. While the dataset includes information on sickness and injuries, there is no information on whether these were work-related or not.
9. The Ghanaian education system currently entails 12 years pretertiary education: six years primary, three years junior secondary, and three years senior secondary. Students then enter tertiary education. There are also various types of technical, vocational, and non-formal education. Basic education – which consists of the first nine years of pretertiary education – is compulsory (and free) in Ghana. See Blunch (2005a) for more information on the Ghanaian educational system.
10. The exact question is: "Has [Name] been working full-time (roughly 5 full days a week) or part-time during the past 4 weeks?," where "part-time" implies either working less than five days per week or less than 8 hours per day.

11. There are 27 missing observations as compared to the analysis sample: this is due to the responses to the "part-time–full-time" work question for these children not being recorded.

12. The children living in the household may not necessarily be biologically related to the household or the household head. Apart from including this variable to capture this potentially important determinant of child work status – and thus also help ensuring valid inference on the other explanatory variables – the issue of child fostering is beyond the scope of this analysis. See Ainsworth (1996) for more on child fostering in West Africa.

13. Household expenditures are estimated based on a multitude of poverty predictors, e.g., how frequent the household gets meat to eat, whether the household uses toothpaste and toilet paper, and so on. See Fofack (1997) for details.

14. The exact question is: "If [Name] is not currently in school, explain why." The possible responses are: "Not of school age/Completed school," "Too far away," "Too expensive/Cannot afford," "Is working," "School is useless/uninteresting," "Illness," "Pregnancy," "Failed exam," "Got married," and "Other." Multiple responses are allowed.

15. Again, this is also one of the major reasons why I do not model the work and schooling decision simultaneously in a bivariate probit or multinomial logit, say: when the work-school decision in practice involve a choice of engaging in *either* work *or* schooling – and since most of the sample (almost 80%) attends school, anyway – it seems more worthwhile to focus on the work decision.

16. To conserve space, the results for these are not included in Table 4; they are available upon request.

17. Results are not shown here but are available upon request.

ACKNOWLEDGMENTS

I wish to thank Bruce Fuller and Emily Hannum for their support and encouragement of this work. Comments and suggestions from David Ribar and two anonymous referees helped greatly to improve this manuscript. Remaining errors and omissions are my own. The data were collected by the Ghana Statistical Service in collaboration with the World Bank and kindly provided by the Ghana Statistical Service. The views and opinions expressed here, however, are entirely those of the author and should not be attributed to the Ghana Statistical Service or the World Bank.

REFERENCES

Ainsworth, M. (1996). Economic aspects of child fostering in Côte d'Ivoire. In: T. P. Schultz (Ed.), *Research in population economics* (Vol. 8, pp. 25–62). Greenwich, CT and London: JAI Press.

Bass, L. E. (2004). *Child labor in Sub-Saharan Africa*. Boulder, CO: Lynne Rienner Publishers.
Basu, K., & Van, P. H. (1998). The economics of child labor. *American Economic Review, 88*(3), 412–427.
Becker, G. S. (1964). *Human capital*. New York: National Bureau of Economic Research.
Beegle, K., Dehejia, R., & Gatti, R. (2004). *Why should we care about child labor? The education, labor market and health consequences of child labor*. NBER Working Paper no. 10980. National Bureau of Economic Research, Cambridge, MA.
Bergstrom, T. C. (1996). Economics in a family way. *Journal of Economic Literature, 34*(4), 1903–1934.
Blunch, N.-H. (2005a). *Recent economic, political and social developments in Ghana: A background note*. Mimeo, Department of Economics, The George Washington University.
Blunch, N.-H. (2005b). *Skills, schooling and earnings in Ghana*. Mimeo, Department of Economics, The George Washington University.
Blunch, N.-H., Dar, A., Guarcello, L., Lyon, S., Ritualo, A., & Rosati, F. (2005). Child work in Zambia: A comparative study of survey instruments. *International Labour Review, 144*(2), 211–235.
Blunch, N.-H., & Verner, D. (2000). *Revisiting the link between poverty and child labor: The Ghanaian experience*. World Bank Research Working Paper no. 2488. World Bank, Washington, DC.
Buchmann, C. (2000). Family structure, parental perceptions, and child labor in Kenya: What factors determine who is enrolled in school? *Social Forces, 78*(4), 1349–1379.
Canagarajah, S., & Coulombe, H. (1997). *Child labor and schooling in Ghana*. Policy Research Working Paper no. 1844. World Bank, Washington, DC.
Canagarajah, S., & Nielsen, H. S. (2001). Child labor in Africa: A comparative study. *Annals of the American Academy of Political and Social Science, 575*, 71–91.
Chao, S., Agyemang-Mensah, N., Bhushan, I., Canacoo, V., Demesmaker, L., Grieko, M., Hancock, G., Kilo, M., Manalo, M., Mason, A., Mensah, P. Olawoye, J., & Steel, W. (1999). *Ghana: Gender analysis and policymaking for development*. World Bank Discussion Paper no. 403. World Bank, Washington, DC.
Clogg, C. C., Petkova, E., & Haritou, A. (1995). Statistical methods for comparing regression coefficients between models. *American Journal of Sociology, 100*(5), 1261–1293.
Clogg, C. C., Petkova, E., & Shihadeh, E. S. (1992). Statistical methods for analyzing collapsibility in regression models. *Journal of Educational Statistics, 17*(1), 51–74.
Dessy, S. E., & Pallage, S. (2005). A theory of the worst forms of child labour. *Economic Journal, 115*, 68–87.
Fofack, H. (1997). *Using poverty predictors as expenditure proxies for ranking households for poverty analysis*. Washington, DC: Mimeo, Institutional and Social Policy Division, Africa Region, World Bank.
Fuller, B., & Rubinson, R. (Eds) (1992). *The political construction of education: The state, school expansion, and economic change*. New York: Praeger.
Hausman, J. A. (1978). Specification tests in econometrics. *Econometrica, 46*, 1251–1271.
Huber, P. J. (1967). The behavior of maximum likelihood estimates under nonstandard conditions. In: *Proceedings of the 5th Berkeley symposium on mathematical statistics and probability* (Vol. 1). Berkeley, CA: University of California Press.
ILO. (1997). *IPEC at a glance*. Geneva: International Labour Organization.
Jensen, P., & Nielsen, H. S. (1997). Child labour or school attendance? Evidence from Zambia. *Journal of Population Economics, 10*, 407–424.

Lavy, V. (1996). School supply constraints and children's educational outcomes in rural Ghana. *Journal of Development Economics, 51*, 291–314.
Maitra, P., & Ray, R. (2002). The joint estimation of child participation in schooling and employment: Comparative evidence from three continents. *Oxford Development Studies, 30*(1), 41–62.
Manser, M., & Brown, M. (1980). Marriage and household decision-making: A bargaining analysis. *International Economic Review, 21*(1), 31–44.
McElroy, M. B., & Horney, M. J. (1981). Nash bargained household decisions: Toward a generalization of the theory of demand. *International Economic Review, 22*(2), 333–349.
Mincer, J. (1974). *Schooling, experience and earnings.* New York: National Bureau of Economic Research.
Mizon, G. E., & Marcellino, M. (Eds) (2002). *Encompassing.* Oxford: Oxford University Press.
Nieuwenhuys, O. (1996). The paradox of child labor and anthropology. *Annual Review of Anthropology, 25*, 237–251.
O'Donnel, O., Van Doorslaer, E., & Rosati, F. (2002). *Child labour and health: Evidence and research issues.* UCW Working Paper no. 1. Understanding Children's Work Project, Florence.
Rogers, C. A., & Swinnerton, K. A. (2002). *A theory of exploitative child labor.* Mimeo. Department of Economics, Georgetown University.
UNICEF. (1999). *The state of the world's children.* New York: Oxford University Press.
White, H. (1980). A heteroskedasticity-consistent covariance matrix estimator and a direct test for heteroskedasticity. *Econometrica, 48*(4), 817–830.
Wu, D.-M. (1973). Alternative tests of independence between stochastic regressors and disturbances. *Econometrica, 41*, 733–750.

APPENDIX A. DEFINITION OF DEPENDENT AND INDEPENDENT VARIABLES

Dependent Variable
Works   1 if main occupation is work, 0 otherwise

Independent Variables

Individual child characteristics
Female   1 if female, 0 otherwise
Age   Age
Age squared/100   Age squared
Child of head   1 if child of HH head, 0 otherwise
Disabled   1 if disabled, 0 otherwise

Household characteristics
Female household head   1 if head is female, 0 otherwise
Age of household head   Age of head
Age of household head/100   Age of head squared/100

Education of household head
  No education (reference category) — 1 if head has completed no education, 0 otherwise
  Some primary — 1 if head has completed some primary, 0 otherwise
  Primary — 1 if head has completed primary, 0 otherwise
  Middle/JSS — 1 if head has completed middle or junior secondary school, 0 otherwise
  Secondary or above — 1 if head has completed secondary or above, 0 otherwise
  Vocational, technical or other — 1 if head has completed vocational, technical or other education
  Log (per capita household expenditures) — Log (per capita household expenditures); for details, see Fofack (1997)
  Owns land — 1 if household owns land, 0 otherwise
  Owns cattle — 1 if household owns cattle, 0 otherwise

Community characteristics
  Water 30 min or more — 1 if nearest water source is 30 min or less, 0 otherwise
  Primary school 30 min or more — 1 if nearest primary school is 30 min or less, 0 otherwise
  Secondary school 30 min or more — 1 if nearest secondary school is 30 min or less, 0 otherwise
  Log (mean per capita household expenditures in community) — Log (mean per capita household expenditures in the community)
  Urban — 1 if urban location, 0 otherwise
  Western — 1 if Western region, 0 otherwise
  Central — 1 if Central region, 0 otherwise
  Greater Accra (reference category) — 1 if Greater Accra region, 0 otherwise
  Volta — 1 if Volta region, 0 otherwise
  Eastern — 1 if Eastern region, 0 otherwise
  Ashanti — 1 if Ashanti region, 0 otherwise
  Brong Ahafo — 1 if Brong Ahafo region, 0 otherwise
  Northern — 1 if Northern region, 0 otherwise
  Upper East — 1 if Upper East region, 0 otherwise
  Upper West — 1 if Upper West region, 0 otherwise

APPENDIX B. SUMMARY STATISTICS FOR ESTIMATION SAMPLES

Table B1. Descriptive Statistics for Estimation Samples: Full Sample and by Gender and Location.

	Full Sample		Girls		Boys		Rural		Urban	
	Mean	Standard Deviation	Mean	Standard Deviation	Mean	Standard Deviation	Mean	Standard Deviation	Mean	Standard Deviation
Individual child characteristics										
Working	0.132	0.338	0.145	0.352	0.120	0.325	0.162	0.368	0.053	0.225
Female	0.478	0.500	1.000	0.000	0.000	0.000	0.465	0.499	0.513	0.500
Age	10.814	1.984	10.769	1.992	10.856	1.975	10.734	1.973	11.026	1.998
Age squared/100	1.209	0.435	1.199	0.436	1.218	0.433	1.191	0.431	1.256	0.441
Child of HH head	0.769	0.422	0.749	0.434	0.788	0.409	0.781	0.414	0.737	0.440
Disabled	0.007	0.082	0.006	0.076	0.008	0.086	0.008	0.088	0.004	0.062
Household characteristics										
Female HH head	0.250	0.433	0.264	0.441	0.236	0.425	0.221	0.415	0.325	0.468
Age, HH head	49.532	12.739	49.669	13.085	49.406	12.413	49.657	12.893	49.203	12.321
Age squared/100, HH head	26.157	13.847	26.382	14.321	25.950	13.396	26.321	14.095	25.727	13.165
No education, HH head	0.458	0.498	0.459	0.498	0.457	0.498	0.503	0.500	0.339	0.473
Some primary, HH head	0.064	0.246	0.055	0.228	0.073	0.260	0.072	0.258	0.046	0.209
Primary, HH head	0.080	0.272	0.074	0.262	0.086	0.280	0.085	0.279	0.067	0.251
Middle/junior secondary, HH head	0.281	0.450	0.289	0.453	0.274	0.446	0.266	0.442	0.323	0.468
Secondary and above, HH head	0.052	0.223	0.060	0.237	0.046	0.209	0.025	0.156	0.125	0.330
Vocational/technical or other, HH head	0.064	0.244	0.063	0.243	0.064	0.245	0.050	0.217	0.101	0.301
Log (per capita HH expenditures)	11.835	0.473	11.852	0.487	11.821	0.460	11.734	0.409	12.101	0.524
HH owns land	0.465	0.499	0.450	0.498	0.479	0.500	0.543	0.498	0.261	0.439
HH owns cattle	0.105	0.307	0.098	0.297	0.112	0.315	0.132	0.339	0.034	0.181

Community characteristics										
Water 30 min or more	0.192	0.394	0.187	0.390	0.197	0.398	0.232	0.422	0.087	0.282
Primary school 30 min or more	0.192	0.394	0.182	0.386	0.201	0.400	0.217	0.413	0.124	0.329
Secondary school 30 min or more	0.834	0.372	0.825	0.380	0.842	0.365	0.897	0.305	0.669	0.471
Average log (per capita HH expenditures) in community	12.137	0.303	12.147	0.309	12.127	0.296	12.016	0.215	12.455	0.267
Urban	0.276	0.447	0.296	0.456	0.257	0.437	0.000	0.000	1.000	0.000
Western	0.118	0.323	0.124	0.330	0.112	0.316	0.134	0.341	0.076	0.266
Central	0.092	0.289	0.093	0.290	0.091	0.287	0.095	0.293	0.083	0.276
Greater Accra	0.098	0.298	0.108	0.311	0.089	0.285	0.013	0.112	0.323	0.468
Volta	0.100	0.300	0.100	0.300	0.100	0.300	0.119	0.323	0.051	0.220
Eastern	0.129	0.335	0.126	0.331	0.132	0.338	0.136	0.343	0.109	0.312
Ashanti	0.133	0.339	0.137	0.344	0.129	0.335	0.122	0.327	0.161	0.368
Brong Ahafo	0.106	0.308	0.099	0.299	0.112	0.315	0.118	0.323	0.074	0.262
Northern	0.138	0.344	0.125	0.331	0.149	0.356	0.155	0.362	0.092	0.289
Upper East	0.055	0.228	0.056	0.229	0.054	0.227	0.071	0.257	0.013	0.113
Upper West	0.032	0.176	0.032	0.176	0.032	0.177	0.038	0.191	0.017	0.130
Number of observations	11,968		5,854		6,114		8,163		3,805	

Note: "HH" denotes "household." Estimations incorporate sampling design (weights and clustering).

DEMAND FOR SCHOOLING AMONG ORPHANS IN ZIMBABWE

Craig Gundersen, Thomas Kelly and Kyle Jemison

ABSTRACT

We examine the effect of orphan status on school enrollment in Zimbabwe, a country strongly impacted by the HIV/AIDS pandemic with a rapidly growing population of orphans. Using data from 2002, after controlling for other determinants of enrollment we find that orphans are less likely to attend school than non-orphans. Two additional results have implications for targeting: we find that the effect of being an orphan is especially large for older children and that, after controlling for previous education, the effect of being an orphan on school enrollment sharply declines.

INTRODUCTION

The HIV/AIDS crisis has had an enormous impact on sub-Saharan Africa. Of particular import is the resulting dramatic increase in the number of orphans. In the early 1980s, few children were orphans due to HIV/AIDS; in 2004, over 12.3 million children in sub-Saharan Africa were orphans (UN-AIDS, 2004). The situation is not expected to improve anytime soon. By 2010 the number of children orphaned by AIDS is expected to exceed 35 million (Deininger, Garcia, & Subbarao, 2003). Further compounding these problems is the ever-present deep poverty in sub-Saharan Africa and the toll the HIV/AIDS crisis has taken on their economies (Dixon, McDonald, & Roberts, 2001). One possible consequence of this surge in the number of orphans is a decline in school enrollment. In light of the well-established direct and indirect benefits from schooling, a decline in school enrollment would have enormous consequences for the futures of these countries.

The situation in Zimbabwe is even more critical than in the other countries in the region. There the rate of orphaning is growing rapidly. The best estimates are that 20–30% of all children are now orphans, over three-quarters of whom have been orphaned due to HIV/AIDS (Catholic Relief Services, 2004; UNAIDS, 2004). This substantial number of orphans occurs in a country with recent dramatic increases in poverty due to the lingering effects of drought, triple-digit inflation, political strife, and international isolation. The decline in life expectancy from over 50 years in the mid-to-late 1990s to 43 years in 2003 is evidence of the toll the HIV/AIDS crisis and poverty has taken on Zimbabwe in just the previous five years.

The dire situation in Zimbabwe warrants a close examination, both in its own right, but also to ascertain what may happen in similarly situated countries if their death toll due to HIV/AIDS continues to escalate, especially if it occurs alongside other economic and non-economic challenges. (Other countries facing conditions similar to Zimbabwe include Botswana, Lesotho, and Swaziland.) Because of its status, we concentrate on the determinants of school enrollment by orphans in Zimbabwe.

While becoming an orphan is obviously an extremely emotional event for children and impacts the restructuring of households to accommodate orphans, the effect of orphan status on school enrollment is not immediately clear. As a consequence, the literature has reached mixed conclusions about the school enrollment status of orphans versus non-orphans in sub-Saharan Africa (Yamano & Jayne, 2005; Kobiané & Marcoux, 2005; Evans & Miguel, 2004; Case, Paxson, & Ableidinger, 2004; Ainsworth & Filmer, 2002; Shapiro & Tambashe, 2001; Lloyd & Blanc, 1996; Foster et al., 1995; Nankhuni, 2005).[1]

In this paper, we contribute to the understanding of the effect of orphan status on school enrollment in a country with a disproportionately high number of orphans by answering three broad questions. First, controlling for other factors, are orphans less likely than non-orphans to attend school? For this baseline question, we use a sample composed of households with orphans and households without orphans. While we can control for observed characteristics, we cannot control for unobserved characteristics that would influence the decision to care for an orphan. If these characteristics vary in some systematic way across households, our estimates of the effect of being an orphan on the probability of attending school will be biased.

To address these potential biases, we pose our second question: Among families with their own children and orphans, are orphans more or less likely to attend school than a family's own children? Along with addressing the biases in what types of households take in orphans, we are able to address the extent of favoritism parents have for their children over those taken in as orphans (Bishai et al., 2003; Case et al., 2004; Ntozi, 1997).

Our final question: Is the enrollment of orphans a function of previous investments in education? One possible reason why orphans have differential enrollment rates is because their schooling was interrupted in order to care and/or provide for their dying parents. If their schooling was interrupted, the economic returns to a year of education may also be diminished. To test whether school interruption matters for the enrollment of orphans, we restricted our sample to children who attended school the previous year. Doing so also allowed us to consider in greater detail the possible favoritism shown by parents toward their own children versus orphans.

We begin this paper with a review of how the HIV/AIDS crisis has influenced the education system in sub-Saharan Africa and then place this in the broader literature of the determinants of education. We then turn to a description of our data and a survey conducted by Catholic Relief Services (CRS) with the support of the U.S. Agency for International Development (USAID) in 2002. This is followed by a section on the methods we use to estimate our primary model and the two extensions to this model.

After some summary statistics, we answer the three primary questions posed in this paper. We find, controlling for other factors including economic status (employment status, current consumption, and assets), characteristics of the household and child, and place-of-residence, that orphans are less likely to attend school than non-orphans. The difference between the likelihood of orphans and non-orphans attending school is especially large for older children. This holds for both the full sample and for the sample restricted to households with own children and orphans. There is some evidence, however, that after controlling for previous education, orphans and non-orphans *within the same household* are equally likely to attend school.

BACKGROUND

The household's decision-making process regarding the demand for education for children is a complex one. A number of the factors affecting this decision are relatively well understood in the literature. For instance, the effect of household composition (Al-Qudsi, 2003; Fuller & Liang, 1999; Lloyd & Blanc, 1996; Parish & Willis, 1993), community characteristics (Binder, 1999; Connelly & Zheng, 2003), the quality of schooling (Filmer, 2003), and wealth (Deolalikar, 1997; Filmer & Pritchett, 1998; Glewwe & Jacoby, 2004; Lloyd & Blanc, 1996; Nielsen, 2001) have important and predictable effects on the demand for education.

There are other determinants of the demand for education that are less well studied and understood, however. Principal among these are factors that the HIV/AIDS crisis has thrown into sharp relief, especially the impact of orphaning on children. We now turn to the possible effects of various factors on the school enrollment of orphans in Zimbabwe and in sub-Saharan Africa.

The presence of orphans in a family constitutes a serious financial burden (Baylies, 2002). Since most schools in Zimbabwe require fees and related expenses to cover school maintenance, utilities, and school activities,[2] these costs alongside the opportunity cost of having a child in school, may lead to non-enrollment. But if household size is controlled for, this alone should not imply a lower probability of enrollment for orphans. Education is costly, but it is equally costly for orphans and non-orphans – or at least, there is no a priori reason to expect it to be more costly for orphans.

While the costs of educating an orphan may be the same as educating one's own child, a caregiver may put a higher priority on their own children's education in comparison to an orphan's education. The notion that caregivers' actions are motivated by biological relatedness is both intuitively appealing and consistent with Hamilton's Rule in evolutionary biology, which states that investment in children is determined by the closeness of biological relatedness (Hamilton, 1964). Even without any "biological preference" for their own children, caregivers who perceive education as an investment good (one that will pay off when the child remits income at some future point) may favor their own children if the parent believes these remittances are more likely to be received from one's own children than from an orphan. This would lead to higher rates of school enrollment by non-orphans.

Even if caregivers believe they will reap the same percentage of future income from their own children as they would from orphans, they may believe the rates of return will be higher for their own children. This may hold true especially if an orphan's schooling was interrupted out of the need to care for their parents, to work to replace a parent's lost income and funeral expenses, to increase household production, or for some combination of these.[3] Additionally, when the expected bereavement occurs due to a parent's death, the children are often mentally, physically, and emotionally unprepared to deal with its consequences. The cultural taboo of talking about death in many African settings – including Zimbabwe – means that children tend to be unprepared for a parent's death, despite the long period of illness usually associated with HIV/AIDS (UNAIDS, 2003; UNICEF, 2003; UNAIDS, 2001; Gilborn et al., 2005). This lack of preparedness heightens their distress, and combined with a lack of emotional support and guidance from adults, compounds their uncertainty about their future and often contributes to children dropping out of school.

The effect of orphan status may also be influenced by other factors. For instance, Ainsworth (1996) offers evidence from Cote d'Ivoire that families often take in orphaned younger children to gain additional labor for their household, including childcare and other domestic work. The relationship of the orphan to the household head may also matter. For instance, Shapiro & Tambashe (2001) report some limited evidence that at older ages (15–19), foster children may have greater access to education when they enter a household where the household head is an older brother or sister. Programs specifically designed for the benefit of orphans may also lead to higher enrollment rates among orphans. Alongside these two possible reasons for similar school enrollment rates for orphans and non-orphans, there is a long tradition of child fostering in sub-Saharan Africa (Foster et al., 1995; Kamali et al., 1996).

The evidence as to whether orphans are less likely than non-orphans to enroll in school in sub-Saharan Africa is not conclusive. Shapiro & Tambashe (2001) found that children who are being fostered have lower educational achievement than other children in the household in Congo; Yamano & Jayne (2005) and Evans & Miguel (2004) reported that parental death has a significant impact on school participation or enrollment in Kenya; and Case et al. (2004) found that orphans are significantly less likely to be enrolled in 10 sub-Saharan Africa countries. On the other hand, there is also evidence from other studies that orphans are no less likely to attend school. Lloyd and Blanc (1996), for instance, found that the death of a parent has little impact on children's educational chances in a range of African countries. Ainsworth & Filmer (2002) reported that while there is a significant difference between orphan and non-orphan enrollment, this gap is relatively unimportant and is dwarfed by the gap between rich and poor households.

In Zimbabwe the results about the effect of orphan status on school enrollment have been mixed as well. Foster et al. (1995) found that in families of similar economic status, orphans in peri-urban Zimbabwe were not particularly disadvantaged in comparison with non-orphans. Conversely, Case et al. (2004) found, ceteris paribus, lower rates of school enrollment for orphans based on 1999 data from the Zimbabwe Demographic and Health Survey (DHS), although data from 1994 was less conclusive.

DATA AND METHODS

Data Description

The data used in this paper come from a 2002 survey conducted by CRS, with funding from the USAID. The collection of this new data was necessitated by the rapid deterioration of conditions in Zimbabwe since 1999 when the DHS was conducted.

The survey was constructed from the sampling frame of the 2002 Zimbabwe census. From this frame, the following provinces were selected to represent both urban and rural areas: Manicaland, Midlands, Masvingo, Matabeleland South, Bulawayo, and Mashonaland West. Within the districts in these provinces, a sample of households with children under the age of 18 was selected through the following steps: (a) sampling of wards within these districts; (b) sampling of villages within each ward; (c) sampling of Enumeration Areas (EAs) within each village; and (d) sampling of households in each selected EA. (Wards, villages, and EAs were selected with probability proportional to size.) For each household, the household head provided information on the sociodemographic characteristics (age, sex, illness status of parents and/or parental survival, orphan status, education, food security status) of all household members. The final sample consisted of 3,645 children between the ages of 6 and 16 in 1,416 households. The survey instrument was administered in Shona and Ndebele by trained enumerators.

The orphan status of a child is, of course, central to our analyses. We define an orphan as a child whose parents are both deceased, or as a child with one deceased parent if the child does not live with the surviving parent. In our data, however, we do not observe why each child was orphaned (i.e., whether it was due to his or her parent dying from AIDS or from some other cause). On the advice of Zimbabwean and international stakeholders, this information was not gathered due to the extreme stigma attached with HIV/AIDS in Zimbabwe. (For additional information on the reasons for reluctance to reveal HIV/AIDS status in Zimbabwe, see Gilborn, Nyonyintono, Kabumbuli, & Jagwe-Wadda, 2001.) Although we cannot say which children were orphaned by AIDS, UNAIDS (2004, p. 26) estimates the figure to be about 78%.

We note two further issues about our study's sample as it pertains to orphans. First, the sample frame excludes children who are living on their own or in orphanages. Presumably these children are worse off than orphans in households. Second, some children in our sample may be living with other relatives to accrue certain advantages, as for instance the opportunity to attend superior schools, which suggests they would live with other relatives even if both their parents were living. (See Lloyd & Blanc, 1996, to learn more about why children live away from their parents.)

We are unable to identify these orphans in our data, and presumably they are different from children who are in households solely due to the death of one or both parents. In light of the relatively high enrollment rates across Zimbabwe, the need to send children to live with relatives is perhaps less than in other countries. Based on this, we expect the number of children in this category to be fairly small.

Model Description

In order to answer our first question, "Are orphans more or less likely than non-orphans to attend school?" we estimate the following probit MLE model:

$$\text{ATTEND}_k = 1 \text{ if } \text{ATTEND}_k^* > 0; \text{ATTEND}_k = 0 \text{ otherwise}$$
$$\text{ATTEND}_k^* = \beta X_i + \gamma Y_i + \lambda C_k + \alpha \text{ORPHANCHILD}_k + u_k \quad (1)$$

where k denotes a measure of school attendance (described below); k denotes a child; i denotes a household; X is a vector of covariates reflecting a household's economic resources; Y is a vector of covariates reflecting a household's demographic characteristics; C is a vector of covariates reflecting a child's characteristics; ORPHANCHILD = 1 if the child is an orphan, 0 otherwise; and u is an error term. In this model, we are primarily concerned with the sign, magnitude, and statistical significance of α.

There is reason to believe, however, that the estimate of α might be biased due to the correlation between ORPHANCHILD and u. If, say, orphans are more likely to be in families with (unobserved) resources that lead to higher probabilities of attending school, the estimate will be biased upwards. Conversely, if, say, there are unobserved resource constraints affecting families taking in orphans, this would lead to a downward bias.

We control for these unobserved factors by reestimating Eq. (1) with a sample restricted to households with their own children and with orphans.

In other words, households with only orphans or only their own children are removed from the sample. By restricting our sample in this manner, we eliminate the unobserved factors influencing a household's decisions. This sample restriction allows us to address our second question: "Among families with their own children and orphans, are orphans more or less likely to attend school than a family's own children?"

There is also reason to believe that the coefficient α (in either the model containing all children or the one containing households with their own children and orphans) is influenced by the previous educational attainment of orphans. This motivates our third question: "Is the enrollment of orphans a function of their previous investments in education?" For example, if orphans were not enrolled in school previously while still resident in their parents' household because they had dropped out of school to assist their parents, foster caregivers may decide not to enroll the orphan children in school. In this context, the caregiver's decision may be due to factors unrelated to any preferential treatment caregivers give to their own children – that is, unrelated to the child being an orphan.

To make this possibility more concrete, consider the case of the caregiver who has enough resources to enroll either her own child *or* an orphan in school. Suppose further that she considers education to be an economic investment, and that her share in the future return from the investment will be the same for either child – i.e., she believes both children will "repay" her in similar amounts out of their future income. If the children are of the same age and the orphan was forced to miss school for some time due to the type of interruptions detailed above, he would have to repeat grades, making him enter the labor market at a later date than the other child. This would delay that child's "repayment" to the caregiver. Thus, even without showing any favoritism to her own child, this scenario would motivate the caregiver to enroll her own child rather than the orphan. To test the effect of past schooling attainment on school enrollment, we estimate Eq. (1) on samples restricted to children who attended school the previous year.

RESULTS

Descriptive Statistics

In this section we provide our results for the basic descriptive statistics, and in the following section we report those for our multivariate models. The results from the multivariate models serve as the basis for our answers to the

Table 1. School Enrollment Status of Orphans and Non-Orphans.

	Orphan	Non-Orphan
Attending school, ages 6–16 (%)	77.05	86.73
Attending school, ages 6–10 (%)	81.67	86.00
Attending school, ages 11–16 (%)	73.85	87.27
Girls attending school, ages 6–16 (%)	76.81	86.87
Girls attending school, ages 6–10 (%)	80.80	87.08
Girls attending school, ages 11–16 (%)	74.06	86.73
Boys attending school, ages 6–16 (%)	77.92	86.56
Boys attending school, ages 6–10 (%)	82.69	85.01
Boys attending school, ages 11–16 (%)	74.60	87.76

three primary questions we posed at the outset of this paper. In Table 1 we display the school enrollment rates for orphans and non-orphans.[4] We limit the sample to children between the ages of 6 and 16, since these are the ages children are most likely to attend school in Zimbabwe.[5]

For all children of school-going age, orphans are less likely to attend school and the gap is large – 77.0% of orphans attend school versus 86.7% of non-orphans.[6] The enrollment rates of orphans are lower than those reported in earlier studies on Zimbabwe which used nationally representative data (Ainsworth, Beegle, & Koda, 2000; Fig. 2). The increased impact of the HIV/AIDS crisis in Zimbabwe combined with deteriorating economic conditions and political unrest discussed above may be two of the most likely reasons for this decline.

We further break our sample into two age groups – children aged 6–10 and children aged 11–16. We do so to reflect the drop-off in school enrollment that often occurs as the opportunity cost of remaining in school increases (Filmer & Pritchett, 1998). Among orphans, the school enrollment rates fall from 81.7 to 73.9% as children age. Among non-orphans, however, there is not a similar drop-off. This decline in school enrollment among older orphans is consistent with orphans not attending school due to gaps in their previous school enrollments while caring for their parents. Fig. 1 shows in greater detail the difference in school enrollment for orphans and non-orphans as children age. As can be seen, the gap generally widens beginning at age 11, and increases appreciably at ages 15 and 16.

As discussed above, in other countries there is evidence that girls whose parents suffer from HIV/AIDS are especially likely to drop out of school to assume household and market duties. However, we find that within the

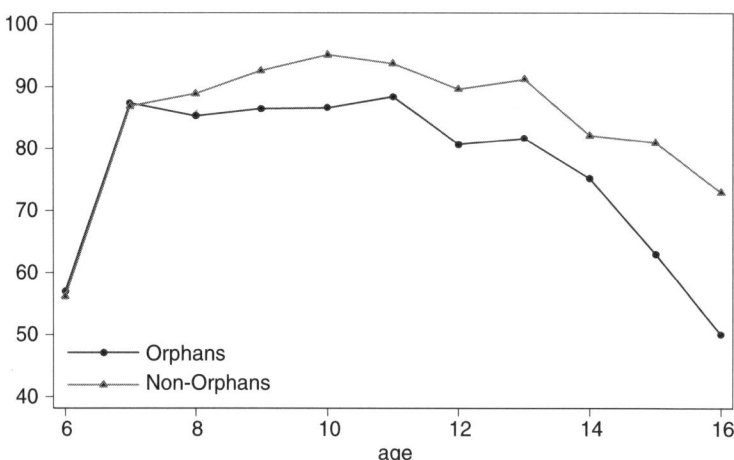

Fig. 1. School Attendance Rates in Zimbabwe by Orphan Status and Age.

categories of orphans and non-orphans, boys and girls, independent of their age, are about as likely to attend school (Table 1).

We now consider whether differences in the economic well-being of households is a possible explanation for differences in school enrollment rates of orphans and non-orphans (Table 2). In our data are numerous variables reflecting the economic status of households. The primary categories reflecting the employment status of the household head are no formal employment, employment as a general worker, subsistence farmer, informal trader, and skilled worker. As seen in column 1 of Table 2, the majority of the sample has no formal employment, with the second most prevalent category being subsistence farmer. (As in Table 1, the sample is restricted to children between the ages of 6 and 16.)

The type of dwelling is a measure of a household's assets and, in order of wealth, these can be categorized as brick and corrugated roof; brick and thatch roof; and pole and dagga.[7] We use three measures of food security: the usual number of meals eaten per day; the adequacy of the household's food intake as perceived by the household head; and whether members of the household eat anything between meals. Based on the data, the average household eats two meals a day, never has an adequate amount of food, and never eats anything between meals. The inclusion of information about employment, assets, and current consumption provides an advantage over other data sets, which do not contain information on all three of these dimensions of economic status.[8]

Table 2. Comparisons of Children by Orphan Status.

	All Children	Orphans	Non-Orphans
Employment			
No formal employment	0.578	0.653	0.535
General worker	0.058	0.049	0.063
Subsistence farmer	0.154	0.133	0.166
Informal trader	0.062	0.049	0.070
Skilled worker	0.070	0.032	0.092
Type of land use			
Communal	0.565	0.540	0.580
Small holder farmer	0.020	0.023	0.018
Urban	0.355	0.369	0.347
Peri-urban area	0.020	0.031	0.014
Resettlement	0.025	0.028	0.023
Type of dwelling			
Brick and corrugated roof	0.568	0.591	0.554
Pole and dagga	0.303	0.282	0.315
Brick and thatch roof	0.119	0.116	0.120
Number of meals per day			
Three	0.261	0.237	0.275
Two	0.554	0.586	0.535
One	0.184	0.176	0.188
Adequate amount of food			
Always	0.101	0.052	0.129
Sometimes	0.321	0.338	0.312
Rarely	0.168	0.157	0.175
Never	0.408	0.452	0.383
Eat anything between meals			
Always	0.020	0.006	0.028
Sometimes	0.102	0.075	0.118
Rarely	0.053	0.061	0.048
Never	0.748	0.777	0.731
Household characteristics			
Household size:			
Two to four persons	0.210	0.246	0.190
Five to eight persons	0.449	0.405	0.475
Nine or more persons	0.166	0.181	0.158
Age of household head	47.304	51.600	44.832
Head of household is female	0.483	0.428	0.577
Characteristics of child			
Child is female	0.509	0.517	0.505
Age of child	11.253	11.204	11.339

Table 2. (*Continued*)

	All Children	Orphans	Non-Orphans
Province			
Bulawayo	0.323	0.347	0.309
Manicaland	0.244	0.239	0.247
Mashonaland West	0.235	0.253	0.224
Masvingo	0.052	0.052	0.052
Midlands	0.094	0.073	0.106
Matebeleland South	0.050	0.033	0.059

Note: Sample is restricted to children between the ages of 6 and 16.

In our sample orphans are much more likely to live in households whose head has no formal employment (Table 2, column 2). They are also less food secure insofar as they are less likely to always have an adequate amount of food and are less likely to always or sometimes have something to eat between meals. These results suggest that, on average, orphans are living in households that are not as well-off as households with no orphans. This contrasts with earlier work in other countries that speculated that better-off households are more likely to foster orphans (Barnett & Blaikie, 1992).

Our findings are consistent, however, with more recent work by Ainsworth and Filmer (2002, Figs. 11 and 12) which found orphans in Zimbabwe to be concentrated among households in the lower end of the wealth distribution. Whether the concentration of orphans in their study and in this paper is part of a broader trend in sub-Saharan Africa or is only specific to Zimbabwe is worth pursuing in future research.

The measures of household characteristics we used are similar to those in these other analyses – household size, the age of the household head, and whether the household head is female. As seen in column 1, the average household has five to eight persons, has a head who is 47 years old, and is about equally likely to have a female or male head. The comparison in columns 2 and 3 indicates that, in comparison to non-orphans, orphans are, on average, much more likely to be in households headed by a male – 57.2% versus 42.3% – and to be in households headed by an older person – 51.6 years of age versus 44.8 years of age. The effect of these on school enrollment is not immediately clear, although some evidence suggests that older caregivers are likely to have less education than younger caregivers which, due to the intergenerational transmission of educational attainment, may lead to lower probabilities of attending school (National AIDS Council, 2004). Table 2 also indicates whether a child is female, the age of the child, and the province of residence.

Model Results

The descriptive statistics found in Tables 1 and 2 indicate that orphans are less likely to attend school, and tend to be in less affluent families than non-orphans. Using the model in Eq. (1) and the subsequent restrictions on the sample, we now consider whether the more limited resources of households with orphans is responsible for their lower school enrollment rates, or if being an orphan still has explanatory power after controlling for other factors. The results are found in Table 3.

Question 1: Estimates of the Effect of Orphan Status – All Children. For the results in the first column of Table 3, our sample includes all children from 6 to 16 years of age.[9] Our results indicate that the effect of being an orphan on school enrollment is both statistically significant and important. All else equal, an orphan has a 9.1% lower probability of school enrollment than a non-orphan.

In order to determine whether the determinants of schooling differ systematically by age, we next divided our sample in two. The results in columns 2 and 3 of Table 3 are for the subsamples of children with ages from 6 to 10 and from 11 to 16. For older children, the effect of being an orphan on school enrollment is particularly large; ceteris paribus, older orphans are 13.8% less likely than older non-orphans to attend school. For younger children, being an orphan has no effect on school enrollment. The effect of being an orphan appears to be largely associated with older children.

Among the variables associated with household characteristics, we found that only the age of the head of household was significant, and only for older children. As is true in other countries throughout the region (World Bank, 2001), the data on the children themselves showed that older children – both orphans and non-orphans – are less likely to attend school in Zimbabwe. The effect of age appears to be primarily relevant for older children (columns 2 and 3, Table 3).

In addition to the usual reasons for the strong effect of age on school attendance among older children – viz., leaving school to increase time spent in household production or the labor market – the possibility of greater exposure to HIV/AIDS in a school setting might deter some parents or caregivers from sending their children to school (Kelly, 2000).

While of the expected inverse relation with the probability of school enrollment, the effect of being a girl is insignificant. The sex of the household head also has no statistically significant effect on school enrollment.

Table 3. Estimates of the Impact of Orphan Status and Other Variables on School Enrollment.

	Children from 6 to 16 Years	Children from 6 to 10 Years	Children from 11 to 16 Years
Orphan	−0.284**	−0.097	−0.446**
	(0.063)	(0.097)	(0.081)
Age of child	−0.018**	0.309**	−0.205**
	(0.009)	(0.032)	(0.020)
Child is female	−0.029	−0.003	−0.049
	(0.052)	(0.084)	(0.070)
Head of household is female	−0.085	−0.092	−0.129
	(0.066)	(0.099)	(0.084)
Age of household head	0.003	−0.003	0.006**
	(0.002)	(0.004)	(0.003)
Household size	−0.012	0.004	−0.024
	(0.018)	(0.025)	(0.022)
Sometimes or always adequate food	0.194**	0.200**	0.226**
	(0.069)	(0.099)	(0.092)
No formal employment	−0.004	−0.026	−0.007
	(0.065)	(0.095)	(0.085)
Brick and corrugated roof	0.077	0.133	0.025
	(0.082)	(0.113)	(0.108)
Brick and thatch roof	−0.029	0.006	−0.049
	(0.111)	(0.166)	(0.145)
Lives on land used for farming	−0.115	−0.065	−0.065
	(0.093)	(0.203)	(0.111)
Bulawayo	−0.092	−0.427	0.039
	(0.166)	(0.285)	(0.199)
Mashonaland West	−0.363**	−0.656**	−0.243
	(0.154)	(0.269)	(0.186)
Masvingo	0.224	0.296	0.170
	(0.213)	(0.331)	(0.272)
Manicaland	−0.165	−0.383	−0.124
	(0.157)	(0.269)	(0.186)
Midlands	0.012	−0.316	0.196
	(0.178)	(0.297)	(0.218)
Number of observations	3645	1525	2120

Notes: Standard errors in parentheses. The sample in the first column is restricted to all children between the ages of 6 and 16.
**$p<0.05$.

Our measure of current consumption, whether a household sometimes or always has adequate food, was positive and statistically significant. This is one indication that the opportunity cost of keeping children in school for these households is lower than for other households. While not completely offsetting the effect of being an orphan, orphans in better-off households (as measured by food adequacy) are almost as likely as non-orphans in worse-off households to attend school. This is consistent with the findings of Ainsworth et al. (2000) for Tanzania where orphans in "better-off" families do not see delayed enrollment. However, it contrasts with our finding regarding household dwellings, which found no statistically significant difference in school enrollment among families based on the structural quality of their house.

Question 2: Estimates of the Effect of Orphan Status – Children in Households with both Orphans and Own Children. In Table 3, our sample consists of three types of households: those with their own children and orphans; those with only orphans; and those with only their own children. When we interpret the coefficient on orphan status in these tables, it is not immediately clear, therefore, whether the coefficient reflects the orphan status of a child or unobserved factors that influence the decision to take in an orphan. To correct for this possible selection bias associated with the decision to take in an orphan, we now limit our sample to households that include both their own children and orphans (Table 4).[10]

The importance of being an orphan decreases once we correct for this selection bias (Table 4). While still statistically significant, orphans are now just 6.1% less likely to attend school, a drop from 9.1% for the full sample. Despite the reduction, the effect of being an orphan remains large. This is important. Even after controlling for the possibility that unobserved factors influencing the decision to adopt an orphan are influencing the decision to enroll an orphan, these children are still disadvantaged by being an orphan in someone else's home. As seen in column (2) of Table 4, the effect of being an orphan is still insignificant for the sample of young children. For older children, however, the effect is diminished only slightly, from a 13.8% probability of school enrollment for the full sample to 11.7%. Insofar as our restricted sample allows us to portray caregiver favoritism for their own children, this effect is present for older but not younger children.

Question 3: Estimates of the Effect of Orphan Status – The Impact of Previous Enrollment. In our final set of estimates, we isolate one additional factor that might influence a caregiver's decision about whether to send an orphan to school: the child's enrollment history. We do this by estimating Eq. (1) on a sample of children who attended school the previous year.[11] In the first panel of Table 5 the sample includes all children, while in the second

Table 4. Estimates of the Impact of Orphan Status and Other Variables on School Enrollment – Households with Orphans and Non-Orphans.

	Children from 6 to 16 Years	Children from 6 to 10 Years	Children from 11 to 16 Years
Orphan	−0.188**	0.011	−0.381**
	(0.082)	(0.123)	(0.115)
Age of child	−0.036**	0.283**	−0.237**
	(0.013)	(0.045)	(0.028)
Child is female	−0.025	−0.050	−0.028
	(0.077)	(0.119)	(0.102)
Head of household is female	−0.069	−0.140	−0.065
	(0.093)	(0.133)	(0.122)
Age of household head	0.003	−0.008	0.009**
	(0.003)	(0.005)	(0.004)
Household size	−0.019	0.007	−0.036
	(0.029)	(0.038)	(0.033)
Sometimes or always adequate food	0.157*	0.053	0.261**
	(0.091)	(0.134)	(0.123)
No formal employment	−0.021	−0.055	−0.031
	(0.090)	(0.129)	(0.121)
Brick and corrugated roof	0.036	0.047	0.049
	(0.118)	(0.155)	(0.167)
Brick and thatch roof	−0.187	0.105	−0.326*
	(0.149)	(0.210)	(0.198)
Lives on land used for farming	−0.044	0.036	0.202
	(0.156)	(0.339)	(0.190)
Bulawayo	−0.095	−0.293	−0.063
	(0.257)	(0.478)	(0.335)
Mashonaland West	−0.289	−0.462	−0.225
	(0.251)	(0.474)	(0.329)
Masvingo	0.299	0.027	0.422
	(0.296)	(0.515)	(0.388)
Manicaland	−0.067	−0.168	−0.082
	(0.264)	(0.476)	(0.345)
Midlands	0.035	−0.140	0.295
	(0.280)	(0.489)	(0.363)
Number of observations	1725	733	992

Notes: Standard errors in parentheses. The sample in all three columns is restricted to children living in households with orphans and non-orphaned children. The sample in the first column is restricted to all children between the ages of 6 and 16.
*$p<0.1$.
**$p<0.05$.

Table 5. Estimates of the Impact of Orphan Status and Other Variables on School Enrollment – Children Attending School, Previous Year.

	Children from 7 to 16 Years	Children from 7 to 10 Years	Children from 11 to 16 Years
	All Children		
Orphan	−0.229**	0.010	−0.309**
	(0.100)	(0.191)	(0.112)
	Children in Households with Orphans and Non-Orphans		
Orphan	−0.163	−0.103	−0.246
	(0.142)	(0.249)	(0.161)

Notes: Standard errors in parentheses. The other covariates in the model (not displayed) are for the same variables as in Tables 3 and 4.
**$p<0.05$.

panel the sample is for children in families with their own children and orphans.[12] (The coefficients on the other variables in the model are suppressed but are available from the authors upon request.) Columns 1–3 mirror the samples from Tables 2 and 3.

For the sample of all children between the ages of 7 and 16, the effect of being an orphan declines somewhat. When our model is estimated for the subsample of households with orphans and their own children, we find that orphan status is no longer a statistically significant predictor of attendance. The effect of orphan status is also statistically insignificant for the sample of older children (column 3) where the effect of orphan status in our previous estimates was particularly strong. So, as long as a child was enrolled last year, whether the child is an orphan or not makes no difference as to the probability of their enrollment in the current year. While this is only one measure of a child's propensity to continue in school, our result is consistent with caregivers not giving preferential treatment to their own children.

This conclusion should be tempered somewhat by a consideration of the timing of when a child becomes an orphan. When we restrict our sample to children who did not attend school the previous year, we include (1) orphans who were not orphans the previous year and (2) orphans who were orphans the previous year. To test our conjectures about the role of previous enrollment, we would have liked to include only orphans who became orphans in the year of the survey. In our data, however, we were unable to identify when a child became an orphan.

Moreover, even for orphans who had been orphaned for more than one year, a subset of these may have been with caregivers whose enrollment decisions were based on the needs of the orphaned child rather than due to preferential treatment for their own children. Future research may wish to examine whether our results about the diminished effect of orphan status among households with their own children and orphans still holds when the timing of orphaning is available.

CONCLUSION

In comparison with most developing countries, the absolute levels of school enrollment in Zimbabwe are high. However, our results suggest reasons to be concerned about the future as the AIDS epidemic continues. Zimbabwe has a rapidly growing population of orphans, the overwhelming majority of whom have been orphaned due to AIDS.

Across several specifications, we find that older orphans are less likely to enroll in school than non-orphans. This, coupled with the fact that the percentage of children who are orphans is growing rapidly, suggests that high average enrollments may not continue in the future. Of further concern is that this rapid growth in orphans can be traced to the HIV/AIDS pandemic. Attendance in school has been shown to be among the most successful and cost-effective means of preventing HIV/AIDS infection (Meyer, 2003). For example, in Zimbabwe secondary education has been shown to have a protective effect against HIV infection for girls that extends at least into early adulthood (Gregson, Waddell, & Chandiwana, 2001).[13]

If children at risk are failing to attend school, an opportunity to break the cycle of infection is being missed. Interventions to increase enrollment among orphans are therefore critical not only for the educational benefits that accrue to the child and those that benefit the broader society, but because they are a critical tool in controlling the pandemic. Given Zimbabwe's relatively extensive system of school facilities, supply is not the key constraint to providing quality universal education. Rather, interventions designed to maintain and improve enrollment should be focused primarily on ensuring that orphans and other vulnerable children have the resources to enroll in school.

We find that current consumption is an important determinant of demand in Zimbabwe. As such, school subsidies or loans may be expected to help increase enrollment. However, the economic crisis in Zimbabwe makes the adoption of new internally funded, large-scale blanket subsidies extremely unlikely, which is why interventions must instead be targeted.

Two of our results should help to inform targeting strategies in Zimbabwe. First, while orphans are less likely to enroll overall, young orphans do not seem to be particularly disadvantaged. It is among the 11–16 age group that orphans can be shown to fare worse than other children, even in households with both orphans and non-orphans. This finding is consistent with the prior argument that caregivers expect lower returns on their investment in orphans' education.

For young children, the opportunity costs of education are relatively low. But as children grow older and more capable of engaging in productive activity, the opportunity costs of time spent in school will increase. As children age, these opportunity costs evidently begin to exceed the expected benefits for orphans more often than for caregivers' own children. This suggests that the expected benefits to investing in education are lower for orphans, either because caregivers expect to receive a higher share of the additional income due to education from their own children, or because the psychic income associated with seeing their own children educated are higher.

Second, previous enrollment matters critically for keeping orphans in school. Among children in families with both their own children and with orphans who were enrolled in school the previous year, orphans are no less likely than non-orphans to be currently enrolled. The policy implication is clear: the key to getting orphans in school is to keep all children affected by HIV/AIDS in school by providing them with the support they need so that they never drop out in the first place.

Our results suggest several directions for future research. The economic approach to the household's decision-making process has proven to be a powerful tool to understanding how HIV/AIDS has affected the demand for education. It does of course have limitations. Additional relevant determinants of schooling – like the stigma associated with HIV/AIDS in many contexts – have not been well incorporated into this approach. However, even within its parameters, much more could be said if better data was available. For example, a critical issue that we highlight is the importance of a child's educational history on the likelihood of current enrollment. Future datasets that include questions regarding the current health status of parents and the subsequent demands placed on children due to a parent's illness would be useful.

More substantively, future research may wish to link the economy-wide (or at least broader labor market) effects of the HIV/AIDS crisis more closely to the household's decision-making process. One promising line of inquiry involves the perceived returns to education. The household's expectation of the returns to education is fundamental to how it calculates the cost benefits, and therefore a critical determinant of the demand for education. While our results allow some inferences to be made regarding how caregivers expect to share in the returns to education, still the rate of return is taken as a given.

Yet there are reasons to expect that the HIV/AIDS crisis may well affect these returns. On the one hand, graduates will be entering an economy that may be less productive due to the effects of the pandemic. These lower rates of productivity for workers would imply lower returns to schooling. Similarly, the pandemic may also affect expectations of life span and therefore returns to schooling. On the other hand, the loss of millions of prime-age earners may cause wages to bid up, much as they were after the great plagues in Europe. Importantly, these effects may not be economy-wide, but may affect different sectors of the labor market in different ways. Consequently they may impact the cost returns on different levels of education in different ways. Understanding better these hypothesized effects on the broader labor market at a disaggregated level, and linking them to household perceptions of the return to education, would provide an important advance in our understand of how the HIV/AIDS pandemic is likely to affect the demand for education.

NOTES

1. For similar empirical work in the Asian context, see for example, Liu, Wyshak, and Larsen (2004).

2. There are two general fees that are paid for school: the School Development Association levy (SDA) (public school) or School Development Association Committee levy (private school) and a general-purpose fund (GPF) fee. The former covers general school maintenance and utilities, and the latter covers things such as sports, field trips, and other school activities.

3. The opposite may also hold: If orphaned children had more years of schooling due to being in a wealthier family, the economic returns to the family taking in an orphan may be higher than for other children.

4. There are some obvious limitations to the use of enrollment as our measure of educational attainment. For example, our results do not indicate the number of years of schooling, or the grade level completed by the students. Less obviously, our results do not permit any inferences to be drawn about the quality of education received, either about the institution (how good the school is), or about the student (our data only includes information on whether a child attends school, not how frequently or with what diligence or enthusiasm). Our data also do not include other indicators of educational attainment. Given the likely impact of HIV/AIDS on both institutional quality and the lives of nominally enrolled students, future research using other measures of education would be useful.

5. In Zimbabwe the educational system is split into primary and secondary schools. The primary schools mainly serve children from the ages of 6 to 12. The secondary schools are further split into the ordinary level and the advanced level. The former primarily serves children from the ages 13 to 16, while the latter primarily serves children from the ages of 17 to 18. While all children are eligible for the ordinary level, not all children qualify for the advanced level. As a consequence, we restrict our sample to children between the ages of 6 and 16, those ages for which education is not restricted.

6. Overall, school enrollment rates in Zimbabwe are higher than in many other developing countries. This is due, in part, to the country's focus, during its war for independence, on the need for free education for all. After independence, one of the government's top resolutions was to ensure free quality education.

7. Pole and dagga huts are cylindrical, single-cell houses with a conical thatched roof, often called rondavels.

8. We use food insecurity as a measure of current consumption in that food consumption is closely tied to food insecurity (e.g., Gundersen & Oliveira, 2001), and food consumption is often used as a measure of current consumption (e.g., Gundersen & Ziliak, 2003).

9. Our samples are defined at the child level rather than the household level. As a consequence, our samples contain children who live in the same household. In the estimates found in Tables 3–5, we correct the standard errors for this clustering at the household level.

10. In comparison to the full sample, which includes all children and was used to address the previous question, our sample restriction results in a 46.7% reduction due to the exclusion of households with only their own children and a 11% reduction due to the exclusion of households with only orphans.

11. To be consistent with our previous results, we limit our sample to children between the ages of 7 and 16. In other words, our sample consists of children who would have been in school between the ages of 6 and 16 in the previous year.

12. When we restrict our sample to children who attended school the previous year, there is a 15.1% drop in the number of children for the sample of all children and a 16.4% drop in the number of children for the sample of households with their own children and orphans.

13. While, on balance, education is expected to produce declines in the incidence of HIV infection among girls, there are aspects to education which may lead to increases in HIV infection. Among these aspects is the possibility of sexual relations between girls and male teachers which would lead to a spread of the disease.

ACKNOWLEDGMENTS

Gundersen and Kelly gratefully acknowledge financial support from the U.S. Agency for International Development (USAID) and Catholic Relief Services (CRS) through USAID Cooperative Agreement Number 690-A00-02-00056-00. The views expressed in this paper are not necessarily those of either organization. Kyle Jemison was the Head of Operations Research for CRS-STRIVE in Zimbabwe when the majority of the work for this paper was done. We thank an anonymous referee and the editors for their excellent comments, along with those who participated in a session at the 2004 African Development and Poverty Reduction in Cape Town, South Africa. Mike Merten provided excellent research assistance.

REFERENCES

Ainsworth, M. (1996). Economic aspects of child fostering in Cote d'Ivoire. *Resource and Population Economics*, 8, 26–52.

Ainsworth, M., Beegle, K., & Koda, G. (2000). *The impact of adult mortality on primary school enrollment in northwestern Tanzania*. World Bank Policy Research, Working Paper. World Bank, Washington, DC.

Ainsworth, M., & Filmer, D. (2002). *Poverty, AIDS and children schooling: A targeting dilemma*. World Bank Policy Research, Working Paper no. 2885. World Bank, Washington, DC.

Al-Qudsi, S. (2003). Family background, school enrollments, and wastage: Evidence from Arab countries. *Economics of Education Review*, 22, 567–580.

Barnett, T., & Blaikie, P. (1992). *AIDS in Africa: Its present and future impact*. New York: The Guilford Press.

Baylies, C. (2002). The impact of AIDS on rural households in Africa: A shock like any other? *Development and Change*, 33(4) 611–32.

Binder, M. (1999). Community effects and desired schooling of parents and siblings in Mexico. *Economics of Education Review*, 18(3), 311–325.

Bishai, D., Brahmbhatt, H., Gray, R., Kigozi, G., Serwadda, D., Sewankambo, N., Suliman, E., Wabwire-Mangen, F., & Wawer, M. (2003). Does biological relatedness affect child survival? *Demographic Research*, 8(9), 261–278.

Case, A., Paxson, C., & Ableidinger, J. (2004). Orphans in Africa: Parental death, poverty and school enrollment. *Demography*, 41(3), 483–508.

Catholic Relief Services. (2004). *Turning the Tide: Sound Practice, Lessons Learned and Corrective Action in OVC Programming*. Harare, Zimbabwe: Catholic Relief Services.

Connelly, R., & Zheng, Z. (2003). Determinants of school enrollment and completion of 10 to 18 year-olds in China. *Economics of Education Review*, 22, 379–388.

Deininger, K., Garcia, M., & Subbarao, K. (2003). AIDS-induced orphanhood as a systemic shock: Magnitude, impact, and program interventions in Africa. *World Development*, 31(7), 1201–1220.

Deolalikar, A. (1997). *The determinants of primary school enrollment and household schooling expenditures in Kenya: Do they vary by income?* Mimeo.

Dixon, S., McDonald, S., & Roberts, J. (2001). AIDS and economic growth in Africa: A panel data analysis. *Journal of International Development*, 13, 411–426.

Evans, D., & Miguel, E. (2004). *Orphans and shooling in Africa: A longitudinal analysis*. Working Paper. University of California, Berkeley.

Filmer, D. (2003). *Determinants of health and education outcomes: Background note for world development report 2004: Making services work for poor people*. Washington, DC: World Bank.

Filmer, D., & Pritchett, L. (1998). *The effect of household wealth on educational attainment around the world: Demographic and health survey evidence.* Washington, DC: World Bank.

Foster, G., Shakespeare, R., Chinemana, F., Jackson, H., Gregson, S., Marange, C., & Mashumba, S. (1995). Orphan prevalence and extended family care in a peri-urban community in Zimbabwe. *AIDS Care*, 7, 3–17.

Fuller, B., & Liang, X. (1999). Which girls stay in school? The influence of family economy, social demands, and ethnicity in South Africa. In: C. H. Bladsoe, J. Casterline, J. Johnson-Kuhn & J. Haaga (Eds), *Critical perspectives on schooling and fertility in the developing world* (pp. 181–215). Washington, DC: National Academy Press.

Gilborn, L., Kluckow, M., Dube, L., Jemison, K., Apicella, A., Smith, T., & Snider, L. (2005). *Assessing Psychosocial Well-being of Youth in Zimbabwe: An Exploratory Study of Stressors, Strengths and Program Approaches.* Washington, DC: Population Council.

Gilborn, L., Nyonyintono, R., Kabumbuli, R., & Jagwe-Wadda, G. (2001). *Making a difference for children affected by AIDS: Baseline findings from operations research in Uganda.* Horizons Program, Working Paper.

Glewwe, P., & Jacoby, H. (2004). Economic growth and the demand for education: Is there a wealth effect? *Journal of Development Economics*, 74, 33–51.

Gregson, S., Waddell, H., & Chandiwana, S. (2001). School Education and HIV Control in Sub-Saharan Africa: From Discord to Harmony? *Journal of International Development*, 13, 467–485.

Gundersen, C., & Oliveira, V. (2001). The Food Stamp Program and Food Insufficiency. *American Journal of Agricultural Economics*, 83, 875–887.

Gundersen, C., & Ziliak, J. (2003). The Role of Food Stamps in Consumption Stabilization. *Journal of Human Resources*, 38, 1051–1079.

Hamilton, W. (1964). The genetical evolution of social biology. *Journal of Theoretical Biology*, 7, 1–52.

Kamali, A., Seeley, J., Nunn, J., Kengeya-Kayondo, A., Ruberantwari, A., & Mulder, D. (1996). The orphan problem: Experience of a sub-Saharan Africa rural population in the AIDS epidemic. *AIDS Care*, 8, 509–515.

Kelly, M. (2000). Standing education on its head: Aspects of schooling in a world with HIV/AIDS. *Current Issues in Comparative Education*, 3(1).

Kobiané, J., & Marcoux, R. (2005). Parental death and children's schooling in two Sahelian countries (Burkina Faso and Mali). What's wrong with the extended family system? Paper presented at the 2005 Population Association of American Annual Meetings.

Liu, J., Wyshak, G., & Larsen, U. (2004). Physical well-being and school enrollment: A comparison of adopted and biological children in one-child families in China. *Social Science and Medicine*, 59(3), 609–623.

Lloyd, C., & Blanc, A. (1996). Children's schooling in sub-Saharan Africa: The role of fathers, mothers, and others. *Population and Development Review*, 22(2), 265–298.

Meyer, D. (2003). HIV/AIDS and education in Africa. Rand Afrikaans University, ASWE.

Nankhuni, F. (2005). Household deaths and children's schooling: Quantifying the effects of HIV/AIDS on adolescents' work-schooling choices in Malawi. Paper presented at the 2005 Population Association of American Annual Meetings.

National AIDS Council. (2004). *The HIV/AIDS epidemic in Zimbabwe: Where are we now? Where are we going?* Ministry of Health and Child Welfare.

Nielsen, H. (2001). How sensitive is the demand for primary school education to changes in economic factors? *Journal of African Economies, 10*, 191–217.

Ntozi, J. (1997). Effects of AIDS on children: The problem of orphans in Uganda. *Health Transition Review, 7*, 23–40.

Parish, W., & Willis, R. (1993). Daughters, education, and family budgets: Taiwan experiences. *Journal of Human Resources, 28*(4), 863–898.

Shapiro, D., & Tambashe, O. (2001). Gender, poverty, family structure and investments in children's education in Kinshasa, Congo. *Economics of Education Review, 20*, 359–373.

UNAIDS. (2001). *Investing in our future: Psychosocial support for children affected by AIDS. A case study in Zimbabwe and the United Republic of Tanzania.* New York: United Nation's Children Fund.

UNAIDS. (2003). *Report on the technical consultation on indicators development for children orphaned and made vulnerable by HIV/AIDS.* New York: UNICEF.

UNAIDS. (2004). *Children on the brink 2004: A joint report of new orphan estimates and a framework for action.* New York: United Nation's Children Fund.

UNICEF. (2003). *Hope never dries up: Facing the challenges. A situational assessment and analysis of children in Zimbabwe: 2002 update.* Harare, Zimbabwe: United Nation's Children Fund.

World Bank. (2001). World development indicators. (CD-ROM).

Yamano, T., & Jayne, T. (2005). Working-age adult mortality and primary school attendance in rural Kenya. *Economic Development and Cultural Change, 53*(3), 619–653.

CHILDREN'S WORK, HEALTH, AND SCHOOL DEMAND

COMMENTARY ON BLUNCH AND GUNDERSEN ET AL. PAPERS

Bruce Fuller

When governments build and development agencies finance new schools, they assume that children will eagerly arrive at the front door. Under modern rules of statecraft and human capital formation, unbounded faith in mass schooling has swept across the globe. But at times families do not share this religious fervor for education, or other demands, such as for the labor power of their children, impinge upon demand for schooling. This, in turn, results in disparities in educational attainment, reinforcing inequalities across ethnic groups and social classes, and often between girls and boys.

SCHOOLS AT THE EDGE OF TOUGH CHILDHOODS

These tandem papers – authored by Niels-Hugo Blunch and Craig Gundersen, Thomas Kelly, and Kyle Jemison – add to a long line of work that identifies the features of childhood and family that influence youngsters' propensity to enter and stay in school. What's intriguing from the start of both reports is the variability in conditions in which children are growing up, evident in both Ghana and Zimbabwe. In these societies, between one-sixth and one-fifth of children, roughly between the ages of 6 and 16 years, are not attending school.

It is remarkable how many children remain in school despite the economic uncertainties, deteriorating health conditions, and political unease that recurrently besets east and west Africa. Still, against the backdrop of modern progress is the fact that many children do not attend school, and we learn that this excluded subgroup is not a representative slice of all children, either in Ghana or Zimbabwe.

Childhood in Ghana

Blunch focuses on how child labor undercuts youngsters' propensity to stay in school. The International Labor Organization (ILO) estimates that about one quarter-billion children, under 14, remain in the labor force, as Blunch details. He then presses on the issue of whether all work is bad for children.

In Ghana, for example, over 90% of children "working" are largely doing their chores around the house or compound, enlisted by parents who need more hands to survive economically and raise younger children. It remains ironic that wealthy nations in the West bemoan how adolescents often seem ill equipped to take on adult roles, isolated from work and full-fledged responsibilities until after finishing college or graduate school. Whereas, child labor activists in developing countries tacitly reify the virtues of full-time schooling, while assuming that all work yields negative consequences for children. Blunch urges us to get beyond these polarized viewpoints.

He pushes further to ask whether the family's economic well-being and spending levels are exogenous to decision-making about children's school attendance. If parents, especially those in poor rural parts of Ghana, tacitly assume that children must work around the compound, especially girls, then we must reconsider our understanding of parents' reasoning and causal events related to school attendance. But Blunch is not naïve about these issues: he goes about testing whether children's (mostly non-cash) work competes with time spent in school. He also asks, which children are most affected by labor demands pressed by their parents?

The notion of opportunity costs – that many parents in poor communities cannot forgo the market value of their children's labor and allow them to stay in school – continues to shape how many scholars estimate children's demand for schooling. Yet going back to economist Albert Fishlow's (1966) historical work on how conditions related to school demand can vary between agricultural versus urban areas, we have known that deep-seated cultural values, including variable religious commitments to literacy, moral socialization, and apprenticeship traditions, also influence family demand for schooling (also, Morgan & Morgan, 2004). So, Blunch directly tackles this question of whether children's time working takes away from time in school, or whether discretionary time is sufficient to engage both activities.

Blunch's findings are eye-opening in several respects. First, he finds that among children, age 8–14 years, about two-thirds of those saying they help around the household see this as significant work even though it remains unpaid. This holds significant implications for how we measure children's activities in such ambitious household surveys which inform development policies.

Blunch also finds that children who report more time working to support their household tend to be older, female, live in rural parts of Ghana, and live farther from schools or sources of fresh water. This brings into the focus the interplay between demand factors, emanating from the conditions of childhood, with institutional conditions. Earlier work, taking advantage of multilevel modeling techniques, has shown that the proximal supply of schools can moderate the influence of child- or family-level demand factors (e.g., Fuller, 1999; Glewwe & Jacoby, 2004).

Blunch also finds that children work less when the entire community is better-off economically, rather than the income of the youngster's own household. This represents a provocative sociological effect, where either extended kin are supporting children's schooling, or local norms regarding formal education have changed within better-off rural communities.

He then digs deeper to examine the underlying motives of children who have left school. Of the fifth of kids who are not in school, about a fifth said that school is "too expensive" or they "cannot afford" to attend. Another two-fifths reported that "school is useless, uninteresting," according to Blunch. Here we arrive at the nexus between economic constraints, perhaps worsened by school fees, and the fact that local norms regarding the comparative desirability of staying in school have not changed. Children's work and their contribution to the family homestead remain the priority. Less than one percent of children report trying to combine school and work, although we wonder whether measurement error is again present.

The author advances our thinking about how to conceptualize and measure the family's social class and economic position in non-western parts of Ghanaian society. Assuming, for the moment, that work and school are the main options available to youth (which, empirically, is the case for most of the sample), the results suggest that household spending is positively related to the probability that the focal child remained in school. But land ownership is not. And when families own cattle, children are less likely to be attending school. So, it's not simply the level of income, but also the structure of work available to children, that appears to drive school demand. This goes back to the earlier theoretical point that the dynamic of opportunity costs, including economic and cultural dimensions, varies across local settings, even among low-income communities.

Overall, the Blunch paper poses important questions about how we conceptualize work during childhood and how the nature of work differs across Ghanaian communities, holding direct consequences on the intensity of demand for schooling. How the supply of new schooling is distributed, presumably in exogenous fashion by central or provincial governments, plays a significant role in moderating family-level drivers of demand. For many, youngsters in Ghana, the school institution remains on the periphery of their rendition of childhood.

Family, Health, and Childhood in Zimbabwe

Gundersen and his colleague tell a story, set in Zimbabwe, which starts in a similar way: about four-fifths of all children, age 11–16 years, were enrolled in school in 2002, when a similar household survey was conducted. Yet a sad and dramatic shock characterizes this and other African societies: the HIV-AIDS epidemic that continues to hit families and young children very hard. The United Nations estimates that over 12.3 million African children have been orphaned by this dismal disease. Life expectancy has dropped in Zimbabwe from over 50 to about 43 years of age in less than a generation.

Gundersen and colleagues go about trying to understand how prior household-level sources of school demand operate, along with this new reality of having thousands of children in Zimbabwe moving into adopted families.

The authors incorporate earlier demand factors identified in this literature, similar to Blunch's analysis. These include family composition, hunger levels, culturally situated measures of social class, and region of residence. Then Gundersen moves into intriguing theoretical territory, blending the ability of diverse families to integrate orphaned children and mount support for their schooling while educating their own offspring. Orphans have often left school to care for a sick parent, perhaps suppressing the likelihood of returning to school after joining a new household. Again, we arrive at this tangled ball of economic and social determinants of school demand. Gundersen's analysis helps to unravel this intriguing set of forces.

His team starts with the a priori question of which families are more likely to take in orphaned children. This is related to the parallel issue, which the authors might address in future work, of what kinds of children are more likely to become orphaned. We might assume that better-off families have the resources to take-in new children. Yet early work, also conducted in Zimbabwe, showed that many families adopt orphans and put them to work, gaining another pair of hands for child care and domestic chores (Ainsworth & Filmer, 2002).

Gundersen does a thoughtful job of conceptualizing such selection processes, then guards against selection bias when estimating enrollment rates for orphans, compared with parents' own children residing in the same household. He recognizes that fostering-out has long been widespread in parts of Africa, long before the shock of AIDS (for review, Lloyd & Blanc, 1996). And the survey's designers excelled in developing culturally valid measures and delivering the interview in both Shona and Ndebele.

Gundersen finds that orphans were less likely to be attending school (77%), compared with non-orphans (87%), before moving to the restricted sample of households in which orphans and parents' own children reside. Enrollment rates for orphans fall about eight percentage points as they age, from 6 to 16 years, presumably as the opportunity cost of staying in school rises. Yet no fall-off in enrollment rates is observed for non-orphans.

The Gundersen team found a slight tendency for orphans to live in poorer households, consistent with earlier work. They detect a slightly lower probability of being enrolled among girls, compared with boys, but this difference is not statistically significant. Importantly, orphans in better-off households are almost as likely to be attending school as non-orphans. So, the attendance gap is wider in poor homes, suggesting that the labor power of orphans is readily tapped by their new guardians.

When moving to the restricted sample of households in which orphans and natural offspring were co-resident, the gap in school attendance narrows. This offers an important adjustment for selection effects, that is, certain households might be more or less inviting of orphans; these displaced children may come from a non-random distribution of families. That said, orphans remain six percent less likely to be enrolled in school, compared with parents' own children in the same household. This gap is insignificant for young children, growing to almost 12 percentage points by the time children reach 16 years of age.

This gap disappears entirely when isolating on children who were enrolled in school in the prior year. This result suggests that prior interruptions in school, perhaps due to the original family's deteriorating health, may hold lasting consequences for children who are then orphaned.

THE SOCIAL DYNAMICS OF CHILDHOOD

One distinct contribution shared by both papers is the recognition that the family institution acts with some agency in mediating the exigencies of poverty or disease. For Blunch, the nature of work and the ability of children to perform these tasks, most frequently outside the cash economy, influences family decision making when it comes to keeping children in school. Gundersen's team focuses on the family's capacity to integrate new children into the household, sometimes exploiting their labor and other times blending work and school attendance. In both cases, the family unit is sifting through economic and normative demands and shaping the nature of childhood for individual youngsters.

I did keep looking for more textured information about these families, especially how parents reasoned through the need for labor and production, against the modernizing norm of keeping children in school. Do parents experience these pressures as a painful dilemma? Why don't Zimbabwean parents discriminate more sharply between their own offspring versus the orphans they have taken in? Why have gender differences all but disappeared, even in poor rural communities, when it comes to demand for schooling? I kept hoping these fine economists would simply hang out inside a few villages or compounds and learn more the inner-workings of families and parents' aspirations for their children.

Blunch found that close proximity of an elementary or secondary school meant that children were less likely to be working and more likely to be in school. Measures of proximity to schools were absent from the Gundersen paper. It is a fundamental theoretical point: to push for a clearer understanding of the interplay between parents' demand for school and how it may be constrained by the simple lack of supply. Yes, this is linked to the classic identification problem in economics. But in real life, as governments and international donors consider how to allocate new schools or classrooms, we should be learning more about demand responses across differing kinds of families.

Both researchers push forward to devise measures of household poverty or wealth, and the family's social-class position which hold meaning in a local society. This is a crucial step in more carefully apportioning variance in school demand between family and school factors. Without these advances in measurement, scholars will likely overestimate the effects of school quality, after failing to fully take into account the influence of family resources and difficult to gauge parenting practices.

Indeed, these papers illuminate little about parents' own practices, including how they balance the importance of children's labor power and longer-term benefits of keeping their children in school. The erratic economic conditions that characterize both Ghana and Zimbabwe, as well as political and institutional uncertainties, may signal diminishing returns to more education in the eyes of parents. Here too, we have so much to learn about how parents are thinking about these competing pressures, when the norms of modernization and mobility grow disconnected from day-to-day material realities.

These authors open up the intriguing territory situated at the juncture of the household economy, new schools rising from the ground, and how parents attempt to structure childhood and young adulthood (which arrives quite early for many). Scholars should keep exploring this essential terrain, perhaps adding a sociologist or anthropologist to their teams to discover what parents are feeling as they cope with, and respond to, these economic and cultural forces.

REFERENCES

Ainsworth, M., & Filmer, D. (2002). *Poverty, AIDS, and children's schooling: A targeting dilemma*. Washington, DC: World Bank Working Paper series, 2885.

Fishlow, A. (1966). Levels of 19th century American investment in education. *Journal of Economic History, 26*, 418–436.

Fuller, B. (1999). *Government confronts culture: The struggle for democracy in Southern Africa*. New York: Taylor & Francis.

Glewwe, P., & Jacoby, H. (2004). Economic growth and the demand for education: Is there a wealth effect? *Journal of Development Economics, 74*, 33–51.

Lloyd, C., & Blanc, A. (1996). Children's schooling in sub-Saharan Africa: The role of fathers, mothers, and others. *Population and Development Review, 22*, 265–298.

Morgan, S., & Morgan, W. (2004). Educational pathways into the evolving labour market of west Africa. In: B. Fuller & E. Hannum (Eds), *Inequality across societies: Families, schools, and persisting stratification* (pp. 225–245). Oxford: Elsevier.

ALIENATION FROM LEARNING – POOR ETHIOPIAN CHILDREN IN ISRAEL

Gad Yair and Orit Gazit

ABSTRACT

Studies of families and inequality in education have focused on the family as a preparatory institution for school. However, researchers have ignored the dynamic process of engaging with academic learning at home on a daily basis and minimized the importance of homework and instruction in this setting. Home observations of Ethiopian families who immigrated to Israel are used here as a case to describe three distracting factors which alienate children from learning at home in lower-class, poor immigrant households: deprived physical settings, sensory bombardment, and emotional stress. By looking at learning at home, this study points at root causes of alienation from learning and thereby adds another perspective on reproduction in education. Our study casts doubt on the ability of home intervention programs to curb social inequalities in education.

INTRODUCTION

That family poverty and overcrowding have detrimental effects on children's growth and student achievement has long been known (Barton &

Coley, 1992; Biddle, 2001; Lareau & Horvat, 1999; Shonkoff & Phillips, 2000). Diverse studies have expanded the understanding of how families support and prepare children for learning at school; some of them have specifically explained why lower-class children in immigrant families attain lower academic achievement (Bankston, 1998; Dauber & Epstein, 1993; Farkas, Grobe, Sheehan, & Shuan, 1990; Lareau, 1987). However, these studies have rarely focused on the actual process of learning at home as an important ingredient in the explanation of inequality in education (Clark, 1993; Lareau, 2001). Consequently, they have not fully disclosed the concrete mechanisms that frustrate the success of home learning.

Different theoretical schools explain the role that families play in reproducing social inequality. Some studies focus on the differential cultural capital families provide to the young. Authors in this vein argue that lower-class and minority students are excluded from schools since teachers and counselors are oriented toward middle-class values and Western knowledge (Bourdieu, 1986; Bourdieu & Passeron, 1979; Bourdieu & Passeron, 1977; Lareau, 1987; Lareau & Horvat, 1999).

Other studies focus on the limited social capital of immigrant and minority communities. They argue that broken or dysfunctional social networks handicap children's school learning because they do not supply the necessary support and control mechanisms that direct learning (Coleman, 1987, 1988; Stanton-Salazar, 1996; Stanton-Salazar & Dornbusch, 1995).

A further line of study analyzes family organizational structures (e.g., single-parent households), specifically pointing at mechanisms which limit the necessary skills and depress aspirations for succeeding in school (Alexander, Entwisle, & Bedinger, 1994; Blake, 1989; Hanson, 1994; Kellerhals, Montandon, & Ritschard, 1992; Marjoribanks, 1996; Widlak & Perrucci, 1988).

A different approach seeks to model the effects of overcrowding on student attainment in school. For example, evidence from France and India highlights the notable effect of overcrowding on school achievement (Evans, Lepore, Shejwal, & Palsane, 1998), class retention, and student dropout rates (Goux & Maurin, 2001). These studies suggest that siblings who share bedrooms can be at risk in school. However, a recent review of the literature (Office, 2004) has pointed to a dearth of investigations that directly link overcrowding and educational outcomes. The review argued that while the correlation between overcrowding and school failure is significant (see also Conley, 2001), the causal mechanisms are yet to be clearly identified. While some studies point to the effects of overcrowding on parental verbal behavior (Evans, Maxwell, & Hart, 1999), others point to its impact on health and psychological adjustment (Evans et al., 1998). These family processes can later affect children's cognitive skills at school.

All these schools of thought argue that high-SES families inculcate the necessary skills for school learning, while impoverished families fail to do so (Marjoribanks, 1996; Stanton-Salazar, 1996; Widlak & Perrucci, 1988). Overall, however, these studies have not used in-home observations that focus on learning. Therefore, they cannot fully describe the mechanisms that associate overcrowding with achievement deficits.

Notwithstanding their theoretical variety, most of these studies also assume that the family is only a preparatory institution for learning. Hence, while they laid the foundations for understanding the role of family socialization in reproducing achievement inequality, they did not focus on the actual process of learning at home and did not describe how parents help their children to learn or do homework. In other words, since most studies assumed that learning takes place in school, they failed to describe how students actually accumulate part of their academic knowledge at home, and why children who grow up in lower-class and disadvantaged families may find it difficult to learn at home.

This paper addresses that deficiency. It focuses on instruction and learning in lower-class, poor, and culturally marginal Ethiopian families who emigrated from the traditional rural Ethiopian society to the urban and competitive educational setting of modern Israel. Based on ethnographic reports from 22 families, the study provides a realistic look at learning at home, and describes the environments that cause disengagement with learning in poor, lower-class immigrant families. Specifically, it describes three distracting factors that alienate children from learning at home: a deprived physical setting for learning, constant sensory bombardment that frustrates efforts to concentrate, and high levels of emotional stress.

After presenting our theoretical approach on engagement with learning at home, we describe changing Israeli policies of absorption and the context of Ethiopian immigration during the last two decades. We then outline our research setting – using data collected on families that participated in a home intervention program – and detail our observation and analysis strategies. The results are presented in three subsections, each presenting a series of specific conditions that frustrate tutors' attempts to teach and exacerbate children's difficulties with learning at home. Based on these detailed observations, the paper concludes with a discussion of the limits of family support of learning, and the challenges that home intervention programs face in poor immigrant communities.

THEORETICAL ORIENTATION

Students' engagement with instruction is the product of an interaction between opposing forces, some in the immediate context and some more distant (Lewin, 1951). To learn, students must pay attention to whatever transpires in instructional moments. If they do not focus on the immediate instructional context, they will not experience instructional opportunities or gain from the potential effects of these opportunities on their achievement, knowledge, and interests. From a phenomenological point of view, engaging with the "paramount reality" of instruction (Berger & Luckman, 1967) is a necessary condition for learning, whatever strategy a teacher uses. If children do not attend to parents' or tutors' attempts to teach them, they are likely to shut out educational opportunities and therefore jeopardize their achievement in school. If they do engage with instruction at home, they are likely to decrease achievement gaps at school.

Although engagement with instruction may seem to be an easy task, it is indeed an achievement, since children are constantly affected and seduced by non-educational contexts (Alexander, 1997). From this dynamic viewpoint, learning is a function of the interaction between students, their social contexts, and the characteristics of instruction (Sternberg & Wagner, 1994). Metaphorically, students' minds can be seen as constituting a battlefield on which their life worlds and different roles and engagements (such as family, work, and leisure activities) continually demand attention (Lewin, 1951). Each context exerts pressure on an individual's consciousness, even when the individual is not physically present in the context. Furthermore, contexts differ in their ability to seduce or swamp an individual's consciousness. Some contexts are more binding or engulfing – what Coser (1974) called "greedy institutions" – whereas others have only flimsy, temporary effects on attention.

This study draws on Goffman's (1967) work in defining students' engagement versus various forms of alienation from instruction. According to Goffman, precontractual moral codes require people to be fully attentive to others in face-to-face encounters, namely to immerse themselves in interaction. However, as Goffman suggested, actors can be physically present in interactions yet only go through the motions, failing to be actually engaged with the immediate situation. For example, external observers can see students sitting in class, looking attentive to instruction, taking notes, and nodding in agreement. Yet on deeper scrutiny, the students are found to have been staring into space, scribbling their names or writing non-relevant notes.

Goffman (1967) suggested that under certain conditions, individuals become highly susceptible to social distractions. Using this premise, recent articles on student engagement in classrooms (Yair, 2000a, 2000b) have shown that while students' attention is diverted by external factors (e.g., family concerns, working after school, peer pressures), teachers may use different strategies and methods (e.g., relevant instruction or group work) to pull students' attention back to the classroom. According to the empirical results, students were found to be alienated from instruction in academic classes almost half the time. However, it was found that the dynamic tug-of-war between teachers' practices and students' disengaging preoccupations may be decisively won by the former through the use of progressive teaching methods.

The current study extends this approach to studying engagement with learning to the home environment. In contrast to a school environment, which is structured to ameliorate distracting factors through controlled activities and settings (e.g., arranged tables and chairs, a planned schedule, organized curricula, etc.), learning at home may lack this structured environment. Prior studies have indeed pointed out the precariousness of learning at home. For example, in order to learn effectively, children require a special, ordered, and educationally equipped space.

As the literature on overcrowding has shown many children lack these conditions (e.g., Conley, 2001; Evans et al., 1998). Furthermore, a lack of separation of learning from other spheres of family life (e.g., eating, playing, and sleeping) makes concentration for learning more difficult (Teachman, 1987). Unstructured family routines were found to debilitate learning (Flores, Tomany-Korman, & Olson, 2005). Other results further suggest that lack of parental rules over TV viewing may deplete the time needed to learn at home and increase the risk of failure at school (Gorely, Marshall, & Biddle, 2004; Vandewater, Park, Huang, & Wartella, 2005).

The following empirical investigation shows that learning at home consists of a continual tug-of-war between distracting factors on the one hand and instructional factors on the other. Using the tug-of-war metaphor, we define alienation from learning as physical or cognitive absence from an instructional activity. The physical indicator is clear: it consists of children walking away from their tutor, thereby resisting instruction whatsoever. However, resistance can be covert as well. We suggest that while children seemingly do homework or attend a learning activity, they may actually be inattentive. As a result of incessant household distractions, children may forfeit their opportunities to learn at home.

We shall show that due to the structural features that characterize poor families (e.g., family size and density), children often find themselves in a chaotic environment, where the distracting factors debilitate their ability to engage with learning. By detailing the mechanisms involved in this tug-of-war,

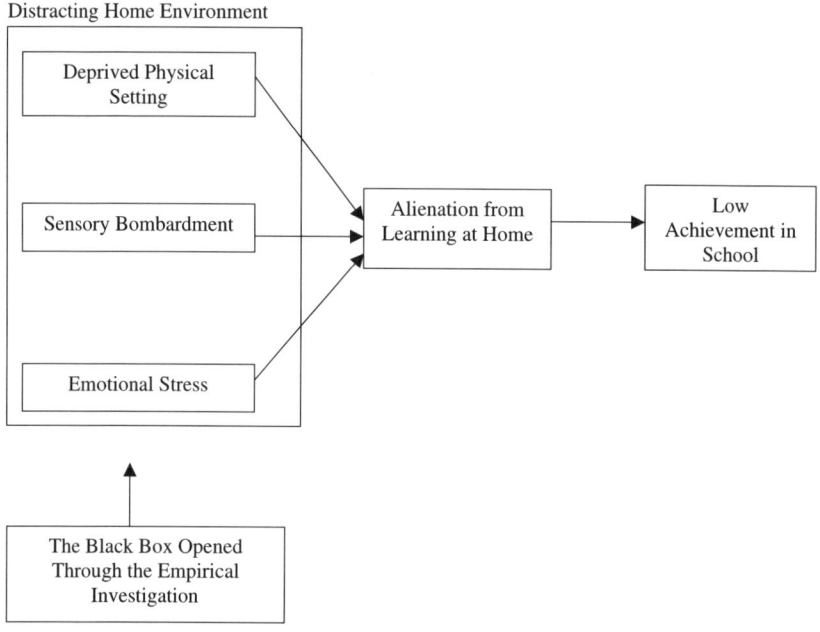

Fig. 1. Disengagement from Learning at Home and Achievement.

and by explaining why alienation from learning prevails in poor families, the current investigation proposes a deeper understanding of the process of learning at home and the way in which this process reproduces social inequality in education. Fig. 1 provides the conceptual rationale that drives this study. It shows that three distracting factors cause alienation from learning, thereby frustrating attempts to complete school assignments. As a result, achievement in school is curtailed. Over time, alienation from learning at home puts children at greater educational risk for expanding gaps in school achievement.

ISRAELI POLICY OF ABSORPTION: HISTORICAL CONTEXT

Israel is renowned for being a society of immigrants. Founded on the Zionist proclamation of "the return to Zion," pre- and early-state immigration policies encouraged every Jew to arrive in Israel and obtain full citizen rights immediately, coupled with short-term economic aid. During the 1950s and the 1960s, the egalitarian Zionist ideology stressed issues of integration ("melting pot") and cultural assimilation, and early studies of Israeli sociology indeed focused on these issues ("desocialization and resocialization"), mostly adopting functionalist perspectives that were closely affiliated with national policies and social agendas (Eisenstadt, 1954; Shuval & Leshem, 1999).

Since the 1970s, critics have begun to decipher gaps between cultural ideals and actual absorption policies, especially vis-à-vis North-African immigrants. This critical perspective adopted a pluralistic discourse that was soon emulated by immigration officers. Since the 1980s, absorption policies have become less rigid, allowing social groups to retain their cultural heritage and collective identity. This transformation from strong, integrative, paternalistic absorption policies to weak, pluralistic, and participative policies constituted the setting for the arrival of Ethiopian Jews to Israel. (For a detailed discussion of these issues see Bar-Yosef, 2001.)

Political and military crises in Ethiopia, together with drought and famine from the mid-1980s to 1990s, caused two massive waves of Jewish refugees.[1] The traumatic journey of the Beta Esra'el from Addis Ababa to Jerusalem constituted a colossal challenge for Ethiopian Jews (Westheimer & Kaplan, 1992). The emigration from Ethiopia proved to be a traumatic experience for individuals, families, and whole villages. Stories are told of long journeys on foot, amongst warring factions, during which émigrés were exposed to recurrent murder, rape, and robberies while staying at temporary havens along the way. The flight to Zion also caused families to undergo separation and breakdown. The 85,000 members of the community now living in Israel (30% of whom were born in Israel) experienced a level of collective suffering that will take years to heal.

The traumatic physical journey to Israel was not the only one that the Ethiopian community had to make, nor was it their last. The move from a pre-modern, largely agrarian, religious, and technologically backward country (Kaplan, 1992) to a highly modern, urbanized, mostly secular, and industrially advanced one constituted a colossal challenge. Most of the immigrants came from small villages, which were characterized by little division of labor and a limited amount of formal schooling. They landed, however, in a modern and extremely differentiated social structure that was largely based on educational credentials, universal criteria of allocation of social rights, and rationalized and bureaucratized social security systems. The cultural and social capital that the immigrants experienced in Ethiopia immediately dissolved, making the transition to Israel extremely difficult.

The Israeli government faced the immense challenge of absorbing these waves of Ethiopian immigrants. This task was exacerbated by the simultaneous arrival of 750,000 Jews from the former Soviet Union. Together, the two immigrant groups – which arrived within the span of a decade – constituted 15% of Israel's population at the time. This necessitated an absorption policy that responded to immigrants immediate needs for housing, employment, language acquisition, and schooling.

Ethiopian immigrants were housed in temporary dwellings (some of which lasted for more than a decade), mainly in peripheral locales. During their first year in Israel, language instruction was coupled with religious and cultural socialization carried out through intensive adult education programs. However, as with all other immigrant groups, school-age children were required to attend regular schools and study in Hebrew (with some extra help during the initial period).

The expectation amongst educators was that within two years, immigrant students would be fully and equally integrated into the Israeli school system and cultural fabric. State agencies provided short and intensive supportive intervention programs within the school system for Ethiopian children. After that, however, they had to cope with any remaining educational and cultural gaps themselves or with the assistance of voluntary organizations.

However, their traditional practices (which they were encouraged by state officials to retain) and oral culture did not provide them with the tools to handle this new challenge. Growing evidence suggests that Ethiopian immigrant families in Israel experience extreme cultural gaps that make it difficult for them to support their children's learning (Bar-Yosef, 2001; Horowitz & Mosher, 1997; Maital, 2000; Weinstein, 1985). Studies show that due to their lack of formal schooling in Ethiopia, immigrant parents find it hard to comprehend the aims, structure, and methods of Israeli schooling. In Ethiopia, schooling was highly structured, hierarchical, based on recitation, and lacked parent involvement (unless in extreme cases of violent behavior). Parents were not informed of school policy, nor were they requested to help with their children's learning (Levine, 1974).

In contrast, Israeli schooling is characterized by a mixture of formal and informal teaching strategies. It is individualistic, and stresses student autonomy; it relies on students doing homework and projects at home; and it also depends on strong parental involvement and home–school linkages (e.g., Goldring, 1997). Consequently, Ethiopian parents often have trouble understanding the requirements that schools place on families and parents, the meaning of homework, and the importance of learning at home in Israel (for similar observations see Portes, 1995, 1996). These parental hardships were exacerbated by parents' lack of facility in Hebrew, which made it extremely difficult for them to help their children do schoolwork (Van-Kauffman, 2004). Hence, most parents assigned responsibility for their children's education to state agencies, and were usually reluctant to play an active role in their children's schooling (Bar-Yosef, 2001).

Given Israel's policy of minimal state intervention in the schooling of Ethiopian children after a two-year transitional period, and given the cultural context of Ethiopians' understanding of the modern Israeli school system, it is not surprising that Ethiopian children are at high risk for school failure. Indeed, a recent report delineated the poor achievement of Ethiopian-origin children in Israel (Fishbein, 2004). For example, dropout rates among Ethiopian children are almost double those for the general Israeli population. At the elementary school level, about 65% of the children of Ethiopian parentage are below average in standardized tests in Hebrew, mathematics, science, and English. This figure climbs to 74% in the middle school years (Fishbein (2004) uses official data reported by the Ministry of Education).

To help combat these rising inequities, voluntary and private sector organizations within Israel have devised different types of intervention programs. Some cater to learning in special education facilities located in the community. Others have a broader vision, and seek to socialize children and their parents within the home environment itself, in order to provide a long-term scaffold for children's learning. This study uses the latter intervention strategy to investigate learning at home under dire social and economic conditions.

Although the current study focuses on Ethiopian immigrant families, it does not look at cultural aspects of learning, a topic worthy of investigation in its own right (for instance, parents believing that children younger than six years old should not be taught formally, or that games cannot be used to teach children). Our study used this group as case of convergence between immigration, low social class, and poverty. We therefore attempt to provide a general picture of the hardship of learning at home under extreme social conditions, which are structural rather than cultural in nature.

RESEARCH SETTING AND DESIGN

This study investigated high-poverty Ethiopian families that participated in a home-intervention program operated by a Zionist organization in 10 impoverished communities with high rates of immigration. This holistic program (involving 120 families at the time of our study) aims to cater to the needs of all children in the household, raise their school achievement, and help their parents adapt to Israeli society and enrich their parenting skills. Families are selected by local coordinators, with three criteria in mind. First, the family is seen as potentially benefiting from a non-expert intervention program; second, the family has no history of mental illness; and third, the family has no known history of violence. With few exceptions, selection criteria were adhered to. The program was administered by a veteran Ethiopian immigrant and was implemented by 18-year-old female tutors from the National Service who worked closely with the children for a year. The proportion of Ethiopian-origin tutors was approximately half.

The project emphasizes the tutors' role in promoting learning, requiring them to help school-aged children at school (during the morning hours) and at home (in the afternoons). These young and semi-skilled tutors arrived at the families highly motivated to supply children with opportunities to learn. Many appeared on the scene with a pre-planned agenda: they brought learning games, memory cards, books, workbooks, and worksheets, as well as materials for creative activities. They also prepared special learning activities for Jewish holidays. (Some of these materials and activities were developed by the central office, by local coordinators, or were shared by tutors who prepared many of them personally.) When necessary, activities were adapted to suit the students' cultural background. However, most activities resembled ordinary Western activities and school assignments, and no unique pedagogical devices were deemed necessary for operating educational activities.

The study is based on observations of a sample of 22 families and their tutors. The families were given the option to decline participation, and the few families that opted out were replaced by families with similar characteristics. The families lived in nine lower-class communities located in southern Israel, most of which are populated by second- and third-generation North-African immigrants. On a scale of 1–10, these communities are ranked by the Israeli Central Bureau of Statistics at the mid-point of the fourth and fifth cluster of locales. Most of these communities have low per-student investments in education, minimal access to educational technology, and experience high rates of unemployment and poor local services. The reason these communities are not ranked in the lowest end of the distribution is that that end is populated by Israeli Arab communities (who occupy the lowest third of the locale-SES distribution).

The families that were sampled in these communities score at the bottom of the social ladder, although they reflect the general characteristics of

Ethiopian immigrant families. Generally, 42.1% of the Ethiopian population is aged 14 or under (compared to 28.9% in the general Jewish population) with 41% growing up in a family with no wage earner. Fully 61% of the children live in families where the head of the household has no education, while 40% of all adult immigrants are unable to hold a simple conversation in Hebrew, and 70% are unable to read or write Hebrew (all the evidence is compiled in Van-Kauffman, 2004).

The distribution in our sample reflects these general figures: 75% of the mothers in the sample are unemployed, as are 47% of the fathers (up to triple the rate for the general population in these communities). A quarter of the families are headed by single parents (mostly single mothers), and the average number of children in these families is 5.8. Most of the parents in our sample lacked a command of the Hebrew language, with few having received a formal education in their homeland. All of the children, however, had a full command of the Hebrew language.

While the households rely on welfare provision for basic needs (e.g., rent, food, and clothing), it is nevertheless common for them to possess two TV sets, as well as other electronic equipment (e.g., cellular phones, audio systems). However, most of the families have no books, encyclopedias, computers or other learning facilities inside the house.

Observations were carried out every other week for a six-month period, between November 2001 and May 2002. Each observation consisted of a one-hour in-house afternoon visit with the tutor and family members. Overall, 150 observations were carried out by a group of 14 research assistants, who were trained by an expert on Ethiopian culture and family problems in Israel. Notes were taken afterwards, usually in the evening following the visit.

We followed a grounded-theory approach (Glaser & Strauss, 1967). Each observation (3–5 pages long) was transcribed through ethnographic reporting of behaviors, activities, and meanings, while also attempting to recover the full complexity of family life. To increase reliability and validity, the researchers reported their observations and initial interpretations on a weekly basis in small discussion groups, and their field reports were distributed to the entire team for comments. A monthly meeting recapitulated major issues, and provided a context for converging and reassessing interpretations.

Next, initial reports were scanned for repeating patterns. Major themes were extracted based on their prevalence, and they were raised in group discussions to add validity to proposed categories. Based on such group deliberations, more focused observations were carried out with the intention of appraising these themes, as well as new ones that were highlighted by more recent data. The major themes that were extracted refer to issues of learning, gender, racism, facilities, living conditions, parenthood and fatherhood, and illness and disabilities. However, for the purpose of this paper, we only selected those excerpts, which refer to learning activities at home. All reported names are pseudonyms.

A final methodological note: the current study is not based on a random sample of locales and families within locales. The tools used for observation were qualitative in nature. Furthermore, families were observed biweekly and for a limited period of time. Therefore, the findings reported below should only be generalized with great caution.

RESULTS

In order to understand the difficulties faced by the children in this study while learning at home, we turn to the context in which learning took place. Generally, the households generated multiple distracting factors, which operated simultaneously and nullified the tutors' efforts to teach the children. While such household environments may have been typical of traditional oral cultures, they constitute an almost impossible setting for learning in text-centered traditions (e.g., reading alone and quietly, concentrating for long stretches of time, memorizing texts, etc.; see Manguel, 1996).

To understand how the typical distractions we observed affect the ability to learn at home, we used the concept of alienation from interaction (Goffman, 1967) as an analytic tool. We suggest that external distractions constantly caused alienation from instruction at the micro level of the household, and therefore nullified the instructional effort expended by the tutors. In the following analysis we focus on three major disengaging factors that emerged through our grounded-theory approach: deprived physical setting, sensory bombardment, and emotional stress. These factors explain why children in immigrant, lower-class poor communities cannot reap the opportunities they are given to learn at home. Table 1 summarizes specific indicators of three causal mechanisms that frustrate attempts to teach and learn at home.

Deprived Physical Setting

The immigrant families' physical setting lacked order and the necessary learning materials; proper lighting for reading was rare; and there was

Table 1. Themes and Indicators of Alienation from Learning at Home.

Deprived Physical Setting	Sensory Bombardment	Emotional Stress
Household disorder	High levels of noise	Sibling envy
Lack of lighting	Many kids, multiple agendas	Parent–child strains
Lack of materials	Tempting alternatives, TV	Parent–parent strains
No niche for learning		

Note: Entries in the table are the indicators discussed in the text.

neither a separate niche for learning nor any other localization of different life spheres within the household. We found that this typical setting frustrated efforts to concentrate on learning by diffusing the children's attention. It also made it difficult for the children to cooperate with the tutor, who herself often found it difficult to sustain a focused educational activity for more than a short time.

Reports from observers showed a repeating pattern of disorganized households that interfered with learning. Attempts to do homework were often disturbed by the haphazard nature of learning. The following quote describes the typical home setting: "Pieces of chocolate are scattered on the floor, with many tissue papers as well as cookie wrappers..." "Toys and markers [are] all over the living room floor, and the old couch is covered with different things. The living room table is also covered with empty bottles and unfinished food plates." Under such conditions, children had difficulty arranging a dedicated space for using books and worksheets, and to focus on learning in general. A typical report describes a girl's repeated disengagement caused by the unorganized surroundings, which constantly distracted her attention:

> Smadar was sitting at the table doing math. Around her were scattered papers in a mess. She managed to finish her homework only after she walked away from the table many times to look for a pencil, an eraser, and other necessary equipment.

As the observer recounted in the group session, Smadar's engagement during the activity was distracted by the disorder surrounding her and she found it difficult to concentrate and learn. The myriad of scattered objects in the setting where Smadar and the tutor attempted to study constantly vied for her attention, alienating her from learning.

No less of a distraction to the learning process was the lack of proper lighting. Reports indicate that the families usually avoided turning on the lights in the house, largely because of parents' low income and difficulties in paying bills. As one observer wrote: "It was already dark outside, but there was only a single lamp hanging above the kitchen table, providing a pale yellow light for the entire house." Many reports indicate that children attempt to study (i.e., complete worksheets, coloring pages, and other activities that require precision) while in partial darkness. The observers repeatedly recounted cases of frustration and inability to concentrate caused by this darkness.

Difficulty with concentrating in the dark is further exacerbated by a lack of necessary learning materials. Although schooling in Israel is free, teachers expect parents to buy the necessary supplies for learning at home (e.g., notebooks, markers, etc.), and assign sophisticated home projects that require the use of computers, the Internet, encyclopedias, etc. While a middle-class family with an average income can afford these materials, the Ethiopian immigrant families usually could not due to the large number of children in their families and their limited economic resources. Consequently, children were often frustrated by their inability to complete learning assignments or engage with learning simply because they lacked the necessary materials. In one household, the observer noted that in the absence of the tutor, little learning could take place:

> Roni and Sarah were very happy to see me, and immediately wanted to play. When I asked them to choose a game, Roni turned to Michal, the tutor. I then observed that there are no games at all in the house, and they therefore waited for Michal to bring them some in her visits. Roni returned with a card game for reading practice. However, when Michal left the house she took the game with her.

These difficulties in engaging with learning occur within the larger setting of the household, where there is no separation between rooms, spaces, and life spheres. Eating, sleeping, playing, and studying usually all occur at the same time and in the same place. The typical Ethiopian household had neither a separation between the bedrooms and the living room nor the safe haven of private spaces (e.g., restrooms). Moreover, children often lacked a personal corner for individual use; some even lacked a bed of their own. Under these conditions, learning often took place on the floor, while all the day-to-day life in the crowded house continued. The following incident was typical:

> Rose, the mother, sat on one bed, while Gali was tutoring one of the girls on the other bed. Abe and another girl were sitting on the floor. They all seemed to be disengaged, with the mother constantly reminding them to behave.

As this quote suggests, engagement with learning is challenged when studying is pushed to the temporarily free corner, and repeatedly moved by frequently changing needs of family members. Such changing conditions affect engagement with learning on a moment-by-moment basis and add to the difficulties discussed above, which together explain the high rates of alienation from learning observed in the households.

Sensory Bombardment

The large number of people in the families, and the households' limited physical space, produced a setting that overburdened the senses of those living in it. Attempts to control the disorder created by the large number of siblings competing for attention or space further exacerbated the difficulty of studying in silence. The researchers often reported a feeling of sensory bombardment, with loud music and television playing constantly, strong food odors, loud conversations, playing, and attempts to teach all occurring simultaneously, and making learning all but impossible. A typical report described a setting where all family members sat in a small room, while the tutor attempted to teach:

> The tutor sat by the table and tried to explain triangles to Mary; Hanna and I [the observer] sat on the bed and talked; Rebecca and Gail (the baby) sat on the floor singing, while loud MTV music was playing on TV.

In another family, the tutor managed to organize the younger children to play a memory learning game. Three children were sitting around the table, taking part in the game. Soon, however,

> One of the kids turned a card before his turn, and in response his brother pushed him, enraged, while the other brother refused to continue playing out of frustration with his failure. Meanwhile, the older sisters strolled around the table talking to their brothers, watching television, and simultaneously arguing loudly in Amharic [the official Ethiopian language]. The tutor tried to gain the children's attention with no success. She tried a different learning activity, but after a short while the children's patience ran out. They started pulling the game board, fighting among themselves, and running all over the house. The tutor seemed desperate.

This incident shows how the large number of children participating in the activity, simultaneous noise from the TV, and the constant tug-of-war between the children, challenged the tutor's ability to engage all the children in learning. Such challenges indeed recurred in most families on a daily basis. Another report describes a typical learning activity with all family members sitting around a single dining room table:

> Studying was stopped every minute, due to the many people at the scene (six attending). Dani offered everybody toasts, but Tami yelled at him to stop distracting her attention. Joshua, who was learning to read at the time, read a letter out loud, and the tutor corrected his mistakes. Suddenly the mother came in. As she entered, anarchy hit, and soon the center of gravity moved to the living room. Jake pulled down the TV cover and

started to watch an Indian film. Tami shouted at him to turn the sound the TV off, but got no response. Dana started crying, and all the other kids moved to the living room ... The tutor kept on sitting near the dining room table teaching young Joshua, who soon left her and walked all over the apartment.

Alienation from learning occurs not only due to the many individuals in the setting, but also from the intermingling of different agendas within the setting. For example, in another family, a tutor attempted to read the children a story while using paper puppets she had prepared in advance:

> The tutor handed each child a paper puppet, and attempted to begin the show. Meanwhile, a girl from next door joined the group, followed by another young girl who handed a sandwich over to Rachel ... The mother walked into the room with a bowl of macaroni and served the boys ... After several attempts to tell the story of the happy prince, the vexed tutor gave up.

Alienation from instruction often seemed to occur when many senses were stimulated simultaneously, as in the following example:

> David threw a 'mock bomb' in the middle of the house. After a few seconds a blast was heard, and white smoke spread throughout the household. The incident created a chain of shouting responses by the mother and the tutor, who until then had been busy playing learning games with the other kids.

Television also proved to be a major attention grabber, both when it was operating loudly and by continually tempting the children (since it was rarely shut down). Indeed TV viewing affects learning, even in middle-class families. However, as one observer noted, the TV in these households acts as a continual "mesmerizing magnet" for all family members. To temper the competition between family members over what to watch on TV, two sets usually operate at the same time, with each one vying for dominance. Furthermore, there were no apparent rules about when, what, and how much TV viewing was allowed. Therefore, TVs remained on throughout the afternoon hours, including when the tutors attempted to teach some of the children. Under these conditions, engaging the children with instruction was difficult at best.

The tutors, for their part, either waited for popular TV shows to end in order to start activities, or were forced to stop in the middle of activities because the children had a program "they had to watch." At other times, TV simply diverted the children's attention while they were participating in a learning activity. For example, as occurred often in many of the households, the tutor arrived while the children were busy watching TV: "She attempted to attract their attention, but repeatedly failed, so she decided to wait and allowed them to watch until the show was over." In another family, "the children were already engaged with learning for 15 minutes, when the 'Dijimons' show started on TV. The tutor and Isaac agreed that he would watch the show first and then return to his studies." In yet other cases, the tutors joined the children and watched TV instead of engaging the kids in learning.

When the sensory bombardment of the television occurs along with other prevailing disturbances in the house, it becomes almost impossible to study. The following incident illustrates the fragility of successful educational activities in the participant families:

> The TV was constantly on at full volume. "Pinky and the Brain" was showing, and one of the girls suddenly erupted, shouting. 'Enough! I've had it! I can't study like this!' The grandmother shut down the TV, but this 'technological' silence didn't stop the grandmother from making background noise. A few moments later shouting in the household erupted again.

Such occurrences were repeated in almost every visit. The evidence paints a picture of a family environment that could hardly sustain an educational activity from beginning to end. It shows that the constant sensory bombardment in these high-poverty families frustrated the tutors and the children, and made engagement with learning a daunting task. The attempt to focus on learning and homework was repeatedly defeated by the multiple stimuli that constantly competed for the children's attention.

Emotional Stress

The large number of siblings, home crowding, and deprived economic conditions also produced high levels of emotional stress among family members. Emotional stress alienated children from learning because parents and tutors had difficulty responding to each child's needs simultaneously and dividing their attention. As a result, envy and sibling rivalry were frequently observed, and ensuing fights and quarrels often disrupted instructional activities. Thus, while tutors attempted to engage children by doing homework or participating in alternative learning activities, the children were often distracted by envy, anger, and other negative emotions.

Interpersonal competition and envy were common in the Ethiopian households – just as they are in any middle-class family (Dunn, 1982). However, the large size of the families and the absence of resources exacerbated levels of envy. As a result, children constantly monitored each other, assessing who benefited too much and who was relatively deprived. For example, with a festival approaching, the tutor arranged an activity where the children were to learn different songs. Her report describes how this activity was disrupted:

> In the midst of the activity, Liran showed signs of anger toward her sister, Merav, whom she suspected received more attention than her. She then hit her with a painful blow to her head. Merav started crying and responded with an equally painful strike. The shouts and crying brought the father into the room to see what the fuss was about ... He took Liran with him, and she did not return to study until the end of the tutor's activity.

This interaction between the children shows that engagement with learning is easily disrupted by emotional distractions. The tutor's attempt to impart new knowledge often failed when envy and interpersonal competition interfered with learning. Other reports support this contention by showing that when children suspected the tutor of paying more attention to others, they deliberately opposed learning with her and alienated themselves from the setting.

Strained parent–children relationships and fragile marriages also contributed to the level of stress in the participant families. Observers frequently noted that parent-to-parent relationships were strained, and that they believed the resulting stress affected the children's ability to engage with learning. Since the phenomenon of single mothers in the sample community is twice the Israeli average, and since mothers in the community often bear children to different fathers, the presence of an adult male in the household was often associated with increased stress. According to a case reported by one of the observers:

> The father was joking with the tutor about being unfaithful to his wife. Shouting between the couple was rampant ... and constant tension was experienced in the household.

In other families, observers reported no interaction between the parents. As mentioned, a quarter of the sample consisted of single-mother families. In the remainder, there was evidence of talk of divorce, parental absence, and adultery. In this emotional climate, children were preoccupied with their parents' relationships and consequently alienated from the learning process.

DISCUSSION

The three distractions discussed above – deprived physical setting, sensory bombardment, and emotional stress – were seen to affect learning at home. All three exemplify how the home environment of poor immigrant families pulled the children's attention away from learning. The semi-skilled tutors could not withstand the influences of such powerful home environments.

Our observations suggest that many tutors lacked the ability to draw children's attention to their academic activities. Most of them did not use appropriate, relevant, and challenging content, even when they had prepared it in advance. Few of them created favorable conditions for an orderly learning environment, which is a prerequisite for teaching children self-direction with learning tasks. In most cases tutors simply ended up acceding to the general turmoil within the household. In this typical scenario, alienation from learning was the norm.

These results suggest that in order to explain inequality in education, researchers need to focus more deliberately on learning at home (Barton & Coley, 1992; Howe II, 1993). Previous studies have highlighted the importance of the family as a preparatory and supporting institution for school learning (Bankston, 1998; Lareau, 2003; Marjoribanks, 1996; Teachman, 1987). They have also pointed to the significant role that families play in producing achievement gaps in school (Coleman et al., 1966). Adding to these prior contributions, this study has shed light on three mechanisms that can be used to explain the difficulties that children in impoverished immigrant families have when trying to use opportunities to learn at home. Specifically, the study has demonstrated that deprived settings, sensory overflows, and emotional distractions constitute the major causes that interfere with organized attempts at providing children with learning assignments at home.

Most middle-class Israeli children grow up in spacious households, and benefit from an environment that provides positive conditions for learning. In contrast, poor children in Israel – exemplified here by those from poor Ethiopian immigrant households – are born into a reality of cramped, shared rooms with little dedicated space for learning or personal use. This study has shown that this context usually harbors a variety of intense distracting factors that frustrate learning at home. This inequality of life chances is echoed in gaps in school achievement; and it is from here that divergent educational careers and adult achievements emerge. These findings therefore imply that a realistic sociology of education should focus more attention on the family as a unique context for instruction and learning. Such a realistic approach may provide a more accurate explanation of the complex processes of social reproduction in education.

This study has made a significant step in that direction. It uses simple theoretical premises as a scaffold for its analysis. It assumes that learning is a cumulative process (Carrol, 1963), and that every utilized opportunity to learn improves achievements (Barr & Dreeben, 1983). Using Goffman's (1967) insight about engagement and Yair's model of student disengagement in classrooms (Yair, 2000a, 2000b), the study provides a close analysis of alienation from such opportunities to learn at home. By focusing on the family as a context rampant with alienating factors, the study investigates the pitfalls of learning at home. This focus on the contexts in homes that produce alienation from learning helps to shed light on why so many opportunities to learn are wasted due to prevailing distracting factors in lower-class, poor immigrant families. It also explains why growing up in such families is prone to lead to ever-increasing achievement gaps.

We have documented the challenges that children face in attempting to learn in Ethiopian immigrant households, as well as the challenges that tutors face in attempting to help them learn. These families experience a critical transition between cultures and social contexts – a transition that Coleman (1995) used to characterize as the great historical transformation in the interplay between society, families, and education. Modern Western requirements to study at home challenge parents and children in poor Ethiopian families on a daily basis, setting them on a track of cumulative disadvantage. Based on Western premises, schools and teachers assign homework, require computers and Internet connections, and assume availability of basic reference books. However, these expectations create unintended, hidden day-to-day challenges that Ethiopian families face in the Israeli setting. We have shown that attempts by various organizations to provide home intervention programs to strengthen Ethiopian families and enrich their educational resources are jeopardized by deprived home environments. In that sense, this study has pointed to the difficulties faced by societies that value democratic, egalitarian ideals in realistically providing all citizens with equal educational opportunities.

Thus, from a practical point of view, the study sheds light on the limited capacity of home intervention programs to expand the life chances of immigrant children growing up in high-poverty families. Similar to the program studied here, "Head Start" (Fenichel & Mann, 2002), "HIPPY" (Baker, Piotrkowski, & Brooks-Gunn, 1999), "America Reads," and other home-intervention programs aim to enrich children and supply them with the resources to benefit equally from school learning.

However, when these programs are implemented within deprived home settings, they confront a myriad of distracting factors that compete for children's attention. This study suggests that such programs need to focus not merely on the content of activities, but also on two other tasks. First, they must exert greater control over the general home environment and arrange the immediate context of learning in order to withhold distracting factors. Second, home tutors and parents should be instructed on how to pull children's attention away from these distracting factors by using highly powerful instructional strategies.

Some tutors – in some observations – exhibited these very requirements. They had mastered the skills of organizing mothers and children to engage in orchestrated activities that persisted for at least an hour. Some exhibited flexibility so that changing distractions were countered by responsive pedagogical strategies. If a program could "clone" these tutors or guarantee their survival organizationally, one could entertain hopes for the success of such home intervention programs. However, such tutors were rare (about 4 out of 22), and at one time or another they too succumbed to the hectic family environments. The burdens of impoverished single mothers who raise 3–5 children by themselves, and have little language facility or educational skills, proved to be too difficult for the 18-year-old girls to bear.

These observations lead us to conclude that while home-intervention programs are valuable and can make a difference in certain circumstances, their day-to-day implementation can only have a limited, short-term effect on the life chances of children living in high-poverty families (Shonkoff & Phillips, 2000). This conclusion is especially true to the extent that schools continue expecting families to provide a significant share of the input into learning (in time, equipment, and social and cultural capital). Under these circumstances, social, ethnic, and racial inequalities in school achievement are bound to be produced and reproduced through the home environment (Downey, von Hippel, & Broh, 2004).

This study's findings, like those of a number other studies, suggest that to counter the reproduction effects of immigration, lower social class, and family poverty, the government cannot be content with inexpensive home-intervention programs for poor immigrants. Rather, it needs to start a new macro-level war against the poverty of immigrant and minority students. Based on our findings, several lines of effort can be pursued.

If home intervention programs are to continue, the government needs to make them more effective. For example, it must supply families with educational kits in order to augment deprived educational resources. Every family should receive age-relevant books that tutors can use with each child. Families should receive financial assistance for electricity so they can extend learning into the evening hours. Families should also be better integrated into communal activities and encouraged to participate in school field trips and other school activities. In particular, this will help parents attain better knowledge of their new society and of the ways of schooling in Israel. In addition, the government can make greater efforts to provide mothers with educational opportunities during the morning hours, in order to empower their ability to support their children's effort to learn at home. Such support is likely to decrease emotional stress at home, and provide parents with the understanding and skills to arrange educational activities at home.

A parallel effort might concentrate on making available public educational spaces that are better suited to curb distractions. Since schools are only open for four to seven hours a day, they can be easily used during the afternoon hours. These educational venues may provide immigrants with focused yet still informal opportunities to learn. Furthermore, instead of the "individualized" strategies used in the home, tutors can work during the afternoon hours in groups and thereby enjoy the benefits of co-teaching, with each tutor capitalizing on her unique talents.

For example, we expect that four tutors working with a group of 12–15 children will be more effective than the separate efforts each of them make in the chaotic home setting. An expert teacher would supervise the tutors on a daily basis. This professional support would make possible greater integration between schoolwork and afternoon activities, and enable the tutors to maximize their teaching skills. To the extent that these home and after-school activities are coordinated with full government funding and support, they are likely to limit growing achievement inequalities in Israel.

However, in contrast to prior eras, current governmental policies and social developments converge on the opposite track, namely the growth of decentralization, budget cuts, and decreasing welfare policies (Nir and Inbar, 2004). These trends lead us to predict that – notwithstanding the heroic efforts of extant home-intervention programs and the growth in private sector involvement in deprived communities – the educational opportunities for children of immigrant families in Israel will continue to lag far behind those of other children.

NOTES

1. The Israeli Government recently decided to allow family members who were left in Ethiopia to move to Israel. This decision is likely to perpetuate the challenges that families and support services experience on a daily basis.

ACKNOWLEDGMENTS

This research emanates from a three-year study of a tutoring program for families in impoverished communities in Israel. We thank Anat Penso and

Radai Tesama for contracting the study. Facilities were supplied by the NCJW Research Institute for Innovation in Education, School of Education, Hebrew University of Jerusalem. The views expressed here are those of the authors'. We thank all research assistants who carried out observations and helped us in collecting the data used in this paper. We also appreciate Charles Bidwell's encouraging comments on an earlier version. Tracy Karp supplied important editorial assistance. Finally, we thank two anonymous reviewers and the editors for their advice.

REFERENCES

Alexander, K. L. (1997). Public schools and the public good. *Social Forces*, 76(1), 1–30.
Alexander, K. L., Entwisle, D. R., & Bedinger, S. D. (1994). When expectations work: Race and socioeconomic differences in school performance. *Social Psychology Quarterly*, 57(4), 283–299.
Baker, A. J. L., Piotrkowski, C. S., & Brooks-Gunn, J. (1999). The home instruction program for preschool youngsters (HIPPY). *The Future of Children*, 9(1), 116–133.
Bankston, C. L. I. (1998). Family structure, schoolmates, and racial inequalities in school achievement. *Journal of Marriage and the Family*, 60(3), 715–723.
Barr, R., & Dreeben, R. (1983). *How schools work*. Chicago: University of Chicago Press.
Barton, P. E., & Coley, R. J. (1992). *America's smallest school: The family*. Princeton, NJ: Educational Testing Service.
Bar-Yosef, R. W. (2001). Children of two cultures: Immigrant children from Ethiopia in Israel. *Journal of Comparative Family Studies*, 32(2), 231–246.
Berger, P., & Luckman, T. (1967). *The social construction of reality*. London: Allen Lane.
Biddle, B. J. (Ed.) (2001). Poverty, ethnicity, and achievement in American schools. In: *Social Class, Poverty, and Education: Policy and Practice* (pp. 1–29). New York: Routledge Falmer.
Blake, J. (1989). Number of siblings and educational attainment. *Science*, 245, 32–36.
Bourdieu, P. (1986). The forms of capital (R. Nice, Trans.). In: J. E. Richardson (Ed.), *Handbook of Theory of Research for the Sociology of Education* (pp. 241–258). New York: Greenwood Press.
Bourdieu, P., & Passeron, J. (1979). *The inheritors*. Chicago: University of Chicago Press.
Bourdieu, P., & Passeron, J.-C. (1977). *Reproduction in education, society and culture*. London: Sage.
Carrol, J. B. (1963). A model of school learning. *Teachers College Record*, 64(8), 723–733.
Clark, R. M. (1993). Homework-focused parenting practices that positively affect student achievement. In: N. F. Chavkin (Ed.), *Families and schools in a pluralistic society* (pp. 85–105). New York: State University of New York Press.
Coleman, J. S. (1987). The relations between school and social structure. In: M. T. Hallinan (Ed.), *The social organization of schools*. New York: Plenum Press.
Coleman, J. S. (1988). Social capital in the creation of human capital. *American Journal of Sociology*, 94, S95–S120.
Coleman, J. S. (1995). Social change and the loss of social capital: Implications for children. In: R. Kahane (Ed.), *Educational advancement and distributive justice: Between equality and equity* (pp. 17–31). Jerusalem: Magness.

Coleman, J. S., Campbell, E. Q., Hobson, C. F., McPartland, J. M., Mood, A. M., Weinfeld, F. D., & York, R. L. (1966). *Equality of educational opportunity*. Washington, DC: U.S. Government Printing Office.
Conley, D. (2001). A room with a view or a room of one's own? Housing and social stratification. *Sociological Forum, 16*(2), 263–280.
Coser, L. (1974). *Greedy institutions: Patterns of undivided commitment*. New York: Free Press.
Dauber, S. L., & Epstein, J. L. (1993). Parents' attitudes and practices of involvement in inner-city elementary and middle schools. In: N. F. Chavkin (Ed.), *Families and schools in a pluralistic society* (pp. 53–71). New York: State University of New York Press.
Downey, D. B., von Hippel, P. T., & Broh, B. A. (2004). Are schools the great equalizer? Cognitive inequality during the summer moths and the school year. *American Sociological Review, 69*(5), 613–635.
Dunn, J. (1982). *Siblings: Love, envy, and understanding*. London: Grant McIntyre.
Eisenstadt, S. N. (1954). *The absorption of immigration: A comparative study based mainly on the Jewish Community in Palestine and the state of Israel*. London: Routledge & Kegan Paul.
Evans, G. W., Lepore, S. J., Shejwal, B. R., & Palsane, M. N. (1998). Chronic residential crowding and children's well-being: An ecological perspective. *Child Development, 69*(6), 1514–1523.
Evans, G. W., Maxwell, L. E., & Hart, B. (1999). Parental language and verbal responsiveness to children in crowded homes. *Developmental Psychology, 35*(4), 1020–1023.
Farkas, G., Grobe, R. P., Sheehan, D., & Shuan, Y. (1990). Cultural resources and school success: Gender, ethnicity, and poverty groups within an urban school district. *American Sociological Review, 55*(1), 127–142.
Fenichel, E., & Mann, T. L. (2002). Early head start for low-income families with infants and toddlers. *The Future of Children, 11*(1), 135–141.
Fishbein, Y. (2004). *The grade – Barely absorbed: A follow-up report on the integration of Ethiopian-origin youth in high school (Hebrew)*. Jerusalem: Israel Association for Ethiopian Jews.
Flores, G., Tomany-Korman, S. C., & Olson, L. (2005). Does disadvantage start at home? Racial and ethnic disparities in health-related early childhood home routines and safety practices. *Archives of Pediatrics & Adolescent Medicine, 159*(2), 158–165.
Glaser, B. G., & Strauss, A. L. (1967). *The discovery of grounded theory: Strategies for qualitative research*. Englewood Cliffs: Prentice Hall.
Goffman, E. (1967). *Interaction ritual*. Middlesex, England: Penguin.
Goldring, E. (1997). Parental involvement and school choice: Israel and the United States. In: R. Glatter, P. A. Woods & C. Bagley (Eds), *Choice and diversity in schooling: Perspectives and prospects* (pp. 86–101). London: Routledge.
Gorely, T., Marshall, S. J., & Biddle, S. J. H. (2004). Couch kids: Correlates of television viewing among youth. *International Journal of Behavioral Medicine, 1*(3), 152–163.
Goux, D., & Maurin, E. (2001). *The effect of overcrowded housing on children's performance at school*. Paris: INSEE.
Hanson, S. L. (1994). Lost talent: Unrealized educational aspirations and expectations among U. S. youths. *Sociology of Education, 67*, 159–183.
Horowitz, T. R., & Mosher, N. (1997). Achievement motivation and level of aspiration: Adolescent Ethiopian immigrants in the Israeli education system. *Adolescence, 32*, 169–180.
Howe II, H. (1993). *Thinking about our kids*. New York: The Free Press.

Kaplan, S. (1992). *The Beta Israel (Falasha) in Ethiopia: From earliest times to the twentieth century*. New York: New York University Press.
Kellerhals, J., Montandon, C., & Ritschard, G. (1992). Social-status, types of family interaction, and educational styles. *Archives Europeannes de Sociologie*, *33*(2), 308–325.
Lareau, A. (1987). Social class differences in family school relationships: The importance of cultural capital. *Sociology of Education*, *60*(2), 73–85.
Lareau, A. (2001). Social class and the daily lives of children: A study from the United States. *Childhood*, *7*(2), 155–171.
Lareau, A. (2003). *Unequal childhoods: Class, race, and family life*. Berkeley: University of California Press.
Lareau, A., & Horvat, E. M. (1999). Moments of social inclusion and exclusion: Race, class, and cultural capital in family school relationships. *Sociology of Education*, *72*(1), 37–53.
Levine, D. N. (1974). *Greater Ethiopia: The evolution of a multiethnic society*. Chicago: University of Chicago Press.
Lewin, K. (1951). *Field theory in social science*. New York: Harper & Bros.
Maital, S. L. (2000). Reciprocating distancing: A systems model of interpersonal processes in cross-cultural consultation. *The School Psychology Review*, *29*(3), 389–400.
Manguel, A. (1996). *A history of reading*. New York: Viking/Penguin.
Marjoribanks, K. (1996). Ethnicity, proximal family environment, and young adolescent' cognitive performance. *Journal of Early Adolescence*, *16*(3), 340–359.
Nir, A., & Inbar, D. (2004). Israel: From egalitarianism to competition. In: I. Rotberg (Ed.), *Balancing change and tradition in global education reform* (pp. 207–228). Lanham, MD: Scarecrow education Publishing.
Office of the Deputy Prime Minister. (2004). *The impact of overcrowding on health and education: A review of evidence and literature*. London: Office of the Deputy Prime Minister.
Portes, A. (Ed.). (1995). Children of immigrants: Segmented assimilation and its determinants. In: *The Economic Sociology of Immigration* (pp. 248–280). New York: Russell Sage Foundation.
Portes, A. (1996). *The new second generation*. New York: Russell Sage Foundation.
Shonkoff, J. P., & Phillips, D. A. (Eds) (2000). *From neurons to neighborhoods: The science of early childhood development*. Washington, DC: National Academy Press.
Shuval, J. T., & Leshem, E. (Eds). (1999). The sociology of migration in Israel: A critical review. In: *Immigration to Israel: Sociological perspectives* (pp. 3–50). New Brunswick: Transaction.
Stanton-Salazar, R. D. (1996). A social capital framework for understanding the socialization of racial minority children and youth. *Harvard Educational Review*, *67*(1), 1–40.
Stanton-Salazar, R. D., & Dornbusch, S. (1995). Social capital and the reproduction of inequality: Information networks among Mexican-origin high school students. *Sociology of Education*, *68*, 116–135.
Sternberg, R. J., & Wagner, R. K. (Eds) (1994). *Mind in context: Interactionist perspectives on human intelligence*. Cambridge, England: Cambridge University Press.
Teachman, J. D. (1987). Family background, educational resources, and educational attainment. *American Sociological Review*, *52*(4), 548–557.
Vandewater, E. A., Park, S. E., Huang, X., & Wartella, E. A. (2005). "No-You can't watch that" – Parental rules and young children's media use. *American Behavioral Scientist*, *48*(5), 608–623.

Van-Kauffman, R. (2004). *Between ideology and practice: Israeli ambivalence toward multiculturalism – The case of Ethiopian immigration.* Unpublished Hebrew, Hebrew University of Jerusalem, Jerusalem.

Weinstein, B. (1985). Ethiopian Jews in Israel: Socialization and re-education. *Journal of Negro Education, 54*(2), 213–224.

Westheimer, R. K., & Kaplan, S. (1992). *Surviving salvation: The Ethiopian Jewish family in transition.* New York: New York University Press.

Widlak, P. A., & Perrucci, C. C. (1988). Family configuration, family interaction, and intellectual attainment. *Journal of Marriage and the Family, 50*(1), 33–44.

Yair, G. (2000a). Educational battlefields in America: The tug-of-war over students' engagement with instruction. *Sociology of Education, 73*(4), 247–269.

Yair, G. (2000b). Not just about time: Instructional practices and productive time in school. *Educational Administration Quarterly, 36*(4), 485–512.

HOME ENVIRONS AND ALIENATION FROM SCHOOLING COMMENTARY ON YAIR AND GAZIT

Daniel Bekele

In an era of massive global migration, many nations are grappling with how to support the social integration of immigrant children. This task is made all the more challenging when these children are impoverished and from a society very different from that of the receiving country. Since modern schooling is the primary vehicle for upward mobility for these children, their ability to successfully negotiate the schooling process is key to their future security in a strange new world.

The article by Gad Yair and Orit Gazit offers a window into the lives of Ethiopian children whose families are struggling to make a better life in Israel, and the view is disturbing. Crowded housing, family conflicts, and lack of quiet space to concentrate are important, practical barriers to the educational success that these children must achieve to have any hope of securing a middle class existence in Israeli society. Here, I discuss insights from the article on three issues: the critical relationship between children's home lives and their educational outcomes; strategies for policy makers and activists; and needed directions for further research.

BRINGING CHILDREN'S HOMES BACK INTO FOCUS

Yair and Gazit argue that many researchers – preoccupied with the effects of schools – ignore the forceful influence of home environs and parenting practices. They build from Goffman's (1967) theory of student engagement and the alternative, alienation from the school institution. As articulated by Yair and Gazit, the theory documents a tug-of-war between teachers' efforts to capture their students' attention and the multiple stimuli that distract students from pursuing their formal studies. The authors convincingly apply this model to the overcrowded and chaotic environments in which many Ethiopian children grow up.

Their rich ethnographic data from 22 households show that these children, in general, live in crowded and stressful households, marked by family demands and conflict, as parents struggle to survive economically within impoverished immigrant enclaves. Yair and Gazit detail common distractions that undercut children's efforts to complete their homework or even have calm, engaging conversations with adults: the television and radio, the chatter and noise emanating from every room in small flats, and the absence of quiet space for children to simply sit and read or tackle their homework.

The authors also attest to everyday emotional stressors that affect the motivation of young children in this Ethiopian community, including conflicts between children and parents and sibling rivalries among large families living in small households. Yair and Gazit contribute a significant new case study to the growing literature on immigration, poverty, and basic housing conditions, and reveal a number of concrete mechanisms by which Ethiopian immigrant children's home lives constrain their ability to engage fully at school.

Many dimensions of this work on Ethiopians in Israel are consistent with recent research on housing and education conducted elsewhere. Sociologists, applied anthropologists, and others investigating the everyday lives of immigrants have long highlighted the debilitating effects of stifling population density and the "ghettoization" of poor families. For example, of 80 studies undertaken in OECD countries, a review by the Office of the Deputy Prime Minister (2004) singled out the work of Goux and Maurin (2003) as the most robust study on the effects of overcrowding on school performance. Goux and Maurin's work indicates that in France, children who grow up in a home with at least two children per bedroom are both held back and dropout from school more often. Most of the other reviewed studies (numbering

40) also provide evidence on overcrowding and physical health. Another 25 studies found evidence for an association between mental health problems and overcrowding. The review identified 17 studies that related facets of overcrowding to children's development and school achievement. These relationships represent "facts that no longer need to be validated," in the view of Goux and Maurin (2003, p. 1).

IMPLICATIONS FOR ACTIVISTS AND POLICY MAKERS

Yair and Gazit's findings suggest the futility of governmental efforts to close immigrant achievement gaps without addressing central issues facing this community – adequate housing, affirmative action to equalize job opportunities, and family planning – which persist as underlying structural constraints that limit children's capacity to achieve in school.

Yair and Gazit link their qualitative findings to possible policy actions and steps that can be taken by community organizers. This section, while useful, is also a bit risky, as the authors acknowledge: caution must be exerted in generalizing from their rich but small dataset. Still, the authors do consider recent budget cuts in education made by the Israeli State; cuts that have reduced immigrant access to tutoring and home visitation programs. They rightfully emphasize the importance of more and safer public space for children, along with the need for more engaging after-school programs. Yair and Gazit also point out that while the state says it wants to welcome Ethiopian immigrants, its current policies may be having the reverse effect: as the state decentralizes social programs, it may well shrink the programs that aid social integration.

Immigrant parents would not be surprised by these new findings. They may be less in the dark than government policy makers. What many immigrant families do not need is another indictment of their ability to provide for their children, or programs that merely address symptoms, rather than deeper underlying problems. Instead, a good place to start might be to initiate an open and candid discussion of race among families, educators, and policy makers. Reading between the lines in the Yair and Gazit paper, we sense that Ethiopian-Israelis have formed a caste-like group, in part because they are Black, and therefore much less able to realize the social integration and shared community that exist among other Israelis.

NEW DIRECTIONS FOR RESEARCH ON THE ETHIOPIAN COMMUNITY IN ISRAEL

Yair and Gazit's work suggests needed directions for research *beyond* overcrowding and poor housing. One needed area of research is family–school relationships. Their interviews suggest that many parents do not understand the inner workings of their children's schools, nor do they feel comfortable engaging teachers, sensing a distance characterized by divergent languages and class distinctions. Some, most notably Pierre Bourdieu, have attributed this sort of phenomenon to the lack of appropriate cultural capital to understand how schools operate within the majority culture (e.g., Bourdieu, 1986; Lareau, 2003). Consider the example of a child who is not finishing homework due to the distractions and uncertainties at home. How does an immigrant parent attempt to explain and negotiate with a teacher who comes from middle-class Israeli society?

Moreover, the emotional strife in many households likely causes children to act out, which probably draws negative evaluations from their teachers. This finding is consistent with the developing literature on overcrowding, in its emphasis on parenting practices, social stress, and resulting behavioral problems (Bradley & Caldwell, 1984; Evans, Saegert, & Harris, 2001; Evans, Maxwell, & Hart, 1999; Shonkoff & Phillips, 2000; Wachs, 1989). Earlier work also shows that immigrant youngsters tend to display more behavioral problems in classrooms and less task persistence (Evans, Lepore, Shejwal, & Palsane, 1998; Saegert, 1982). Immigrant children may be unable to win teachers' attention or steady assistance due to language differences. Some teachers respond negatively to immigrant children because they display class differences, manifest in their language, behavior, and social symbols.

How do mainstream teachers make sense of children's linguistic and social differences – that is, how the nature of childhood and home realities interact with the school's own culture, its particular social norms, and its valued ways of learning? As research in this area develops, additional study will be needed on how teachers in Israel respond to immigrant children and their families, especially in circumstances of class and linguistic mismatch.

Another potentially interesting direction for research is work on immigrant optimism. There are a number of studies elsewhere reporting that many immigrant parents express high educational expectations for their children. These parents also demonstrate significant levels of ambition and time at work and share an optimism that they can get ahead, and in turn can create a brighter future for their children (e.g., Portes & Rumbaut, 2003; Suárez-Orozco & Páez, 2002). The uniformly bleak portrayal of immigrant family experiences detailed in the interviews does not suggest that immigrant optimism and hopes for mobility documented elsewhere are at play here.

A final point is that a cultural perspective in which community practices are portrayed as dysfunctional leaves out questions that are crucial for educational researchers and policy makers. Understanding the deep challenges facing many Ethiopian children in Israel is an important aim, and this piece moves us toward that goal. Yet, presumably, some mobility is occurring, and to address the needs of this immigrant group, it will be important to find out whether this is happening, and under what conditions. Do children's life chances improve over time, or does their alienation simply intensify among second- and third-generation households? In the context of great challenges, what attributes allow some children to persevere against the odds? How do children in this community manage to achieve mobility within such a constrained class structure? There is a critical need for research investigating how immigrant children from poor families manage to succeed in school, despite their numerous disadvantages, and what factors aid this process.

CONCLUSIONS

In closing, Yair and Gazit have performed a wonderful service in shifting our attention back to the basic condition of childhood, as a starting point for both educational research and interventions. Importantly, their work publicly illuminates the distressing housing conditions and overcrowding that mark the Ethiopian community in Israel. The issues they describe have parallels across the world, and their work offers an important and detailed case study to an emerging literature on housing and child welfare.

We need to learn more about sources of mobility and resiliency among these immigrant families. As research on Ethiopian immigrants in Israel develops further, I will look forward to learning more about how students, families, and teachers successfully negotiate issues of culture, class, and ethnicity, and about the attributes and practices linked to success among children in this community.

REFERENCES

Bourdieu, P. (1986). The forms of capital. In: J. G. Richardson (Ed.), *Handbook of theory and research for the sociology of education* (pp. 241–258). New York: Greenwood Press.

Bradley, R. H., & Caldwell, B. M. (1984). The HOME inventory and family demographics. *Developmental Psychology, 20,* 315–320.
Evans, G. W., Lepore, S. J., Shejwal, B. R., & Palsane, M. N. (1998). Chronic residential crowding and children's well-being: An ecological perspective. *Child Development, 69,* 1514–1523.
Evans, G. W., Maxwell, L. M., & Hart, B. (1999). Parental language and verbal responsiveness to children in crowded homes. *Developmental Psychology, 35,* 1020–1023.
Evans, G. W., Saegert, S., & Harris, R. (2001). Residential density and psychological health among children in low-income families. *Environment and Behavior, 33*(2), 165–180.
Goffman, E. (1967). *Interaction ritual. Essays on face-to-face behavior.* New York: Pantheon.
Goux, D., & Maurin, E. (2003). *The effect of overcrowded housing on children's performance at school.* Paris: INSEE. Retrieved on November 15, 2004 from http://www.jourdan.ens.fr/piketty/fichiers/enseig/ecoineg/articl/GouxMaurin2001.pdf
Lareau, A. (2003). *Unequal childhoods: Class, race, and family life.* Berkeley: University of California Press.
Office of the Deputy Prime Minister. (2004). The impact of overcrowding on health and education: A review of the literature. May 2004 http://www.odpm.gov.uk/stellent/groups/odpm_housing/documents/page/odpm_house_028620.pdf
Portes, A., & Rumbaut, R. (2003). *Legacies: The story of the immigrant second generation.* Berkeley: University of California Press.
Saegert, S. (1982). Environment and children's mental health: Residential density and low-income children. In: A. Baum & J. E. Singer (Eds), *Handbook of psychology and health,* (Vol. 2, pp. 24–271). Hillsdale, NJ: Lawrence Erlbaum.
Shonkoff, J. P., & Phillips, D. A. (Eds) (2000). *From neurons to neighborhoods: The science of early childhood development.* Washington, DC: National Academy Press.
Suárez-Orozco, M., & Páez, M. (Eds) (2002). *Latinos: Remaking America.* Berkeley: University of California Press.
Wachs, T. D. (1989). The nature of the physical microenvironment: An expanded classification system. *Merrill Palmer Quarterly, 35,* 399–419.

ABOUT THE EDITORS AND AUTHORS

Emily Hannum is Assistant Professor of Sociology and (by courtesy) Education at the University of Pennsylvania. Her research focuses on education, poverty, and social inequality, particularly in China. Recent publications include "Market Transition, Educational Disparities, and Family Strategies in Rural China: New Evidence on Gender Stratification and Development" (*Demography*, 2005) and "Global Educational Expansion and Socio-Economic Development: An Assessment of Findings from the Social Sciences" (with Claudia Buchmann, *World Development*, 2005). With Albert Park, she co-directs the Gansu Survey of Children and Families, a longitudinal study that investigates family, school, and community factors that support children's education and healthy development in rural Northwest China.

Bruce Fuller is Professor of Education and Public Policy at the University of California, Berkeley. Trained in sociology and social policy, his work focuses on the tensions surrounding state activism, cultural diversity, and the de-centering of public aims and institutions. Fuller has worked for the California legislature, a governor, and as a World Bank sociologist. His recent books include (with Susan D. Holloway) *Through My Own Eyes: Single Mothers and the Cultures of Poverty* (Harvard, 1997) and *Inside Charter Schools: The Paradox of Radical Decentralization* (Harvard, 2000). His new book, *Standardized Childhood* (Stanford, 2007), examines the cultural and political forces that engulf the universal preschool movement.

Jennifer H. Adams is Assistant Professor of Social Science, Policy, and Educational Practice at the Stanford University School of Education. She studies children's schooling and social welfare in China. Her current research focuses on the community and school contexts in which children learn and develop in China's rural areas. Her work shows the persistent and sometimes rising impact of community characteristics on children's education and development. Recent publications include "Children's Social

Welfare in Post-Reform China: Access to Health Insurance and Education, 1989–1997" (*The China Quarterly*, 2005).

Sajeda Amin is Senior Associate in the Policy Research Division of the Population Council, where she has worked since 1995. She is interested in a range of issues related to gender, work, poverty, and family in the developing world. She is currently involved in studies in Bangladesh, Egypt, and Vietnam on young people's livelihood strategies. These studies are part of a larger program on transitions to adulthood. Prior to joining the Population Council, Amin was a research fellow at the Bangladesh Institute of Development Studies in Dhaka. She received a doctorate in demography and sociology from Princeton University in 1988.

Daniel Bekele is a project manager at the Ethiopian Community Mutual Assistance Association in Cambridge, Massachusetts, where he oversees projects on education. His research focuses on literacy, inequalities of access to education, the association of HIV/AIDS and education, and the intersection between culture, demography, and education in sub-Saharan Africa. He is a founder and director of the Ethiopian Center for Educational Information. Bekele interviews local scholars and writes commentaries on issues related to immigration and the lives of Ethiopians for a weekly radio show. He earned his doctorate in human development and psychology at the Harvard University Graduate School of Education.

Niels-Hugo Blunch is Assistant Professor of Economics at Washington and Lee University. His research interests include household economics, economics and sociology of education and health, labor economics, demography, and program evaluation. Recent publications that he has coauthored include, "Child Work in Zambia: A Comparative Study of Survey Instruments" (*International Labour Review*, 2005) and "Asymmetries in the Union Wage Premium in Ghana" (*World Bank Economic Review*, 2004). Current projects include an examination of educational returns in Thailand and a study of characteristics and experiences of laid-off workers in China.

Orit Gazit is a graduate student at Hebrew University of Jerusalem, where she is writing a dissertation entitled "Political Exile in Sociology and International Relations." She is finishing a law degree at Hebrew University. Her main areas of research are poverty, social inequality, and political exile. Her recent work focuses on political exiles escaping military rule in Argentina, Chile, and Uruguay, and is set within the larger context of human rights violations and the exile's identity conflict in the host country, Israel. A recent publication is "Poverty and Education in Israel, 1990–2005." (Institute for Innovation in Education, the Hebrew University of Jerusalem).

Craig Gundersen is Associate Professor of Human Development and Family Studies at Iowa State University. He was an economist at the Economic Research Service of the U.S. Department of Agriculture. His research focuses on poverty, food insecurity, and ameliorative programs, primarily in the U.S. Along with numerous government manuscripts, his work has appeared in the *Journal of Human Resources, Demography, American Journal of Agricultural Economics, Pediatrics, Review of Agricultural Economics*, and *Southern Economic Journal*.

Kyle Jemison is a former Director of Operations Research for Catholic Relief Services in Zimbabwe. His research centers around child and community development, with a focus on child nutrition, education, food security, and children affected by AIDS. Recent publications include "Measuring Care and Support for Orphans and Vulnerable Children in Zimbabwe" (with L. Tinarwo, J. Lentfer, *Monday Developments*, 2004), and "Food Insecurity and Hunger in the Classroom: Its Effects on Kindergartners' Physical and Mental Growth" (with Josh Winicki, *Journal of Contemporary Economic Policy*, 2003). He is continuing his study of children affected by AIDS, including the well-being and educational attainment of children living with chronically sick parents.

Thomas Kelly is an economic consultant based in Johannesburg, South Africa. His research focuses on poverty and inequality in developing and transitional countries. He also acts as an advisor to governments and international organizations on poverty reduction policies and the monitoring and evaluation of these policies. Recent publications include the edited volume, *Social Capital and Economic Development: Well-being in Developing Countries* (with Jon Isham and Sunder Ramaswamy). His most recent research focuses on the impact of orphaning on household decision making in sub-Saharan Africa.

Jing Lin is Associate Professor at University of Maryland, College Park, in the area of international education policy. She has done extensive research on Chinese education, culture and society. In particular, she has systematically studied social change and educational reforms in China since 1978.

She is the author of five books: *The Red Guard's Path to Violence (1991)*, *Education in Post-Mao China (1993)*, *The Opening of the Chinese Mind (1994)*, *Social Transformation and Private Education in China (1999)*, and *Love, Peace, and Wisdom in Education (2006)*.

Simeen Mahmud is Senior Research Fellow at the Bangladesh Institute of Development Studies in Dhaka. Her research has focused on citizenship and participation, education and gender, and women's work and empowerment in Bangladesh. Among her recent publications are "Citizen Participation in the Health Sector in Rural Bangladesh: Perceptions and Reality" (*IDS Bulletin*, 2004), and "Globalization, Gender and Poverty: Bangladeshi Women Workers in Export and Local Markets" (with Naila Kabeer, *Journal of International Development*, 2004). Currently, she is working on social policy with a focus on health and education; the construction of citizen identity and practice; and the effect of health and micro credit interventions on women's well-being.

Hyunjoon Park is Assistant Professor of Sociology at the University of Pennsylvania. He is interested in social stratification, education, health, and the transition to adulthood in different countries. His dissertation examined how national contexts of public policy and educational systems shape the way in which family background influences children's educational achievement (University of Wisconsin-Madison, 2005). Recent publications include "Age and Self-Rated Health in Korea" (*Social Forces*, 2005) and "Intergenerational Social Mobility among Korean Men in Comparative Perspective" (*Research in Social Stratification and Mobility*, 2004). He is currently investigating the consequences of changing family structure for children's well-being in East Asia.

Heidi Ross is Professor of Educational Leadership and Policy Studies at Indiana University, where she has worked since 2003. Ross has served as Director of Asian Studies and Chair of Educational Studies at Colgate University, and was President of the Comparative and International Education Society from 2001 to 2002. She is co-editor of the *Comparative Education Review*, Chair of the Research Committee of the World Council of Comparative Education Societies, and will be Indiana University's Director of East Asian Studies beginning July 2006. Ross has published widely on education in China and qualitative research methodologies, and is currently conducting a longitudinal study of girls' education in Shaanxi Province. Ross received her doctorate from the University of Michigan.

Jennifer Rothchild is Assistant Professor of Sociology and Women's Studies at the University of Minnesota, Morris. Her main research interests include gender, sociology of education, social inequalities, and the nexus between education and family. For several years, she has been examining the complexities of gender within the context of Nepal's rural educational systems, and her book entitled *Gender Trouble Makers: Education and Empowerment in Nepal* will be published by Routledge this year. She is also developing a project involving the intersections of race, caste, gender, and social class in the experiences of displaced, abandoned, and orphaned children in Nepal.

Gary D. Sandefur is Dean of the College of Letters and Science and Professor of Sociology at the University of Wisconsin-Madison. Recent publications include, "Off to a Good Start? Postsecondary Education and Early Adult Life," in *On the Frontier of Adulthood: Theory, Research, and Public Policy* (with Jennifer Eggerling-Boeck and Hyunjoon Park, University of Chicago Press, 2005), and "Transition to Adulthood in Japan and Korea: An Overview" (with Hyunjoon Park, *Sociological Studies of Children and Youth*, 2005). He is currently studying educational inequality and the role of families and social contexts in adolescent and early adult obesity.

Gad Yair is Senior Lecturer at the Department of Sociology and Anthropology at the Hebrew University of Jerusalem. His academic interests include the sociology of schools and schooling, organizational theory, the sociology of learning, sociological theory and its history, and higher education. Among his recent publications are, "Not Just Location: LEAs and Inequalities among Schools" (*Journal of Educational Administration*, 2005), and "In a Double Bind: Conflicts over Education and Mayoral Election Outcomes" (*Local Government Studies*, 2005).

SUBJECT INDEX

Activists and policy makers, implications for 267
Africa, child labor, orphanhood, and educational opportunities in 7–9
Asia 133–159, *see also under* families, schools, and reading
   and Latin America, school and family effects on literacy, comparison 6–7, 170–172
   gender, family organization, and education in rural south Asia 6

Bangladesh 5, 10
   girls' schooling and marriage in 71–97, *see also under* girls' schooling
Bangladesh Rural Advancement Committee (BRAC) 79
Beijing 45, 49
Bright Light school 47–51

Catholic Relief Services (CRS) 209
Chapainawabganj 79
Child work
   and schooling 189–190
   child work status, incidence and main correlates of 186–188
Childhood in Ghana 232–234
Children's homes and education 266–267
Children's lives
   and schooling across societies 1–12
   child labor, orphanhood, and educational opportunities in Africa 7–9
   childhood, family, and schooling, comparative force of 3–4

China, community resources and schools in 5–6
differing childhoods, diverse schools, and uneven attainment 4–10
gender, family organization, and education in rural south Asia 6, *see also* Asia
home environment and schooling for Ethiopian immigrants in Israel 9–10
in Asia, families, schools, and communities 163–174
lessons from new studies of 10–11
outside of schools 1–3
Children's work and school attendance in Ghana 177–200
   child work and schooling 189–190
   child work status, incidence and main correlates of 186–188
   data and choice of child work status and explanatory variables 183–186
   data and descriptive analyses 183–190
   empirical strategy and issues 181–182
   methodology and research questions 180–183
   multivariate results 190–197
   theoretical framework 180–181
   work and schooling 188–189
Children's work, health, and school demand 231–237
   schools at the edge of tough childhoods 231–235
China, community matters in 5, 11, 15–39, 164–166
   analytic sample 24

SUBJECT INDEX

analytic strategy 27–29
background and context 17–22
community's effect on schooling, understanding 17–19
community resources and schooling in rural China 20–22
community resources and schools in 5–6, 164–166
data and methodological approach 22–29
Gansu survey of children and families 22–24
measurement 24–27
research findings 29–36
social capital formation, through Chinese school communities 43–68, *see also separate entry*
social status and mathematics score 32–37
village social capital effect on economic resources available in the community 35–36
Chittagong 79, 84
Community's effect on schooling 17–19
Core Welfare Indicators Questionnaire (CWIQ) 183–184

Ethiopian children's education in Israel 239–261, 268–269
deprived physical setting 250–253
emotional stress 255–256
Ethiopian immigrants, in Israel 9–10
Israeli policy of absorption, historical context 244–247
research setting and design 247–250
results 250–256
sensory bombardment 253–255
theoretical orientation 242–244

Families, schools, and reading in Asia and Latin America 133–159
data 140–142
data and variables 140–144

descriptive statistics 145–148
economic and educational indicators in 134
effects of family background 148–150
hypotheses 139–140
individual and family characteristics 142–143
method 144–145
private and public school differences 150–152
reading literacy 142
research questions 137–139
school characteristics 143–144
school climate, effects of 154–156
school's overall socioeconomic status and school resources 152–154
Family, health, and childhood in Zimbabwe 234–235

Gansu, mathematics achievement across rural villages in 29–32
Gansu Survey of Children and Families (GSCF-1) 22–24
Gender
as a social construction 103–105
gendered education 107–108
in home 105–107
Gendered homes and classrooms, schooling in rural Nepal 101–128
gender as a social construction 103–105
gender in the home 105–107
gendered education 107–108
research design and data 109–112
social construction effects of gender 112–123, *see also separate entry*
student profiles 109–112
theoretical framework 103–108
Ghana 5, 7–8, 10, 177–200, *see also under* children's work and school attendance
childhood in 232–234

Subject Index 279

Girls' gross enrollment ratios (GERs) 167
Girls' schooling and marriage in rural Bangladesh 71–97
  community factors 80
  cultural norms and 75
  data and methods 79–82
  discussion 93–94
  household factors 80–81
  individual factors 80
  outcomes 78
  predicting school and marriage outcomes 83–93
  private and state support for education 77
  school attendance, 2001 level and trends 82–83
  theoretical framework 74–78
Girls' schooling in rural south Asia 166–170
Guangxi 46

Hebrew 246–247
'Heyneman–Loxley effect' 171
Hierarchical Linear Models (HLMs) 144
HIV/AIDS crisis 8, 234–235
  in Zimbabwe 207–215, 225–227
Home environs and alienation from schooling 265–269
Hong Kong 135, 139, 147

Independence, Ability, Care, and Elegance (IACE) 55
Indonesia 142, 147
International Adult Literacy Survey (IALS) 142
International Labor Organization (ILO) 232
International Non-Governmental Organizations (INGOs) 102–103
International Socioeconomic Index of Occupational Status (ISEI) 143

Israel, Ethiopian children's education in 9–10, 239–261, *see also separate entry*

Japan 135
Jiangxi 46

Kanyadan 106
'Kishori Abhijan' program 79–94
Korea 11, 135

Latin America 133–159, *see also under* families, schools, and reading

Marriage in rural Bangladesh 71–97, *see also under* girls' schooling
Mexico 142, 147

National Education Longitudinal Study (NELS) 17–18
Nepal 5, 10–11
  schooling in rural Nepal 101–128, *see also under* gendered homes and classrooms

Organization for Economic Co-operation and Development (OECD) 139–142, 146–148, 154

Program for International Student Assessment (PISA) 140–143, 171

School and family effects on literacy, Asia and Latin America compared 170–172
School Leaving Certificate (SLC) 122
Schooling among orphans in Zimbabwe 207–228
  background 209–212
  data and methods 212–214
  data description 212–213
  descriptive statistics 214–218
  HIV/AIDS crisis 207–209

model description 213–214
model results 219–224
orphan status, estimation 219–224
results 214–224
school attendance rates 216
school enrollment status of orphans and non-orphans 215
Schooling and marriage in Bangladesh 71–97, *see also under* girls' schooling
Sherpur 84
Social capital formation, through
  Chinese school communities 43–68
  and educational opportunity 61–63
  Bright Light school, 'First World' urban private school on the privileged periphery 47–51
  portraits of four school communities 45–60
  social capital and educational opportunity 61–63
  West Bend and Willow Path, private schools for the rural poor 51–55
  Yu Cai-Shanghai #3 Partnership 55–60
Social construction effects of gender 112–123
  social construction of gender at school 116–125
  social construction of gender in the home 113–116
Social dynamics of childhood 236–237
Social status and mathematics score 32–35

Socioeconomic Status (SES) 133, 137–145, 148–156

Thailand 142
TIMSS (Third International Mathematics and Science Study) data 136

United States Agency for International Development (USAID) 105

West Bend school
  assessment 54–55
  community without bridges 51–53
  private school for the rural poor 51–55
Willow Path, private school for the rural poor 51–55
  assessment 54–55
  school community with bridges 53–54
World Bank 4, 102
Wu–Hausman-type test for collapsibility 195

Yu Cai-Shanghai #3 Partnership 55–60

Zimbabwe 5, 7–8, 10
  family, health, and childhood in 234–235
  schooling among orphans in 207–228, *see also separate entry*
Zionist ideology 244–245, 247

SET UP A CONTINUATION ORDER TODAY!

Did you know that you can set up a continuation order on all Elsevier-JAI series and have each new volume sent directly to you upon publication? For details on how to set up a **continuation order**, contact your nearest regional sales office listed below.

To view related Educational Research series, please visit:

www.elsevier.com/education

The Americas
Customer Service Department
11830 Westline Industrial Drive
St. Louis, MO 63146
USA
US customers:
Tel: +1 800 545 2522 (Toll-free number)
Fax: +1 800 535 9935
For Customers outside US:
Tel: +1 800 460 3110 (Toll-free number).
Fax: +1 314 453 7095
usbkinfo@elsevier.com

Europe, Middle East & Africa
Customer Service Department
Linacre House
Jordan Hill
Oxford OX2 8DP
UK
Tel: +44 (0) 1865 474140
Fax: +44 (0) 1865 474141
eurobkinfo@elsevier.com

Japan
Customer Service Department
2F Higashi Azabu, 1 Chome Bldg
1-9-15 Higashi Azabu, Minato-ku
Tokyo 106-0044
Japan
Tel: +81 3 3589 6370
Fax: +81 3 3589 6371
books@elsevierjapan.com

APAC
Customer Service Department
3 Killiney Road #08-01
Winsland House I
Singapore 239519
Tel: +65 6349 0222
Fax: +65 6733 1510
asiainfo@elsevier.com

Australia & New Zealand
Customer Service Department
30-52 Smidmore Street
Marrickville, New South Wales 2204
Australia
Tel: +61 (02) 9517 8999
Fax: +61 (02) 9517 2249
service@elsevier.com.au

30% Discount for Authors on All Books!

A 30% discount is available to Elsevier book and journal contributors on all books *(except multi-volume reference works)*.

To claim your discount, full payment is required with your order, which must be sent directly to the publisher at the nearest regional sales office above.

Callahan Library
St. Joseph's College
25 Audubon Avenue
Patchogue, N.Y. 11772-2327